Is There No Other Way?
The Search For
A Nonviolent Future

_____

Michael N. Nagler

BERKELEY HILLS BOOKS
BERKELEY, CALIFORNIA

Published by
Berkeley Hills Books
P. O. Box 9877
Berkeley, California 94709
www.berkeleyhills.com
(888) 848-7303

Comments on this book may also be addressed to: jpstroh@berkeleyhills.com

Cover design by Elysium, San Francisco.

Manufactured in the United States of America.
Distributed by Publishers Group West.
ISBN: 1-893163-16-4
First Printing March 2001
Second Printing March 2002

Library of Congress Cataloging-in-Publication Data

Nagler, Michael N.
  Is there no other way? : the search for a nonviolent future / Michael
N. Nagler.
      p. cm.
Includes bibliographical references and index.
  ISBN 1-893163-16-4 (alk. paper)
  1. Nonviolence. 2. Violence. I. Title.
HM1281 .N34 2001
  303.6'1--dc21
                                    2001000206

Contents

To my beloved teacher, Sri Eknath Easwaran
January 2, 1911 — October 26, 1999

Acknowledgements

It took many years and much help for me to write this book, and I apologize in advance if I fail to acknowledge everyone who lent a hand.

As my dedication makes clear, first thanks go to Sri Eknath Easwaran, who took me under his wing when I was long on passion but dangerously short on wisdom, and who is still and always shall be the guide of my life. I thank him and his wife, Christine, in the same breath, always.

Of the many others I am pleased to recall, first mention goes to my research assistant, Julie Anderson, who, armed only with modest research grants from the University, helped me hunt down many references (often on the obscurest leads) and corrected the irrational punctuation that accompanies the creative process, in my case. Julie was a sensitive reader before she turned tireless researcher. Barbara Gee, who had just the skills I lacked and the free time to put them at my disposal, did everything from the sublime to the mechanical in the last hectic weeks. Veronica Bollow (not even armed with research grants), saved Julie and me from the effects of our computer illiteracy, and finally Christine Nielson and Suraya Breen did the last needfuls.

Glenn Paige was among the first of my peace research colleagues to give this manuscript, or one of its ancestors, a critical read. I wonder how much Glenn will recognize in this published product, or whether he will realize how helpful his comments, negative and positive, have been. The most recent in the same collegial category is Elise Boulding, who has helped everyone in the peace world at one time or other. Where would we be — where would the world be today — without her? Colman McCarthy, the nation's only nonviolence journalist, was always there to mentor me in one pithy phrase that would save me a lot of floundering. ("Don't try to say everything at once, Mike.")

Years ago Candice Fuhrman read this manuscript when it was in dreadful shape, and had the courage to say so. In fact I have been blessed all along with outspoken readers and editors: Mary Lamprech of University of California Press liberated me from the notion that I was writing another academic book (she called this project "Walden Three"), the sharp-eyed Bernadette Smyth, went out of her way to be encouraging even as she was slashing away at typos and idiosyncracies, and so did Gail Larrick. My editor-publisher John Strohmeier has been intellectual foil, friend, capable businessman and visionary rolled into one — a joy to work with. This is publishing as it was meant to be: human-scale, personal, responsive, and driven by meaningful values.

My friends at my nonprofit, METTA, especially Jim Phoenix, Megan McKellogg, and Barb again, and in the nonviolent peace force project — David Hartsough, Mel Duncan and the whole gang (you know who you are). Through you I have been "plugged in" to the most important social work on the planet and supplied with information and hope for decades.

I thank my two grown children, Jess and Josh, and especially Jess and Rick's nearly-grown children, who at times had less of a grandfather they might have had for the sake of this effort, and of course my spiritual brothers and sisters at our community, the headquarters of the Blue Mountain Center of Meditation, who have shared their life and struggles with me for over thirty years. Carol, for one, not only challenged me when I was getting intellectually complacent but had to chase me down when I was deep into some subtleties of nonviolence when I should have been deep into some hot, soapy dishwater. I think too, always, of the children of our community, who remind me of all the world's children, who are the reason for everything. Without my community, children and adults alike, not only this book but everything I have become would not have been possible.

Lastly I think back on the innumerable people with whom I have thrashed out these ideas down the years, and first and foremost the students (more than a thousand now) who have taken PACS 164 with me at Berkeley, some of whom are today risking their lives to bring about the kind of world aimed at in this book. I honor them more than I can say.

And a special thanks in this number to Lauren and Jason, who put me up in a hotel room in Los Angeles so I could finish the references to this book one marathon day before their lovely wedding.

My heartfelt thanks to all who have, in whatever way, poured themselves into the greatest project now confronting humanity, the project of putting an end to violence, to which I hope this book may make a small contribution.

Introduction

On an unlikely, treeless savanna miles from any-where, Paolo Lugari Castrillón planted his dream. It was 1971. Off in the Eastern *llanos* of Colombia, sixteen hours from the nearest city, he and an idealistic band of followers founded what is now Gaviotas, a thriving, self-suffi-cient, sustainable, and in many ways model community — socially, eco-logically, economically — which caused Colombian novelist Gabriel García Márquez to dub Lugari "the inventor of the world." At Gaviotas (named for the nearby river gulls, *las gaviotas*) kids shriek as they pump each other up and down on seesaws, but at Gaviotas there's an extra edge to their satisfaction, for they are also pumping the water for the irrigation system. The music hall's curved stainless steel roof is also an intensely efficient water heater; in fact, solar collectors of a special Gaviotan design are providing heat for tens of thousands of buildings in Bogotá and through-out Colombia.

By dint of much research, diligence and insight the Gaviotans dis-covered that a particular type of Caribbean pine that was doing well in nearby Ecuador would take on the barren *llano*. Patiently, they planted seedlings, they tended them, and today millions of these pines adorn — and transform — the local ecosystem. For from the soil underneath them, much to everyone's surprise, a richly diverse primordial rain forest has sprung up, evidently from seeds that were hiding in the shallow soil, waiting who knows how many eons for the right conditions to bloom again.

This book will be about a renewal which, if we can make it happen, will resemble the miracle of the pines at Gaviotas, for it also will evoke forces that lie hidden in the thin soil of our impersonal, "bottom line," violence-prone civilization where human meaning has faded and human bonds are often scattered like the dust. As with Gaviotas' unexpected forest, the seeds of this renewal do not have to be created; they are waiting there in the soil of our own existence — waiting for us to create the conditions to awaken them. Like those of the new-sprung rain forest of Gaviotas, they are primordial, I will argue; far more native to the human condition than the world of abrasive relationships we have surrounded ourselves with in this industrial era. And, again like the Gaviotans' surprise rain forest, we don't have to know ahead of time what the renewal we hope to achieve will look like. At least not exactly. What we have to be very clear about is how to create the right conditions; then we can let nature — in this case human nature — do the rest.

My own renewal began in the fall of 1966, where a lot of renewing, and hoped-for renewing, was going on in those days: Berkeley, California. That was when I met my spiritual teacher, Sri Eknath Easwaran, who was teaching the form of meditation he himself had perfected and practiced to any and all interested parties right on my campus, in what was then in fact known as the Meditation Room of the Student Union building. A friend of mine, Javier Castillo, knowing that I was looking for *something*, some kind of answer to the emptiness left in many of us by the Free Speech Movement, which had started with such hope and ended in such dissatisfaction, suggested we go and "check him out." I needed some renewing. There was an inner emptiness that Javier may have sensed, perhaps more than I did. I had just been "regularized," i.e. advanced from Acting Assistant Professor to the real thing on the completion of my dissertation, invited from the vestibule into the halls of academe; so there I was teaching Classics and Comparative Literature at Berkeley — the career to die for. I had a family with two angelic kids in a cozy little house across the street from a regional park redolent with eucalyptus trees and laced by twisty paths, one of which took you down to a perfect lake for a before-dinner dip after a hot California day on campus. I thought I was on top of the world; but where was that world taking me?

One day, a few years earlier, I had stood in the living room of my Berkeley apartment looking at my newborn daughter when the news came over the radio that strontium-90 released into the atmosphere by atomic bomb testing was poisoning the spring rain, thus lacing the milk supply with a heretofore unknown, altogether invisible and cunning poison. At that moment I knew from the depths of my being we were going to have to "stop the machine" (as Mario Savio would later say); but how? Many people my age who had the same disillusionment were "dropping out" and trekking to India — or at least New Mexico — to find some way out of the oppressive, boring materialism of a culture that was weirdly inimical to life. For some lucky reason all I had to do was walk across Sproul Plaza from my office to the Student Union Building's Meditation Room.

Some time soon I will write the story of my meeting with Sri Easwaran and all it has meant to me and to many others; for now, what matters is how it turned one particular compartment of my life from anguished frustration to creative action. I had hated violence since long before this fateful meeting, almost as far back as I can recall anything about myself. By the time I came to Berkeley, already a "peacenik" with the rhetoric of the Civil Rights Movement echoing in my ears, I had of course heard of Gandhi — but like most Americans I knew little enough about him. A few days after my eleventh birthday the cover of *Life* magazine had pictured the scene of the Mahatma's cremation and the wild grief of the mourners, leaving a distinct impression of otherness, even weirdness, about the man and his culture which the little I later heard — about his fasts, his asceticism — did little to dispel. I admired his achievements, but they seemed almost more than human. I felt that he was probably a great man, and I was not, and there was an end to it.

But when Sri Easwaran began to weave his own reminiscences of Gandhi into his inspiring talks, slowly and from many angles shedding light on who Gandhi really was, an entirely new picture emerged. I began to see that Gandhi was at once much greater and yet more relevant — even to my own little life — than I had imagined.

This was, of course, only one of many changes, and not even the deepest wrought by those early talks. Sri Easwaran was gradually making it clear to me that the emotional anguish I was passing through was not unique to me and, more important, that it had a cure, that my political dissatisfaction — with all its passionate intensity — was really spiritual and could be given a more meaningful direction. With his combination of expertise, patience and boundless commitment (he sometimes quipped that his initials stood for "Endless Enthusiasm"), he inspired me to make meditation the mainstay of my life; with his values, his compassion and his vision, along with his personal experience of growing up in Gandhi's India, he enabled me to grasp who the Mahatma was and to sense the practical meaning of his legacy.

So it came about that no sooner had I gotten my foot on "the ladder" (academic jargon for a tenure-track teaching post) than I began trying to set it over to a different perch — something rather difficult to do with a ladder when you're standing on it! I used my faculty credentials to sponsor my new teacher in an experimental course on the "Theory and Practice of Meditation," a magnificent experiment that drew over a thousand students and yet could find no place to roost in the formal structures of the University and was discontinued after two goes. I tried being the chair of Religious Studies for a while, but that was doomed — the academic approach to religion and mine were on different planets. And finally I began teaching my course on nonviolence and Gandhi. That worked. It grew into a spate of articles, the beginnings of peace studies at Berkeley, this book — a career. More important, it grew into many life-long friendships with the extraordinary young people who have taken the course over nearly a quarter of a century. Only someone who has taught, perhaps, will appreciate how much these students engaged me with their enthusiasm, challenged me with their intelligence, and above all inspired me with their demand for a better world.

That is the background, and this is the conviction that led me to write this book: that after several decades' exploration of nonviolence I have no doubt whatever that we can bring a loving community to birth out of the civilizational crisis we are passing through. Precisely what such a future would look like is difficult to specify just yet, and perhaps we don't need to spell it out completely at this stage, but two things are certain. One is that, like the "miracle" of Gaviotas, it's going to take one heck of a lot of work. Most miracles do. Planting a million trees might end up looking easy by comparison.

Second, the Gaviotans give us a lead that is more than metaphorical. Like them, we know that though the results of our efforts may lie off beyond the mists of an uncertain future, if it is to be a future that we really want, we will have to make one right choice very similar to the one that brought Gaviotas into existence: the choice for constructive action over, and in the face of, an enormous prevailing negativity. Paolo Lugari chose the godforsaken *llanos* because, "If we can do this in Colombia, there's hope that people can do it anywhere." In that same spirit we can choose to craft a life of security and vitality even here, perhaps especially here, where a culture of violence seems to dominate everything. I am not being quixotic. A surprising number of the projects we'll be looking at in the ensuing pages led to results — good results — that the actors themselves didn't anticipate. Often their best and most enduring successes were not quite what they intended, indeed sometimes what they intended to do failed; but in every case they did one right thing: they chose persuasion and inclusion over threat power and hatred and domination. They chose nonviolence.

1   Hard Questions, Hard Answers

All major natural and human systems are in crisis or
transition. The signs of this change range from the
crash of fisheries around the world, the depletion of
rainforests, the declining credibility of government,
the growing inequality between rich and poor, and
the crisis in meaning and sense of emptiness that
comes with an overemphasis on material consumption.
— *Positive Futures Network newsletter*

For pain does not spring from the dust
or sorrow sprout from the soil:
man is the father of sorrow,
as surely as sparks fly upward.
— *Job*

Afront page photo in the Sunday *New York Times*
on August 17, 1997, showed a grieving woman,
Linda Reid, putting flowers on the gravestone
of her son, who had hanged himself at the age of seventeen. He was the
sixth teenager from that community to hang himself or herself that year.
Why? The article describing the suicides in this South Boston area talked
about the pressures of community pride, about racial tensions, lack of
economic opportunity — all things we are well aware of but which hardly
explain why a young person in a country like ours would take his or her

life. The real explanation must lie much deeper than community pride and economic opportunity. In 1998 the Surgeon General reported that children between the ages of ten and fourteen are twice as likely to take their own lives as they were fifteen years earlier. What is the explanation? As though sensing that all the talk about community pride and the like was a smoke screen, the writer finally quoted a local priest: "There really aren't any answers."

I refuse to accept this. I refuse to believe in the journalistic cliché "meaningless violence." I refuse to believe that there are no answers to the cheapening of life and the rise of violence against it. Two young men murder their own parents to get their money; a murder-suicide leaves a celebrity and his wife, apparently happy for years, dead in their palatial home; a teenager is shot dead in the street for his running shoes — why? It may be easy to say that there's no answer; but it's not acceptable. If we have no answers to such a basic matter as why we can't live in peace with one another, often can't go on living at all, maybe we're asking the wrong questions.

And in one respect, it's only too clear that we are doing just that. It's even clear why: violence is "reported" to us every day by the mass media in a wash of meaningless detail. "Joe X, 26, was shot three times with a 9mm handgun purchased the previous Tuesday for $23." Or, "This month the homicide rate in Dayton was 1.8% lower than last month." Frequently, we are solemnly told the trivial "reasons" offered by flustered survivors who hardly understand what is happening to them, and there is no limit to how absurd, how downright insulting to human nature these can be. In what would be called today a frivolous lawsuit, the wife of James Oliver Huberty, who killed twenty-one people in the McDonald's San Ysidro massacre in 1984, claimed his murderous rampage was caused by the excessive MSG in McDonald's hamburgers. The way violent events are reported (and this is a large part of what we read and think about today) is virtually always trivializing. It comes to us as a barrage of incidental details, often of cold statistics. Engrossed in one sensational detail or another, one particular violent episode or another, we never think about violence itself.

The right questions, then, are not, why are very young students turning their schools into battlefields, or why is there an increase in hate crimes right now against gays in Florida or a decrease in sex offenses in New England? They are:

What is violence?

Why is it getting worse? *and*

How do we make it stop?

Stirrings of Change

Despite discouragement by the mass media, there is evidence that people *want* to confront these questions. They are becoming more dissatisfied with the "No answer" school and other forms of dismissal — rightly, for to dismiss something as dangerous as rising violence is treacherous. The tendency to deny violence has been with us for a long time, to be sure, but there are signs that it is weakening. Considering the enormous role played by violence throughout history, Hannah Arendt wrote in her classic study, *On Violence*, in 1969, "It is . . . rather surprising that violence has been singled out so seldom for special consideration." She is reflecting the fact that a new awareness is dawning, that many feel the time to get past denial and face the issue head on is right now. It has been half a century since Gandhi observed that the world was "sick unto death with blood-spilling," and at about that same time, French philosopher Jacques Ellul made the shrewd observation that our era "is not at all the age of violence; it's the age of the *awareness* of violence."

In other words, what really characterizes our time is not so much that there is so much violence — there have been such times before — but that we are challenged, possibly as never before, to deal with it. This being true, the mass media could not have chosen a worse time to make violence appear trivial and incomprehensible. It is a singular and untimely disservice to human civilization.

Confronting violence is a little like turning around to face a bright light that's been projecting all kinds of fascinating images and shadows out in front of us. (Yes, I've been influenced by Plato.) It's hard to peer into that glare, but when we succeed we find ourselves going through a kind of Alice's looking glass. Suddenly we feel like the character from that popular 'sixties poster, with his head stuck into a whole other universe — or that convict in a cartoon staring wistfully through the bars at a little patch of sky while all along the door to his cell stands wide open behind him.

It is a much wider world we suddenly behold; the light is harsh at first, but when we face it problems that seemed impossible to cope with now appear teamed with all kinds of solutions — solutions with unexpected good side effects, instead of bad ones.

The prevailing method of dealing with violence has a dreadful tendency to create more problems than it solves. For example, we try to stop young people from bringing guns to school by installing metal detectors. It does cut down on the number of guns they bring in, of course — *and* it demoralizes the students because of the distrust it implies; it intensifies the excitement of the "game" of sneaking guns into school; and most of all it normalizes the violence. It blunts the shock. How could we have allowed a situation like this to happen, where young people have guns at all, much less carry them to school? And without that shock, where's the motive to solve the problem? Where's the impetus to probe the real problem, of which children with guns in school is only one form: the problem of violence?

Moving Toward the Truth

I have been identifying the mass media as a major source of our problem, and I'm going to continue, for one simple reason: they are where it would be most effective to make a change. In all honesty, however, we cannot put all the blame on them. When Hannah Arendt says it is "rather surprising" that violence has not been given special attention before now, she is giving us a scholarly hint that we have a natural inclination to avoid thinking directly about violence, which is understandable. We would be thinking about the most negative side of human nature, which means the most negative side of *ourselves*. I don't like this any more than you do. But although it must be done, it doesn't have to be done destructively. That is, we can peer into the depths of human nature — of ourselves — in a balanced way, seeing what is good as well as what's discouraging about us. Today, by emphasizing the shadow side of humanity — and "emphasizing" may be too mild for our obsession with the ugly and violent today — our culture seems to be making us more and more ignorant of our human stature. Let me throw that claim into relief by quoting a brief passage from an era, namely the fourteenth century, when that was not yet true.

> Beneath you and external to you lies the entire created
> universe. Yes, even the sun, the moon and the stars. They are
> fixed above you, splendid in the firmament, yet they cannot
> compare to your exalted dignity as a human being.

It seems almost fantastic to us that a writer could matter-of-factly describe humanity in these glowing terms; but it would have seemed just as fantastic to him that we matter-of-factly bill ourselves as "natural born killers" — just as fantastic and much more dangerous.

The obsession with negativity we take for granted paradoxically makes it nearly impossible to understand our negative side. It has blocked us from getting down to the causes of violence, those that lie within us, by creating a sense that *only* causes of violence lie within us. As we shine our light into the murk, therefore, it is essential to be watching for the seeds of change and regeneration that surely lie hidden there along with the drives, the impulses and blindness that make us violent. Opposites can strangely be the same.

The other day as I was walking across Sproul Plaza, made so famous in the 'sixties as the scene of the Free Speech Movement, I saw a cluster of students handing out leaflets around a hastily knocked-together kiosk. Nothing unusual, for Berkeley. They were clearly agitated (also not too unusual), and I went over to read their large, hand-lettered sign: *Anti-Asian Hate Crimes on the Rise.* I was shocked and hurt. At Berkeley, so many of my students and friends and colleagues are Asian that this hit me personally and hard, quite apart from the fact that this kind of thing should not be happening in Berkeley or anywhere in this century. But I've learned something over the years: if I wanted to do something about this, something effective, something that would last, I would have to get my initial reactions under control. I would have to take a step back and try to see the bigger picture.

To be more precise, in this case, three steps. Like letting ourselves down a chain into murky waters, hand over hand, we would have to back down in our thinking, from

anti-Asian hate crimes

to hate crimes

to hate.

Hate is the real problem. The more hate there is, the more it will express itself in whatever form. *Some* of those forms will be illegal — crimes, in other words — and some of *those* will be directed against Asians. But the underlying reason anti-Asian hate crimes are on the rise — in Berkeley or anywhere — has nothing to do with Asians or even racism: it is that hate is on the rise. Today it might be Asians, tomorrow it could be Jews, it could be blacks, homeless people, gays and lesbians; yesterday it was communists. But since these are all only the *targets* of some people's hate, only forms that hatred takes, trying to cope with each victimized group individually is like trying to fix one leak at a time in a rusted-out plumbing system. Wouldn't it be more effective to shut off the water? Or to modify that image, hatred is a tide that raises all boats. We won't get far trying to rescue the boats — or even groups of boats — one at a time.

These students were not the only ones trying to deal with one problem of victimization in isolation. We are all doing this, because it's become our culture-wide style when it comes to most serious issues. As John Burton, former Secretary of Australia's Department of External Affairs and now a well-known scholar of conflict, writes, "In so far as specific problems are being tackled by authorities as though they were separate problems, there can be no lasting cures for any of them." What civilizations are passing through, he points out, is in reality a clash between the systems we've built and the actual human needs they were supposed to address. Not, that is, an isolated clash between group and group.

The trouble with trying to stop one leak at a time is, first of all, that we do nothing about the others. Have a teach-in, raise consciousness, or if you really want to be unimaginative, provide Asians with more "security" measures. You may see some reduction of anti-Asian hate crimes (I'll be arguing later that even this isn't guaranteed), but what about anti-black, anti-lesbian, anti-Caucasian hate crimes? What about explosions of road rage? What about war?

On the other hand, if you could somehow do something to control hate, *all* the manifestations of hate would subside to that degree. The effect on specific hate crimes might be less obvious at first because it would be indirect, but in the long run it would be much, much more reliable. You simply cannot have anti-Asian hate crimes if you don't have hate. On the whole, this is so obvious that the only reason to repeat it is that as soon as some particular form of violence gets in our face, so to speak — witness my first reaction at the kiosk — it puts all our attention on its particulars. Emergencies are great motivators; but they create a terrible atmosphere for really solving problems. To solve problems you need to have a little control, a little distance, a lot of patience. You need to see, for example, that the problem is not hate against group A or B: it's hate.

Incidentally, as I headed back to my office, whom should I run across but a well-known Berkeley personality haranguing the passersby in a voice I recognized all too well. It's the kind of voice that makes you wince before you even hear what it's saying. I'm not sure what his problem is or why he chooses to bring it on campus, but he's extremely angry and attacks people for hours in a voice raucous with bitterness. He's popularly called the "Hate Man." I had the odd feeling that I might be the only one on campus noticing the connection.

Science and Serendipity

It sounds simple, but once we have worked our way down the chain from anti-Asian hate crimes to hate crimes, to hate — which is not easy to do when you're caught up in a hateful situation — we have not only an answer to the question of why this kind of crime, but the beginnings of a way to solve it. Once we've gotten down to the emotional cause, we start seeing a pragmatic measure that we'll be able to apply, *mutatis mutandis,* to just about every form of violence. Since the underlying cause of the violence is hate, we could fix the problem if we had a way to turn hate into something else. And there is evidence that this trick may not be as impossible as it seems.

In a remarkable experiment first reported in the *Journal of Abnormal Social Psychology* some time ago, school children of the same age were divided into two groups and treated equally, except that one group was encouraged to be aggressive and the other to be cooperative. Within a few weeks they were behaving quite differently. Our culture trains most children, before they even reach school, to be aggressive, but it's fairly easy to overcome that training with a little encouragement to their innate tendency to share, cooperate, think about each others' welfare. Then both groups were brought together and subjected to an acute frustration: they were sat down in a nice big room with a projector that was flanked by several cans of film. For good measure, each child was given a candy bar but told not to start in on it just yet. The room was darkened and the first film started — when suddenly, without a word of explanation, the experimenters snapped on the lights, shut off the projector, confiscated the candy bars and packed the children off to their respective classrooms. Science is rough! But the issue was important — to see if cooperative training would hold up under such unmerited mistreatment — and the results, duly filmed through the classrooms' one-way glass, were extremely suggestive. The children with pro-aggression training were of course hell on wheels; their frustration boiled over in fights, arguments and general mayhem more than ever. That's not very surprising. But the children who had been systematically encouraged to cooperate with each other were *more cooperative than ever.* Apparently they were not just protected from the bad effects of the frustration: they throve on it. They were able, that is, to divert the negativity it released within them into constructive channels. Psychic tension, it seems, is neither good nor bad in itself; it can be thought of as raw energy that can be made to flow through aggressive *or* through cooperative channels. Peace could be a simple matter of training.

As you may have guessed from the cans of film and the projector, this study by Joel Davitz was published nearly fifty years ago, at a height of the Cold War. Many political commentators were saying back then that if we made it through that year, 1952, we could survive anything. It might be thought that at such a time the question of what human beings can and cannot be trained to do with their aggressive drives would be of first importance. But Davitz's study was by and large ignored. This was the heyday of the "innate aggression" theory. At that time the idea that human aggression is biologically programmed and there is nothing you can do about it, an idea now largely discredited (but still uncritically believed by the mass media and the general public), was about to break over the public in a series of pseudo-scientific publications by Robert Ardrey (*The Territorial Imperative* would come out in 1966), Raymond Dart and several others. The heyday of that sensationalistic "science" is now behind us, however, and we are free to imagine that there may indeed be ways to turn hate and other negative energies into something else, that human nature may contain the cure as well as the cause of the violent trend steadily engulfing us.

Science has not stood still since 1952, and we know a good bit more about cooperation. Mediation training in schools has become a growth industry, for example; but the implications of the Davitz study are still far from fully realized. The study itself is known among peace-oriented psychologists, but its implications have not been systematically explored despite their potential importance. With or without popularizers like Robert Ardrey and their "swashbuckling" theory of innate aggression (I borrow that adjective from philosopher Mary Midgley), pessimism about human nature is the norm in public opinion, and, I'm afraid, in mainstream science. People study the shadow side. We have to look hard to find the side we most need to see.

The Thrill of Prevention

Berkeley students, among whom I've studied and taught for more than thirty years and who will always be in my heart, are, as I say, only one example of the need to let ourselves down the chain of causality. If you really want justice for your own or any group you identify with, you have to step back in your vision and your emotions, not for the purpose of caring less, but to create a space for better-aimed passion. This is what all of us have to do if we are ever to see a life secure from violence, even if we're non-minorities living in a comfortable community like South Boston. Whether we are activists angered by some form of injustice or we just want to get from our car to our house without being mugged, we are going to have to change our way of thinking. We have to slow down our initial reactions — not by any means in order to lose the intensity of our feelings about the problem, but on the contrary, in order to convert those valuable feelings from fear, panic or resentment into determination. The more of the underlying causes we can see, the better we'll be able to identify the long-lasting, and only real, solution.

But there's an important point we only just began to mention: why wait until you're being mugged, or until people with ugly attitudes have started insulting your community? Obviously, it's tons more effective not only to be working at the root of the problem instead of the leaves, but to be working there *steadily* instead of being caught by surprise every time there's a violent incident. How can we? We've already had one clue: this process begins to work the minute we stop being taken in by the details which the media think it is in their best interests to deluge us with and start reflecting about what is going wrong, the minute we step back from the hurt and anger about what's happening to us personally and start to think about inhumanity itself.

In the summer of 1998, a dedicated teacher and school principal in South Africa, Sister Theodelind Schreck, was slain while driving to pick up her niece. Although KwaZulu Natal province has a long history of political violence, the slaying of a nun in an apparent robbery shocked many people. "Sister Theodelind Schreck was dedicated to her teaching and religious duties," said Ben Ngubane, premier of the province. Then he made an observation that rose above the fuss about why *her*, about *this* murder being unacceptable, and provided useful insight for all of us. "Violence remains violence, irrespective of motivation."

This is a fundamental insight about the nature of violence, and it implies a strong positive message that is just as clear: since violence is violence, anything we do to reduce violence anywhere will do something toward reducing violence everywhere.

Premier Ngubane's insight is borne out by scientific research. One of the papers read before the British Psychological Society in 1994 was about the negative impact of television news bulletins. By then it was well known to social scientists that the parade of bad news that people see on the media depresses them. What was surprising, however (but perfectly logical, when you think about it), is that the anxious and depressed states people get into from watching this news – or various forms of "entertainment," that portray the same dismal picture of human nature – have a general impact: we start seeing *everything* more negatively. Evidently the negativity we take in — and other studies show that it doesn't much matter whether you think you're seeing news or fiction — "tend[s] to promote a negative frame of mind in which negative events, thoughts and memories *are likely to be dwelled on and positive ones filtered out and ignored."*

Clearly, that could lead to a vicious circle — and clearly, in fact, it has. There is a lot of bad stuff in the world. By seeing it up close, out of proportion, we come to expect things to be worse and worse, and when we have negative expectations, life obligingly fulfils them. That part of the circle is easy to understand: negative expectations mask from view our positive potentials, which are the very ones we need if we're going to avoid and resolve problems like violence.

Note that the London psychologists compared the effects of bad news to what they called "neutral" news — not with actual good news. Maybe there wasn't enough good news out there to build a sample. But this is the main point: the principle that they were dealing with, the principle that negativity generalizes in the viewer's mind, is one of the most important things to know about violence. Think how differently we would form policies and regulate our own viewing habits if we became aware what it's doing to our outlook on life, what it's costing us emotionally and spiritually, to take in so many violent, depressing images and stories.

In practical terms, though, the real importance of the London study comes out when you turn it around. To take in uplifting images and stories must have exactly the opposite effect. Logically, that would make things better as surely as seeing violence makes them worse. But somehow we never think to explore the bright side of the principle. A recent news story on "emotional literacy," for example (a current term for the kind of cooperative training Davitz was talking about fifty years ago), had the byline, *Today's Lesson: Curbing Kids' Violent Emotions.* You could put it that way. But what if, just for the argument, we were to title that article, *Today's Lesson: Unleashing Kids' Compassionate Emotions.* Unthinkable, but actually more correct. It is a better description, I believe, of what is really happening in those young people. Their natural drive to cooperate, keyed to positive emotions like compassion, is taking up some of the energy that had been fueling their aggressions. The results of this simple process took the Davitz experimenters quite by surprise — like the Gaviotans when they created the conditions for a rain forest they didn't know was there.

I've just come from my daughter's house where I watched a PBS documentary on the aftermath of colonialism in the second half of the twentieth century. The film brought out extremely well the contrast between the aftermath in India and the aftermath in other colonial areas, primarily Africa. It pointed out how despite India's many problems she remains the most populous democracy on the planet, with robust institutions to keep her that way, and enjoys rewarding relationships with the former colonial power — all this in contrast to names that make us wince today, such as Somalia, Rwanda, Liberia, the Congo, Ghana, Algeria. The film, as I say, brought this out very well. What it didn't think to mention was, *why.* It is as though the filmmakers did not dare to say that nonviolence (which was, with a few lapses, the liberation method chosen in India) led to one result while violence (which predominated in Africa with a few exceptions) led to quite another. By the end of this book you will see why I dare to say exactly that.

Let me emphasize the simple but important step we've already taken in this direction. As journalist Daniel Schorr wrote recently, "Television, celebrating violence, promotes violence . . . By trivializing great issues, it buries great issues. By blurring the line between fantasy and reality, it crowds out reality." But if television and other media celebrate, promote and trivialize violence, we don't need to. My hope is that after reading this book you'll never hear a news report or see a violence-packed film in quite the same way again. While the details of that crime report are being reeled off — what caliber was the gun, where was the wound, what was the motive, if any — something in you will cry out, "This is violence. Forget everything else and figure out what's going wrong!"

That step taken, we can take the next: to see through events to an underlying story that contains scintillae of hope, and a few examples of that follow.

Strength is Strength

As part of wrapping up the second Christian millennium, *Time* magazine ran profiles of one hundred key people who, in the editors' estimation, had left their mark on the twentieth century. It was not inspiring. What they did with Gandhi was shockingly bad, but they did manage to relate an eye-opening story about Nelson Mandela. When the young Mandela stepped onto the quay with a boatload of other prisoners at the infamous Robben Island, where he was to spend so many years of his life, guards shouting, "Huck! Huck!" tried to herd the new arrivals like cattle, to make them trot up to the prison and submit them to other humiliations. Mandela and a friend refused and kept on walking calmly though the guards threatened "Do you want me to kill you?" Once inside, one of the warders, a certain Captain Gericke, went a little too far, calling Mandela "boy." "Look here," Mandela calmly told the startled Gericke, "I must warn you, I'll take you to the highest authority and you will be poor as a dormouse by the time I finish with you."

"Incredibly," *Time* says, Gericke backed off.

But is this so incredible? Don't bullies frequently cave in when they meet with unexpected resistance? We've all seen examples of this, and in the next chapters we'll not only see a few more, but will work out a scientific explanation for the phenomenon.

Let's follow the lead the *Time* writers missed. First connection: intuition leads us to a famous event a quarter of a century later, when Mandela is now in a position of strength, in fact the first president of a free South Africa. As most of us remember, during his inauguration speech he paused, turned to his arch enemy, F. W. de Klerk, took his hand and said, "I am proud to hold your hand — for us to go forward together. . . . Let us work together to end division."

What is the connection between these two events? In the ordinary way of seeing things, nothing. In the ordinary way of thinking, every conflict, if not every interaction, has to have a winner and a loser. Did de Klerk win or did he lose when Mandela made his gesture of reconciliation? Absurd question. What about Mandela? As an individual, Nelson Mandela may not have liked F. W. de Klerk, but he used his strength of character to overcome his personal dislike; and we can clearly trace, through his change of roles, the thread from prisoner Mandela's strength on Robben Island to President Mandela's strength in Johannesburg. This intriguing connection does not appear in the ordinary way most of us think about conflict and human relationships, but in the emerging new way of thinking about conflict and relationships it's clear enough: The capacity to stand up to a bully and the capacity not to act like one — the strength of character to rise above anger, even if that anger is perfectly justified — are closely connected. These qualities not only can coexist, they explain each other: strength is strength.

We miss this whole fascinating connection if we think "strength" means the ability to prevail, to dominate, period. Mandela's great role-model, Gandhi, would by contrast often confess his blunders in public; he seemed to enjoy it, much to the consternation of his coworkers. Once his sister was alarmed at what seemed to her a particularly damaging confession, and he said, "Tell sister there is no defeat in the confession of one's error. The confession itself is a victory."

That strength means so much more than power over another explains the strange conversions of angry, violent people that keep cropping up in the annals of peace. When segregationist George Wallace became governor of Alabama, he kept his campaign promise and literally "stood in the schoolhouse door" to block black students from entering the University of Alabama in 1963, making himself a national symbol of defiance in the cause of segregation. But in the course of time, something apparently lifted the fog of hatred from his mind, and on March 11, 1995 he came in his wheelchair to a celebration of the anniversary of the Selma-to-Montgomery civil rights march to apologize to the marchers, black and white, whom his state troopers had clubbed and fire-hosed thirty years before. That took guts — but then, so did the way he defied the whole country back when he saw things differently. From an icon of segregation he became, on the front cover of *Life*, an icon of reconciliation. No wonder Gandhi often said that there's hope for a violent man to become non-violent, but not for a coward. In nonviolent logic, this makes perfect sense: what we're seeing is the same courage and strength, put to better use.

Second connection: now link both these events in Mandela's life, the defiance and the generosity, with his impressive leadership — his ability to pilot a brand new state that had just emerged from horrendous conditions with still unresolved tensions of frightening magnitude. This is a little subtler than the courage to defy and/or forgive: Is someone who forgives his enemies, in public, a good leader? Of course. She or he will tend to have access to creative resources for order which we'll have a chance to explore later (especially in chapters five and six). For now, let's consider one more nonviolent event misunderstood — and this time not just by the press.

In August 1991 a counterrevolutionary coup that would have pushed

Russia back to Stalinism was thwarted by a popular uprising. This is how one important liberal magazine characterized the event (my emphasis): "The coup failed. The regime collapsed. *For once, the world was lucky.*" But the successful popular resistance to the August coup was not "lucky"; it was the result of deliberate acts carried out by courageous nonviolent resisters who had been systematically studying nonviolent tactics for months, in part through workshops run by experienced American trainers. (One friend of mine had done an average of two such workshops a day all over Russia throughout that summer.) All of this was totally unknown to the press. "The August coup was not a surprising event," wrote conscientious objector Alexander Pronozin shortly after it occurred. "The real surprise was how quickly the coup was brought down and that the 'weapon' that won the day was nonviolent social-based defence."

We will say more later on about this remarkable form of defense (chapters four and seven), and when we do I hope to clarify what it could mean for the majority of us, who are not likely to participate in a "people power" resistance. What I want to emphasize now is that the rapid success of the resistance to the coup, which seemed so inexplicable, so "lucky" to the news media and general public — and, I have little doubt, the political leadership of the time — was neither. It was the result of hard work and sacrifice; it followed the rules of the game with perfect predictability. You do not have to follow news about nonviolence on special listserves to be more aware of these rules. Anyone who has a hunch that life is not so haphazard as it appears, that everyone responds to love or hatred when it's offered to them, will know what I'm talking about.

My colleague and friend Sergei Plekhanov, then Deputy Director of the Soviet Institute for U.S. and Canadian Studies, was not in Moscow on the critical day the coup was thwarted. A year later I heard him describe what he had gone through when he saw the starkly juxtaposed television images of the Kremlin, ringed by grim walls and armored vehicles, and the Russian parliament building in white marble and glass guarded only by unarmed people, almost a mythic image of civil authority besieged by violence. I still remember the quiet passion in his voice that so gripped the international scholars gathered around him: "And what do you have against them?" he said. What can you wield against those tanks and armored personnel carriers? "Nothing. Nothing but spirit, a sense of legitimacy, and the willingness of some people to risk their lives." I hope the irony was not lost on my colleagues, for this "nothing" is the classic recipe for successful nonviolence: spirit, a sense of legitimacy (that one's cause is just), and the willingness to sacrifice — if necessary to lay down your life. Those are precisely the three things that make resistance to an unjust regime successful. Basic. Nonviolence 101. To miss this is to be unable to explain what forces were at work in the confrontation of August 1991 — and why the people won.

The Purloined Answer

This side of the Iron Curtain there was a land called Yugoslavia, where people of different cultures and ethnicities lived side by side. They worked together, despite their tensions. They went to schools together. They quarreled. They intermarried. This went on for centuries. Then one day, when the lid of centralized state-socialist control came off, the three major cultural groups (they are not ethnic groups) flew apart. The result was the most appalling violence seen in Europe, and possibly anywhere, since World War II. Many asked, "Why? How could they be putting people in cattle cars all over again?"

As usual, there were those who said there was no answer. Others cited history, as though memories of the famous battle of 1389 had to rankle even though the people who fought it had been dead for five hundred years.

But in all this, one banal factor has been overlooked: the poisonous power of propaganda. The Slav populations of the other formerly Communist East European countries just to

the north, in Hungary and Romania, developed a hearty
skepticism about what they saw on state television or read in
government-run newspapers. For some reason, that kind of
doubt died in Yugoslavia if it ever existed. People here have
always believed, and still believe, what they see and hear on
television.

In a way, this is nothing new; we all know about the "yellow journalism" that put the U.S. into conflict with Spain in 1898. Then it was
mainly newsprint, now it's television (or, in the case of Rwanda, radio).
But the difference between then and now is not just technological, or for
that matter political. It's the difference of half a century's "background"
message of alienation and violence, the cumulative mental poison that
makes all of us more edgy, dispirited and prone to react with violence
along whatever fault-lines present themselves, be it between races, between cultural subgroups in a formerly viable community, or between
two cars on a crowded freeway.

The London study we quoted earlier points to this effect; so did the
wise words of Daniel Schorr; so do these from a twelve-year-old school-
child in Santa Rosa, California:

If there was no violence on the television, less people would
make violence on the streets. Also I think less people would
be shot, murdered, kidnaped and other things.

They sure would. It's as simple as "violence in, violence out," a result
that is obvious to science, common sense, and our own personal experience, and which we nonetheless like to regard in some circles as controversial. It isn't. If we play up violence, we'll have more violence; if we play
up money and greed, there will be more robberies; and in the words of
another wise twelve-year-old: "People get a lot of ideas from sex [on
television] and think it's okay and then they rape people."

It seems so — well — stupid to do this to ourselves that one can understand the bitterness behind these hard words of Wendell Berry.

> Always the assumption is that we can first set demons at large, and then, somehow, become smart enough to control them. This is not childishness. It is not even "human weakness." It is a kind of idiocy, but perhaps we will not cope with it and save ourselves until we regain the sense to call it evil.

If it helps, call it evil. But be careful: there is a world of difference between calling some*thing* evil and calling some*one* evil. The first strategy mobilizes resources against the problem, the second only recycles the ultimate cause of the problem, which is ill-will, resentment, lack of empathy and eventually hatred.

When the members of the European contact group sutured together a "peace" for the remains of Yugoslavia in 1998, they made no provision for reeducation; incredibly, no one paid any attention to the government-run television stations that kept right on whipping up the same hatreds that had started the violence, particularly in Serbia. As one of my colleagues on the scene ruefully told me, "Most people continue to be fed a steady diet of nationalism and propaganda, hatred, half-truths and prejudice." Violence in Kosovo soon followed.

When hatreds are being fanned and sensitivities abused, we have to feel it so deeply that we cannot rest without doing something about this hurt — but calling it "evil" is a tricky way to go. Where there's evil, there has to be an evildoer — someone other than us. Very "other." But in fact, the media are *our* media, we patronize and support them. There is a reciprocity to this process, to be sure: they feed us violence and vulgarity, we then get a taste for it and demand more, which they obligingly supply — a truly vicious cycle. So where shall the spinning finger of blame land?

On the whole, I prefer to think about the unleashing of these demons as a kind of tragically blinkered vision (what Berry calls "idiocy"). Still not very complimentary: but it's a more practical approach.

The Why of Living

The media have purposes of their own; helping us grasp the significance of violent events does not seem to be one of them — much less helping us find our role in eliminating such events. That is why when they run out of superficial answers for one act of violence or another, they have taken to saying that there isn't any answer. But there is. We have seen part of it already. It's that we, collectively, have created such a climate of violence and negativity that life doesn't seem terribly worth hanging onto, yours or anyone else's. At the same time violence seems an intriguing, pseudo-meaningful, "exciting" and normal alternative. Suicide fits into this picture as a kind of inverted violence directed against oneself; or it may be that for some of these young people their own self has come to seem so distasteful that it's radically "other" to them. In any case, the phenomenon of teenage suicides forces us to step *way* back and look at the whole picture. Let me put it as simply as possible:

Life has a purpose. Animals can live without discovering this, but people can't. In the course of historical time, civilizations can get off on a tangent, get fascinated by some side track, and lose sight of why they are alive. When this happens — and it seems to happen periodically — a whole culture can no longer see where it's going. That's when life loses its purpose (or seems to), and individuals, in the grip of a gnawing despair they may not be able to articulate, start to give up on life itself. Then you see teenagers committing suicide as though it were a fad, you see doctors who help people die instead of helping them live, you see the return of the death penalty — all symptoms of what the Pope has called a "death-oriented" civilization. It's not really death-oriented *per se*; it's death-oriented *by default*. When life is seen to offer us no stimulating goal to live for, then, by default, the most repellent things can actually look attractive, because they're the only things that are "exciting." Death and violence take on a lurid appeal. Yet, as an ancient Indian classic puts it, "Those who go after ignorance go to blinding darkness . . . those who get drawn to the shadow side of life go to blinding darkness." To play with the dark side of human nature is to end up in a crisis of violence that seems impossible to understand.

So the violence we're seeing today is intimately linked to the "crisis of meaning" cited by the Positive Futures Network in the headnote to this chapter. They listed it as a symptom; I would argue that the crisis of meaning belongs center stage. If people don't know where the journey of life is leading them, why should they be enthusiastic about continuing? Teenagers can be very direct, and here is what one of them said when President Clinton advocated an educational campaign on the dangers of smoking to dissuade teens from doing it:

> In my opinion, many young people who smoke and say they don't know why are subconsciously choosing death. So telling them over and over that smoking will kill them is not the answer. . . . If the President is serious . . . he's got to find ways to help them imagine a future.

The reason a young person ends his or her life in South Boston, or kills someone along a California freeway; the reason a father turns on his own family or a nation sets off nuclear explosions, is not money or jealousy or traffic. Ultimately it's because life has lost its meaning for them — they cannot imagine a future with any hope or purpose. Money and all those other factors can *precipitate* violence, but only among people for whom, consciously or otherwise, life has lost its value — or more accurately, people who have lost sight of life's priceless value and what a Greek philosopher called its "inexhaustible meaning."

The media are a powerful way we obscure life's meaning, and a way that I'll keep returning to because it's an obvious leverage point at which to begin changing; but it is one way among many. My young friend Sean is taking intensive German to help him with his senior thesis project on the poet Rilke, at Johns Hopkins. After I helped him out a bit with that a while back, we found ourselves talking about what his friends were doing who were studying science at places like Berkeley and MIT. "I can't understand," Sean said. "It's as though there were no controversy about it, as though everyone agrees that there's only the physical body and laws and molecules — haven't they heard of something called the mind?"

I found myself thinking of an article I had read the day before in a newsletter from my own campus about a truly remarkable breakthrough in molecular genetics. My colleagues had been able to photograph the very site on the cell where genes were "switched on" or "off," where DNA is told to go ahead and produce messenger RNA to begin making part of an organism. While I was reading along, marveling how far we have come since my brief stint in medical school (never mind how long ago *that* was), my literary senses were setting off a little alarm. I stopped and counted something. In this brief article, about 600 words, the word "machine" occurred *thirteen times.* This is what's called in literary circles a "subtext." Even while the writer was telling us about a great human achievement, he was also telling us, in that powerful stream of suggestion that runs underneath the literal meaning of our words, "You're a machine, you're a machine, you're a machine . . ."

"For our culture as a whole," Huston Smith recently pointed out, "nothing major is going to happen until we figure out who we are. The truth of the matter is, that today we haven't a clue as to who we are. There is no consistent view of human nature in the West today."

"Who we are" is a question that will be hovering in the background of every argument in this book. Are we separate, material creatures — in which case it's hard to see how we could *not* be doomed to competition and conflict — or are we invisibly connected through what Mahatma Gandhi called "heart unity" underneath all those real-as-far-as-they-go differences of body, culture, likes and dislikes, ideologies and fashions? In that case life may have a profound hidden meaning after all; and in that case, we've got a lot of learning ahead of us.

The dark side of modern science, and unfortunately it has one, does not arise from science itself, still less from any of the facts of nature. It arises from the impression we allow science to give us: the impression that we are merely biological machines in a meaningless material universe. Science has every right to confine its attention to the physical, i.e. the outside world. It has no right to say, when it has done so, that it has given us the whole story.

When scientists, some of them, talk about "the biological basis of violence," they are out of their depth. Science, at least as they practice it, can study the infinitely vast reaches of outer space, but it cannot very well study the inner dimensions of the human being. As a result, in course of time we who turn to science for our answers to life come to feel we do not have such a dimension. We feel empty. Human will, nobility, beauty and life's overriding purpose are all in the category of things scientists do not study and that we eventually come to believe, quite without justification, do not exist.

This drive toward reductionism within science becomes exaggerated in the minds of nonscientists, especially when it is greatly amplified by the mass media. The media report new "discoveries" in material determinism at the rate of about a gene a day: obesity, sexual preference, intelligence, sex appeal and whether you like peanut butter — they've just found the gene or the hormone or the what-have-you that "causes" it. No responsible scientist would actually claim that we can trace something as complex and subtle as anger or cravings or attitudes to a gene or a hormone, but we in the general public are spared such subtlety. We come to feel we do not have a will, that there is no redemptive drama going on in the human being, that we are without meaning or direction, and so, as Dostoevsky said in *The Possessed*, we die of despair.

The one essential condition of human existence is that man should always be able to bow down before something infinitely great. If men are deprived of the infinitely great they will not go on living and will die of despair.

The six South Boston teenagers were examples of that, and today there are many, many others.

When a family becomes "dysfunctional" (a remote euphemism of a word), the children will grow up deficient in security and self-esteem, easy prey to "the crisis in meaning and sense of emptiness that comes with an overemphasis on material consumption" our civilization is passing through. They will find it most difficult to discern the meaning of life, or believe that there is one, and will begin to "die of despair," in a thousand ways — even if they never see a television set.

When I think about the new world of mass media, I'm reminded of something a social worker recently pointed out about child care: "We have no idea how destructive a situation we have created. It is a social experiment on a grand scale with virtually no controls."

But this book is about solutions, not just problems. Some of the stories I told and more that I will tell are really about ordinary people doing in their way what Dostoevsky described in his grand register — people rising toward the "infinitely great" through responses to the reasonably good. For we have arrived at not one, but two answers to the question, "What can be done to keep young people from despairing of their life?" What almost all people can do to create a nonviolent culture is to reduce violence and to find a new sense of purpose. And as we've begun to see, these two grand projects are closely related.

2 Hope in Dark Times

I do admit that the destructive energy is there, but
it is evanescent, always futile before the creative,
which is permanent. If the destructive one had the
upper hand all sacred ties — love between parents
and child, brother and sister, master and disciple,
ruler and ruled — would be snapped.
— M. K. Gandhi

If public opinion would but frown upon violence, it
would lose all its power.
— Leo N. Tolstoy

As of this writing, hundreds of young people
from North America, Europe and elsewhere
have gone to Central America to protect threat-
ened human rights workers with their presence. Their work is still largely
unknown to the American public — the news media shroud this fascinating experiment in profound silence. Nonetheless, they are there.

Karen Ridd was one of them. In 1989 Karen and four other international volunteers were working with a group called Peace Brigades International (PBI) when they were suddenly arrested by Guatemalan military. Three of the five were Spanish nationals, and they were promptly
deported from Guatemala, leaving Karen, who was Canadian, and her
friend Marcella Rodriguez, who was from Colombia, to face whatever
was coming. Fortunately, Karen had had time to call the Canadian consul
and alert another PBI volunteer who happened to call in at the right

moment. This was some comfort, as was the civility — at first — of the soldiers. But no one from the team had had to face arrest before (to date, no international volunteer has been killed in Central America despite the enormous violence all around them) and from another room Marcella heard the soldiers describing them as "terrorists from the Episcopal church." Their spirits did not improve when the two women, along with other detainees, were loaded onto a truck, taken to an army barracks, blindfolded, and subjected to five hours' interrogation about their alleged connection with the guerilla FMLN while sounds of torture and the sobbing of victims came from nearby rooms. Karen knew that PBI would quickly alert their worldwide network about the arrests, but she also knew that time was short — there was no telling what would happen in that barracks if someone didn't get them out before nightfall.

PBI had in fact activated its worldwide network, and before long hundreds of people were sending faxes to the Canadian and Colombian embassies, calling and sending e-mail messages to their representatives to urge Karen and Marcella's immediate release. All this got no response at all from the Colombian embassy, but Canada brought official pressure on the Guatemalan government, no doubt hinting that their extensive trade relations with Guatemala could be compromised if Karen were not released immediately. Whatever it was that got through to whomever was in charge, Karen found herself walking across the barrack grounds towards a waiting embassy official a few hours later, a free woman. But when the soldiers removed her blindfold inside the barracks she had caught a glimpse of Marcella, face to the wall, a "perfect image of dehumanization." Glad as Karen was to be alive, something tugged at her. Feeling terrible, she made some excuses to the exasperated Canadian Embassy official who had come all the way from Guatemala City to get her, turned and walked back into the barracks, not knowing what would happen to her in there, but knowing it could not be worse than walking out on a friend.

The soldiers were startled, and almost as exasperated. They hand-cuffed her again. In the next room, a soldier banged Marcella's head into the wall and said that some "white bitch" was stupid enough to walk back in there and, "Now you're going to see the treatment a terrorist deserves!" No more mister nice guy. But Karen's gesture was having a strange effect on the men. They talked to Karen despite themselves, and she tried to explain why she had returned. "You know what it's like to be separated from a *compañero.*" That got to them. They released Karen and Marcella and the two women walked out together under the stars, hand in hand.

This story speaks for itself, but it will do no harm to spell out what it says. Karen did something that changed the minds of some unsympathetic, indeed pretty dehumanized soldiers. What was it? Is it something *we* could learn to do? It's as though her very vulnerability put in her hands some kind of force which worked a minor miracle, even though Karen had not counted on it. She had not thought through how the soldiers would react when she walked back into that hellish place. She only knew she could not walk out on a friend.

Events like this are virtually never reported in the mainstream media — nor are, for that matter, what international volunteers have been doing in Central America, Hebron, Haiti, Sri Lanka, Northern Ireland, and elsewhere. The fact is, our usual way of thinking about conflicts offers no ready explanation for such an occurrence. When and if we turn against violence we have bumper stickers that encourage us to "practice random acts of kindness and senseless acts of beauty"; but something is going on here that *isn't* random and senseless. There is a kind of logic to events like this with which we simply haven't reckoned.

In the slowly emerging field of peace research, however, people have begun to piece together the dynamic of such events. One of the foremost peace scholars of the twentieth century, Kenneth Boulding, developed a model toward the end of his long, polymathic career which seems to explain the situation very well. Boulding, a Quaker, distinguished economist, poet, and once president of the prestigious American Academy of Arts and Science, who had already made enormous contributions to peace research, wrote a book toward the end of his life called, *The Three Faces of Power*. Human interchanges are not just carrot or stick, he argues in that book. We get things done by three different kinds of suasion we can exert on those around us: (1) *threat power* (do something I want or I'll do something you don't want, (2) *exchange power* (give me something I want and I'll give you something you want), and (3) *integrative power* (which I would paraphrase, "I'm going to do what I believe is right, and we will end up closer.")

All three kinds play their respective roles in Karen's story — and such a mixture, Boulding is quick to add, is how real life usually works. That the Guatemalan soldiers were using threat power is only too obvious. The Canadian Government also relied on threat of a kind, but they relied more on exchange power since they hinted they would pull out of trade agreements unless they got what they wanted. (In addition to economic trade, a subtler medium of exchange, respect and legitimacy, was no doubt also involved.) But Karen used the third, unfamiliar form called integrative power. We need not be too surprised if we are relatively at a loss to explain how this power works. As Boulding points out, "Threat power is particularly the concern of political scientists; economic power, of economists. . . [but] the study of integrative power seems to belong to no particular discipline."

Let's start our own discipline, then. We can start with this reasoning:

Wherever there is a human need, there is a kind of power, insofar as someone is in a position to supply or withhold that need. One of the strongest needs of the human animal is for *integration*, for acceptance, community, fellowship. In her forthcoming book called *Human Nature — Revised*, biologist Mary Clark points out that all human beings strive for three things above and beyond food, clothing and shelter: (1) *bonding* (unconditional acceptance by other human beings); (2) *autonomy* (freedom of individual behavior); and (3) *meaning* (a sense of purpose in life). I think Clark has done well to put bonding first. William Blake put it beautifully in *The Marriage of Heaven and Hell*: "The bird a nest, the spider a web, man, friendship." No one exists without this need. Even "lower" forms of life exhibit a powerful tendency to form communities, as life scientists are well aware. In fact, long before scientists of the modern kind documented this drive, St. Augustine made it the basis of the peace theory he developed in his monumental classic, *The City of God*. In this passage, which to my knowledge is the first time in Western civilization that peace is made the subject of articulate discussion, Augustine observes that even animals form families and societies of a kind, and he goes on:

> It is even more so with man. *By the very laws of his nature* he
> seems, so to speak, forced into fellowship and, as far as in
> him lies, into peace with every man.

It is by this law of nature that an act like Karen's has power, because she both opened the soldier's eyes to Marcella's humanity, and offered them an escape from their own hostility. It is because of this law that we are always moved by stories of reconciliation, the more so when they come after bitter alienation. Think of former governor George Wallace coming to the reenactment of the Selma-to-Montgomery civil rights march to apologize for his former racism, or, a bit earlier, the *Time* cover photo of Pope John Paul holding the hand of Mehmet Ali Agca, the man who had tried to assassinate him two years earlier. Who doesn't thrill to scenes like this? Even though *Homo sapiens* do an impressive job of hating and demonizing one another, apparently there is still some primal need within us for community, for integration, which we can only smother, not utterly destroy. Nonviolence is the science of appealing to that need.

The human being is, as Aristotle named us, a "community animal" who craves fellowship despite himself or herself. That is why solitary confinement is the worst form of punishment for even the most unsociable of men. And why, conversely, anyone who plucks up the courage to offer an opponent a way out of their conflict can find herself or himself wielding an unexpected power.

What is Violence?

Boulding's "three faces" model can be resolved into a still simpler one of two opposed forces. We can call them, conventionally, violence and nonviolence — but to do so is to invoke words that are less than crystal clear.

The word "violence" comes from *violare* in classical Latin. That is useful, for etymologies often allow us to peer into a time when some things were more innately understood than they are now. *Violare* means "to bear in on with force" and in the classical period it came to mean "injure, dishonor, outrage, violate." Like all important words, "violence" has extended, metaphorical meanings. We speak about "a violent storm" or say "I got a violent shock when my car hit the pothole," but that's not the kind of violence we're concerned with in this book. Even the predatory behavior of animals isn't really that kind of violence; a lion may be very hard on a lamb, but that's how nature works (or one way nature works). The lion does not "dishonor, outrage or violate" the lamb that instinct drives it to kill. It just kills that lamb. Another way of looking at it is, there is no bond between the lion and the lamb that is torn asunder when the predator strikes. Animals have a wide range of emotions, but righteous indignation isn't one of them, so far as we can tell.

Violence as we mean the term is a human phenomenon. We are violent when we injure one another, or any part of the subtly interconnected biosphere — of life. Elevate to the highest degree that sense of sacred connectedness which violence harms and you can say, with French resistance fighter Jacques Lusseyran, "God is life, and everything that does violence to life is against God." Animals compete with and prey on each other, but they do so in a mysteriously balanced, harmonious and ordered way that could go on indefinitely — that is, in a word, sustainable. Not so humans. When we prey on each other, something goes shockingly wrong, and it has led to the devastation of whole societies. In that sense of violating the order of things, only humans can, properly speaking, be violent — or nonviolent.

Now, the concept of violence as injury has also to be limited, in two ways. First, even in the case of human beings, it is not violence when we injure someone or something by accident. The law recognizes that. One person can injure another accidentally and they can remain friends — happens all the time. But if one person injures another purposely, one or both of them is going to have to do some work to erase that injury.

Second, once we understand that violence tears the fabric of life, it follows that the real violence lies not in the act but in the very *intention* to injure, and this is exactly the meaning of the Sanskrit word for violence, *himsa*. Here we have to dip into the science of language for one brief but crucial point. Himsa (the "m" here is a nasal sound as in French *dans*) comes from the root *han*, "to strike, slay." But himsa is thought to be a special form of that root. It may well be what linguists call a desiderative; it means not the act but the *desire* or intention to do the act, in this case injure. The mind is very real, to these ancients. "You have heard how it was said to our ancestors: You must not kill. . . . But I say this to you, that anyone who is angry with his brother will answer for it." (Mt. 5.21f) In fact, we at least pay lip-service to this mind-reality also. Does not the UNESCO Charter state, "War begins in the minds of men"? The point, though, is learning to *use* that perdurable wisdom, so it becomes not just a truism gracing some high-sounding documents but a practiced reality.

All violence arises, then, within the mind. By the same token, the hurt caused by violence can be psychological or spiritual as well as material and physical, which brings us close again to the meaning of the Latin word, "violate, dishonor." The news is both good and bad. Bad because it is disquieting to realize that we can be violent when we're just sitting there, harboring bad thoughts but not hurting anyone physically. This is not particularly comforting — but after all, it is better to be aware of it if it's true. Almost all the approaches to violence we are currently taking are a failure. Most of them, even if they contain the problem over here, make it worse over there. Our approach to crime is to put more and more people in prison (while barely denting the crime rate out on the streets). Our approach to world peace seems to be leading to an endless series of wars. The "war on drugs" is a costly, violent failure. So it's a great relief to get our finger, finally, on the pulse of the problem, even if it turns out that we're holding our own wrist.

In recent years, we have all become aware of one further clarification. To say that violence arises in the mind is not to say that all violence is done with our conscious will. There is a kind of violence we commit without being quite aware of it. In fact, a lot of what we'd have to call violence today arises not from any felt hostility but through passive or even unconscious willingness to take advantage of others. Does the nice shirt that I'm wearing come from a comfortable factory in Wisconsin, or a sweat shop in Thailand? Is that homeless man the price of my company's success or my country's defense spending? Was a rain forest razed somewhere to bring the food I'm looking at right now onto my plate? Exploitation built into a social system is called *structural violence*, a term we owe to another great peace scholar, Johan Galtung. Although structural violence is very widespread today because of the way modern economic systems operate, it probably existed as soon as human beings got organized into complex societies. When the Buddha defined a nonviolent person centuries ago he used the telling phrase, *Na hante, na hanyate.* He or she does not kill *nor cause to kill.* He or she does not consciously cooperate in any system that hurts life.

Even in the case of that violence of which we are not quite aware, however, the key issue is intention. There was a saying in Latin, *Quod ultimum est in executione, primum est in intentione.* "What finally comes out as action was there first in intention." Children growing up in a world that's partly built on structural violence may take a long time to become aware of its real nature, and until they do they may unwittingly benefit at the expense of others. No one would call them violent for doing so. Only when they go on cheerfully benefitting *after* becoming aware of this can they be called in some degree violent — which may be one reason people resist being educated about violence. It would be misleading to call unwitting participation in a wrong system violence; in other words, suppressed awareness is not the same as awareness that has not yet dawned.

All these considerations lie within the very useful definition of violence arrived at by Galtung: violence is *avoidable insult to human needs.* This definition keeps in view the hidden, or "structural" violence that we have just been describing, a violence that makes its way into the institutions of virtually all societies. But it also suggests something important about that or any kind of violence. By putting in that word "avoidable," it suggests that life could be lived without such insults; that in an ideal world all violence could be avoided. This is an important article of faith shared by all those who have believed in the possibility of widespread nonviolence down the ages, not excluding our own time. Accidents happen, conflict is inevitable, disputes will normally arise. But none of this necessarily causes *violence.* Even conflicts and disputes can be creatively resolved without violence. Violence is an unnecessary evil.

Here again the model of integrative power can be helpful. At a deep level, whoever commits real violence, i.e. nurses an intention to harm someone, suffers from the very intention — never mind the consequences of any resultant action. Violence cuts both ways. If the web between two parties is torn, both parties feel the tear. Thus violence is a question for psychologists before it becomes a question for lawmakers or criminologists, and St. Augustine, once again, who knew the mind as perhaps few

others in the Western world, put it beautifully: "Imagine someone thinking that his *enemy* could do him as much harm as his own *enmity* that he
harbors against him."

In our modern culture, perhaps the best way we can appreciate this
principle is in the extensive medical evidence on what it does to our health
to hate, to be unable to forgive. Violence, by any meaningful definition, is
a phenomenon that cries out to be repaired, something that in an ideal
world human beings would not do to one another — or to the environment or any of its living inhabitants. More important, it is something
they'd be very likely to stop doing if we could somehow make them aware
that they're hurting themselves along with their victim. Keep this thought
in the back of your mind, because it's the key to an entirely new way to
deal with violence — which means it's the key to the new world we're
looking for.

Three Lenses

Some years ago, the city of Walnut Creek, California ran into an
intractable problem that is still coming up in many American communities. A gay teacher was under attack by parents who had a somewhat
fundamentalist outlook. They did not want their children influenced by
such a "sinful" person. Unfortunately for that community, the people
who wanted to defend this man's right to teach and the people who wanted
him out of the classroom could not communicate with each other. They
were using incompatible models to characterize him and think about
what was at issue. His defenders saw it as a question of the teacher's civil
rights, while the irate parents saw it as a question of the religious well-
being of their kids. In other words, the former were using a *political model*
and the latter a *religious* or a *moral model*. This is a very common kind of
dilemma today, and it can cause immense confusion.

It's clear that the way we think about violence is similarly impractical. One reason for this is that we use the logic of violence itself in our

attempts to control violence: the "war on drugs," the "war on crime" —
one researcher even referred to modern medicine as a "war on bugs." All
this has led to virtually no useful measures for making violence a progressively smaller part of our life.

What we need is a different logic, or, as the Walnut Creek example
suggests, a different window or frame of reference in which to think
about violence. I'm going to outline three such windows, or "lenses" (to
use a term from Howard Zehr's important 1990 book, *Changing Lenses*):
the one that's most commonly in use, a better one that's coming into use,
and the one that I think we should use.

I. The Moral Model. The way we think about violence today is
closely akin to the moral model invoked by the distraught parents in the
Walnut Creek school. We tend to think of violence as a sin (something
that violates the laws of God) or a crime (something that violates the
laws of society, of man). Unfortunately, we no longer have a generally
agreed-upon concept of what "sin" or even "crime" means. How do we
define what's moral — those of us who still call upon the term?

In modern culture human relationships seem to be sliding more and
more into a state of raw competition, more and more of the interactions
between us are thought of in a win/lose framework. As the definition of
what is legal becomes increasingly a matter of negotiation by lawyers, our
agreed-upon concept of natural law, that which formal legislation is supposed to represent, is steadily weakening. The mass media are a bad influence in this unfortunate process. As far as the media are concerned, a
legal process, like the political process itself, is construed as a power struggle
between the participants — and, secondarily, entertainment for the general public. "Mafia Murder Trial Provides Colorful Theater for New York-
ers," ran a recent headline of the *San Francisco Chronicle*.

Looking on violence as a crime or sin when both crime and sin have
become so vague has led to some unfortunate confusion. Recall Jacque
Ellul's observation about the present age, the age in which we have be-

come conscious of violence in a new way. We have now an unparalleled opportunity to take a great step forward in human culture, by taking advantage of this new awareness to *deal* with violence at last. Instead, almost the opposite has happened. Violence has become something we *want.* "The new action thriller which crash-lands at Bay Area theaters has all the modern virtues," said a *San Francisco Chronicle* review on June 6, 1997. And what were those virtues? "*Violence,* volume, stupidity . . ." — all those good things. While this review may have been tongue-in-cheek, check any video store or mass-market bookshelf. You'll find that "violent" now means "thrilling" — the sense of right and wrong is gone.

Using the moral model as a window on violence can also intensify rather than mask the nature of violence — and here the problems involved are, if anything, more serious. Since we still do have a strong emotional response to violence, to label a person or group as "violent" can bring down on them the strongest feelings of hatred and righteous indignation. The next step is to slap polarizing labels on them, like "impure" or "guilty," which make us quickly forget that those people are, after all, human beings like ourselves. This is scapegoating, and although it can arise as a knee-jerk reaction to violence it is, ironically, itself a dangerous form of violence. It is no coincidence that the architects of the Holocaust deliberately used images of dirt and impurity to put their intended victims beyond reach of human sympathy, and they have had many imitators.

When my book *America Without Violence* appeared in 1982 I was interviewed on a major radio station late at night in New York. I was shocked at the reaction of the listeners. It seemed that every caller was blaming the violence on his or her own favorite enemy. "You know perfectly well it's the Puerto Ricans." "Have you read the statistics on blacks under twenty-five?" "It's white men that are causing all the violence," and so forth. This is the same mistake the Berkeley students were making when they focused on hate crimes against Asians, only here it's the victimizers instead of the victims who are being singled out in groups, as though groups, not violence, were the issue. Since that decade, far from taking the necessary steps in our thought from the manifestation to the cause (and no one's denying that some groups of people commit more violence than others, for whatever reason) a more tragic category has been singled out for blame. "It's the teenagers." Racism is bad enough; but if we've reached the point of scapegoating our children, then our approach to violence is going to cost us more than the malady. It could cost us our civilization.

The failures of the moral window are particularly obvious in the area of criminal justice, and we'll be revisiting this area in chapter four. What I propose to do now is just close the moral window altogether. We don't need to find out who is to blame for all the violence; we just need to find out how to make it stop.

2. The Medical Model. A newer model that has been much more effective is the *medical model.* In this way of thinking, violence is not unlike a disease, and peace is a kind of health. This is probably a more accurate way to think about violence than to construe it as a sin or crime. Note how readily medical people are able to cut to the chase and not be caught up in the particulars about violence here in the first issue of *Medical Abstracts Newsletter* for 1993 (their emphasis).

> It is the leading cause of lost life in the U.S. today. It kill
> more people than AIDS or cancer. It has shown no signs of
> cure. It is *violence* . . .

Violence as disease is not a new idea, of course. Augustine made good use of it in developing his famous definition of peace as "the harmony that comes from the ordered relationship of all parts" of, for example, the body, but most of us will remember how, during the antinuclear era, the peace movement was carried to unprecedented heights by doctors, and, in particular, one very eloquent and caring doctor, Helen

Caldicott. What made Physicians for Social Responsibility and its European counterparts so effective was not just the fact that doctors have a deserved authority with most of us, nor even that the extension of their role in preserving people's health one by one to keeping them alive by the millions is only natural. It was the vivid image of the war system as dysfunctional — sick, if you will. That made it much easier for millions of people to work against this system, including many who had uncritically thought of war as highly patriotic and a form of "defense." That new lens made antiwar activists who had been stridently protesting war-preparations quite a bit more effective, since it gave people something sensible rather than recriminatory to do about it. Politicians are people, this model reminded us. If you reason with them you *can* get them to understand you; while as long as you're pointing fingers of blame at them they will only shrink away and harden their stance.

The power of the medical window became very real one summer day in 1993 in the emergency room of a Los Angeles hospital. A distraught woman entered the hospital intending to gun down a nurse she believed was having an affair with her estranged husband. She found the woman she was looking for and shot but did not kill her. The wounded nurse lurched down to the emergency room with her assailant in pursuit. ER nurse Joan Black was on duty. She had heard the code signal that a person with a gun was loose in the hospital moments before her fellow nurse was wounded, and then the woman, .38 in hand, burst through the door. Black, 62, reacted with the instincts of an experienced medical person. "I put my arm around her and started talking to her. She kept saying that she didn't have anything to live for, that this woman had stolen her family. I kept saying, 'You're in pain. I'm sorry, but everybody has pain in their life. . . . I understand and we can work it out.'" (The story about the shooting was front page news; nurse Black's heroic saving of the situation appeared only in a later section. What can you do?) Talking steadily like this, and in the meantime pushing down the gun every time the woman tried to kill herself with it, Black finally calmed her down.

The classicist in me has to point out something here before we go on. Nurse Black instinctively followed, point for point, the pattern laid down by the ancients for calming distraught or inconsolable people. First of all you identify with, rather than blame them. ("You're in pain. . . . I'm sorry.") Then you give them some detachment by reminding them of the first thing we all lose sight of when we're in such a state — that what they're going through is a universal human experience. ("Everybody has pain in their life." Remember Hamlet's uncle: "You must know your father lost a father, That father lost, lost his . . .") You can also remind him or her that the unbearable moment they are experiencing has got to pass, and finally exhort them to snap out of it. ("We can work it out.") The fact that nurse Black was inspired to deliver this perfect imitation of a classical *consolatio* at such a moment illustrates something about the universality of human dynamics that we'll make use of later.

Joan Black must be a great ER nurse. Certainly here she succeeded in quelling an extremely violent situation partly because she *was* a nurse, and on duty in an emergency room. All this allowed her to see the situation quite differently than if she had, say, been confronted with a gunman in a dark alley. She did not see a criminal coming through the door, but a patient. She literally says, "I saw a sick person and had to take care of her." The newspapers almost entirely missed the point. Always wedded to a model of violence which hides the dynamic of events like this, they were quite ready to catch a remark of hers which is completely misleading. "That was probably the stupidest thing I've done in my life." But that's the newspapers' problem, and not ours, as long as we don't believe in them. Joan Black was a hero and she was able to do an extraordinary thing in the face of violence. Why? Because she saw the perpetrator as a patient, a person in trouble, not a criminal.

Three thousand miles away in another emergency room, a medical student named Deborah Prothrow-Stith had a rather different epiphany. This time, she was able to grasp an insight and hold onto it — in fact to turn it into an institution. It happened one night after she stitched up a young man who had just been wounded in a knife fight. While she was getting him ready for release he turned to her and said, "Don't go to bed. The guy who did this to me is going to be in here in about an hour." It was partly meant in jest, partly male bravado; but Prothrow-Stith, a medical person and the mother of a teenage son, pondered what he had said. The futility, the absurdity of patching up the victims of violence, without doing anything about the causes, was borne in on her. It was against everything she was learning in medicine: an ounce of prevention is worth a pound of cure, for the disease of violence as for any other. Later, when Prothrow-Stith went on to become the Massachusetts Commissioner of Public Health, she founded an education and mediation program to prevent teen violence with a curriculum that has been followed in 325 cities in forty-five states. She puts it well.

> The mission in the criminal justice system is to establish blame when there has been a violent episode and to institute the punishment. That's an appropriate mission but it's not a preventive mission. So what we advocate in [my book] *Deadly Consequences* — and in this movement to look at violence as a health problem — is that we start talking about prevention.

Interestingly, Prothrow-Stith also gave a superb definition of structural violence in this widely-aired interview.

> Quite honestly, if you define violence very narrowly as physical injury, then you limit your understanding. . . . A lack of opportunity, an education system that doesn't work, even a family that doesn't work — those are very violent experiences.

Health and illness are very good analogies for peace and violence. To use them is far more practical than trying to use the concept of crime and punishment, however appropriate that may sometimes feel. Thinking of violence as disease takes blame out of the picture; unless you're George Bernard Shaw, you don't blame people for getting sick. For another, it puts our focus where it belongs, where efficiency and compassion want it to go — on prevention. When you can do something creative that addresses the root causes of violence Prothrow-Stith just cited, deep in the societal and family systems, you are doing something vastly more effective than putting more police on the streets or stronger deadbolts on your front door — something which some health professionals, borrowing a term from conflict scholar John Burton, have called "provention."

3. The Educational Model. Despite the utility of the medical window, I am going to open still a third one. If violence is not a sin but more like a disease, it is even more like a kind of ignorance. I believe that a beloved mystic of modern India, Swami Ramdas, meant it perfectly literally when he said:

> Ignorance is the cause of all quarrel and strife in the world. Ignorance is not a crime. It does not deserve to be condemned, but it has to be removed. And by the power of your love, you can remove ignorance.

This seems to me to sum up the nature — and direct us toward the provention — of violence in a nutshell. To look at violence as a kind of ignorance helps immediately to see wisdom and love as the solution.

Once I was in a heated discussion at an impromptu seminar with a group of journalists in San Francisco. A Berkeley colleague turned to me and said, "OK, what is violence?" and I spontaneously replied, "A failure of imagination." While I'm still not entirely sure what I meant, I think I was groping in my own dim way toward Swami Ramdas's insight. If I don't have the imagination to realize that you and I are one despite our physical separateness and the differences in our outlook on life, what's to prevent me from using violence if I think you're getting in my way? You might almost say that there's a kind of violence already in that very failure to see that we're one — violence to the truth.

Ignorance, as Swami Ramdas implies, can be cured. Failures of imagination can be reversed. Love plays some kind of role in both processes.

OK, What is *Nonviolence*?

My friend Alain Richard and I were commiserating with one another as we sat in an unlikely restaurant in San Francisco just before he went back to his native France after many years' work in this country and around the world. The topic of our commiseration was how unhelpful the word "nonviolence" often is, and how no one has come up with a good substitute. But Alain had found a brilliant way to describe nonviolence without calling it that when he was giving workshops in rural Africa some time back. Forget nonviolence, he told me. "I started off by asking them, 'Has any of you (they were mostly village women) ever used inner, moral power against physical force?' Sure enough, hands shot up. One women offered this story: Her husband used to beat her a lot. Once, though, something snapped inside her, and instead of trying to protect herself she stood up and looked him in the eye and said, 'Why don't you just kill me and get it over with?' He never struck her again."

Everything we've just said about the "shadow side," about violence, is a good preparation, but only that, for the real job that we can tackle now, which is to understand the power that so dramatically changed this woman's husband. Violence is dis-integrative, nonviolence is integrative power. It is, like the intention to harm, first of all a question of mind, and only then an expression of a state of mind in action. And it can be *learned*. It is the implications of that learning process that mainly concern us.

As the Davitz experiment showed, it can be surprisingly easy for people to learn positive, cooperative and even self-sacrificing behavior. This is because, upholders of nonviolence argue, what they're really doing is *un*learning aggressive, competitive and other-sacrificing behavior which has been acquired. When we say that nonviolence can be learned we do not mean that it wasn't there already. It was, but for some reason a lot of the conditioning that makes us social humans today seems to obscure that fact. The conditioning comes later, and can therefore be dislodged relatively easily. The biggest problem with civilization-as-we-know-it (and we shall be coming across this repeatedly) is that it has somehow taken the shadow for the light.

Let me begin by calling on etymology, as I did with violence.

The term nonviolence is barely a century old (unlike the term violence!) having first appeared, to be exact, in 1923. "Nonviolence" serves as a literal — but, as it turns out, misleading — translation of the Sanskrit word *ahimsa*, the negation of *himsa*, "desire, intent to harm." In accordance with what we've already seen, ahimsa would mean "the absence of the desire, or intention to harm." But this negative (the *a-* prefix in Sanskrit is basically the same as in English, cf. "amoral") needs a little explanation. Unlike the situation in English, the "non" word, nonviolence, is as old as its opposite. Ahimsa appears in texts even older than Gandhi's venerable "reference book," the Bhagavad Gita (roughly 200 B.C.E.-200 C.E.). And again unlike the English situation, in Sanskrit, abstract nouns often name a fundamental positive quality indirectly, by negating its opposite. Thus "courage" is conveyed by *abhaya*, which literally means, "non-fear"; or we encounter *akrodha* "non-anger" for kindness, and the Buddha's *avera*, "non-hatred," meaning "love." The reason Ancient India's great thinkers expressed themselves in this apparently oblique way was that phenomena like love, absolute courage, and compassion are primordial things that cannot be fully expressed in fallible, conditioned human language. English does not work this way, with the result that "nonviolence" in English does not really convey the meaning of ahimsa in Sanskrit.

Ahimsa is not really a negative term, as to our ears "nonviolence" decidedly is. Ahimsa suggests, where it is not possible to name directly, something profoundly positive. Ahimsa, a kind of double negative, stands for something so original, so positive, that we cannot quite conceive of it with our minds or capture it with our weak words.

I have put you through all this linguistics because — well, for several reasons. First, because it is humbling that modern languages are still struggling for a word to express everything that was enshrined millennia ago in the word ahimsa. Next, because that ancient term was so far ahead of us in prioritizing the mental dimension of violence/nonviolence. And because, finally, in that misleading translation of ahimsa into an English negative we see the most important misunderstanding of violence, the conceptual obstruction that has held at bay the realization which, according to Ellul, our age needs to make in order to fulfil its promise: the realization that nonviolence, by whatever name, is a positive force that holds the solution to most of our major personal, social and global problems.

Gandhi faced this obstruction from the outset of his career in South Africa. When they first met with his disconcerting new form of resistance, Westerners and Western-educated Indians looked for something at least partly familiar that they could compare it to; it must be like the tax-refusal of "nonconformist" denominations back in England, they mused, and particularly like the Women's Suffrage Movement that was raising eyebrows at that time. There, too, a minority was fighting for its rights without using physical violence — but there, alas, the resemblance ended. The superficial similarity was "apt to give rise to a terrible misunderstanding," Gandhi feared, and it was, ironically, a staunch European friend of the movement whose fate it was to fall into the "terrible misunderstanding" in such a way that Gandhi had no choice but to roundly disabuse him of it, in public. In the pivotal year 1906, when the Indians' resistance had shown its mettle and the white settlers were thoroughly alarmed, this friend, William Hoskens, arranged a meeting of prominent Europeans to hear what the Indians were up to, and at that meeting he introduced Gandhi with the following well-intentioned remarks:

The Transvaal Indians have had recourse to passive resistance
when all other means of securing redress proved to be of no
avail. . . . Numerically, they are only a few. They are weak and
have no arms. Therefore they have taken to passive resistance
which is the weapon of the weak.

A modern nonviolence scholar would wince at this classic mistake.
When he heard it, Gandhiji set aside his prepared speech and contra-
dicted his well-meaning friend point for point. He wanted to make it as
clear as possible that the Indians' movement was different in kind from
that of the suffragists, even though both causes were just and neither
relied on physical violence. First of all, Gandhi explained, "The suffrag-
ist movement did not eschew the use of physical force."

But brute force had absolutely no place in the Indian movement in any circumstance, and . . . no matter how badly they
suffered, the Satyagrahis never used physical force, and that
too although there were occasions when they were in a
position to use it effectively. Again, though the Indians had
no franchise and were weak, these considerations had nothing
to do with the organization of Satyagraha.

As we can see, Gandhiji had already invented a new word for what he
was doing — so misleading are both "nonviolence" and "passive resistance." Satyagraha, or "soul force," as he often paraphrased it, is no double
negative. It literally means "clinging to Truth." It is not the "weapon of
the weak," as Hoskens thought, but the weapon of the strong — for there
is a kind of strength that does not come from numbers or from weapons.
It is in favor of this strength, which some think is even greater, that the
satyagrahi (a practitioner of Satyagraha) renounces the use of physical
force, voluntarily and on principle. Later, back in India, instead of being

a minority of 13,000, the resisters would be almost 300 million people, held down by a mere hundred and fifty thousand British colonials. The Indians still used Satyagraha, by choice.

Yet to this day, almost a century after Hoskens' gaffe, we go on repeating it — with no Gandhi around to correct us. A well-known journalist declared recently that Israeli settlers in Hebron, fully one-quarter of whom are heavily armed and fanatically ideological, are using "Gandhian tactics: i.e., passive resistance." He did not know, and most of his readers would not know, that nonviolence and passive resistance can be as different as nonviolence and violence. Satyagraha is not passive and you are not being "Gandhian" when you are full of hatred but happen — for the moment — to be keeping your finger off the trigger. One could quote innumerable examples of this confusion. They would all be laughable if they were not so damaging.

It's often easier to see such confusion on a larger scale. I've mentioned the Dayton accords that were supposed to bring peace to ex-Yugoslavia but contained not a word about what was causing the wars in the region, namely ethnic hatreds stirred up by nationalistic politicians through state television. But at least scholars recognize this today as "negative peace." One of the most egregious examples of this type of confusion was greeted by well-deserved derision by antinuclear organizations when it was put forward, in all seriousness, by the Department of the Navy. They proposed to define peace as "perpetual pre-hostility." This is peace? Who wants it? (Can you imagine Jesus, his hand upraised in blessing, saying, "My perpetual pre-hostility I give unto you?")

But it's just as absurd to think that nonviolence is only the absence of (physical) violence as it is to think that peace is only some kind of interlude between wars. Once again, it is trying to catch a shadow. Don't we want to turn around and see what's casting it?

When I wrote *America Without Violence* back in 1982, the idea of "nature red in tooth and claw" had a firm grip on popular imagination and I had an uphill battle trying to show that the picture painted by certain popularizers of ethology (the science of animal behavior) was an unhappy exaggeration. Only a few scientists and philosophers, like Ashley Montagu and Mary Midgley, were trying to correct what Midgley called this "swashbuckling" view that nature was a violent place and the human being is a puppet pulled by that nature's strings. That has begun to change. Shortly after my book appeared UNESCO convened a seminar of some of the world's most distinguished behavioral scientists to make a public statement on innate aggression. Unheralded, but crucial, the resulting "Declaration of Seville," released in 1986, pilloried the popular view that a complex behavior like human aggression could be programmed by our genes and was therefore ineradicable.

This is not to say that the general run of behavioral scientists — not to mention the general public — would easily give up the "swashbuckling" image. The riptide of cynicism within our present culture pulls many back into the sea of hopelessness just when we have a chance to get up onto dry land; but here and there some scientists are starting to turn that tide.

One day in 1975, about a decade before Seville would appear, the Dutch primatologist Frans de Waal had a career-changing breakthrough in the Arnhem zoo when he suddenly realized that his chimpanzees had an extensive system of reconciliation behaviors, which scientists had never studied.

> Fires start, but fires also go out. Obvious as this is, scientists concerned with aggression, a sort of social fire, have totally ignored the means by which the flames of aggression are extinguished. We know a great deal about the causes of hostile behavior in both animals and humans, ranging from hormones and brain activity to cultural influences. Yet we know little of the way conflicts are avoided — or how, when

they do occur, relationships are afterward repaired and normalized. As a result, people tend to believe that violence is more integral to human nature than peace.

This revelation sounds familiar to anyone working on human violence. The thought that came to me when I read it was how, at a time when five million teenagers were signed up for volunteer service jobs in their communities, and two teenage boys committed a particularly repellant murder, guess who got the coverage.

The important thing to remember is, whatever model we use to think about human potential, whatever we believe we are, will tend very strongly to be self-fulfilling. Not to know that nonviolence is possible, or to think that it's only the province of a few hard-pressed activists on some ragged social fringe, is to be resigned to the ever-increasing violence in our culture, and therefore condemned to endure it without remission. To know that nonviolence is possible, to know that it's not a non-something but a force grounded in nature and exampled in history, is to begin getting our culture back on course.

To say that nonviolence is possible means two things, and both are important. The first is that we have it in us to *be* nonviolent, to "offer Satyagraha," as Gandhians put it, even under tough circumstances. The second is that when we do, it "works." It will become clear why I put "works" in quotation marks later, but let me make some preliminary observations about how nonviolence helpfully affects those around us — or ranged against us.

There is a remarkable bit of evidence from the foundational Satyagraha of our time, Gandhi's great first "experiment with truth," designed to recover the stolen dignity of the Indian community of South Africa. This is from a secretary to General Jan Christian Smuts, head of the South African Government in the Transvaal and Gandhi's chief adversary in this struggle, and it allows us to glimpse what it feels like to be offered Satyagraha by committed, well-trained activists.

> I do not like your people, and do not care to assist them at
> all. But what am I to do? You help us in our days of need.
> How can we lay hands upon you? I often wish that you took
> to violence like the English strikers, and then we would know
> at once how to dispose of you. But you will not injure even
> the enemy. You desire victory by self-suffering alone . . . and
> that is what reduces us to sheer helplessness.

As Midgley says, nature has to be green a long time before she is red. If we read between the lines of this testimonial (and there are similar things on record from the Franco-Belgian invasion of the Rhineland, some twenty years later, and from other events) we can sense something quite compelling at work that we might readily call an appeal to something deep and perhaps not normally visible in human nature. Gandhi's own explanation for the power of such an appeal constitutes, I think, one of the most insightful descriptions of nonviolence ever made.

> What Satyagraha does in such cases is not to suppress reason
> but to free it from inertia and to establish its sovereignty over
> prejudice, hatred, and other baser passions. In other words, if
> one may paradoxically put it, it does not enslave, it compels
> reason to be free.

Talk about an educational model! Any teacher will tell you that this is the kind of education we dream of, in which the student doesn't just learn some facts, doesn't just learn how to put facts together, but awakens to a new realization. It is more a growth experience than learning only with the head, and after *this* kind of learning one does not go back to sleep.

I once had a friend who smoked three packs a day. Bill knew — with his head — all about the effects of smoking on his health, but he somehow went right on smoking. Several times he tried without success to stop. Then one night he had a dream that he was walking through a churchyard. As his dream eye moved over the tombstones, one epitaph caught his attention and he found himself zooming in on it:

HERE LIES BILL.
QUIT SMOKING AT LAST.

He never lit up again.

I submit that a successful nonviolent episode also works at this pre-conscious level. The Guatemalan soldiers suddenly and — as Gandhi implies, and Smuts's secretary confesses — almost in spite of themselves were allowed to see Marcella not as a thing tied to a chair, a victim, but as a person, because of Karen Ridd's act of extreme caring for her, and the brilliant connection she made between that concern of hers and their own comradely feelings for one another — their *compañeros*. Her courage, her love, and her assumption that they, too, were human beings capable of such feelings were the ingredients of her transformative effect on the men, her magic waking potion.

This kind of awakening, this rehumanization, is education of the highest kind, and it is the kind the nonviolent actor aims at. As we'll see from many following examples, nonviolence is a whole-being experience, which has much more long-lasting effects than the otherwise more dramatic results sometimes obtained by threat power. When the German ranks broke in July of 1918, French infantrymen were heard to mutter at the fleeing enemy, *"Ils reviendront."* They'll be back. How right the seasoned soldiers were, much more right, as we know to our devastating cost, than the giddy celebrations of the triumphant world, which only sobered up when, twenty years later, in a hail of shredded treaties, they came back all right, with a vengeance.

Any act of coercion must produce an equal and opposite reaction. In his cell on death row in Georgia State Prison, Brandon Astor Jones saw the following message, literally a handwriting on the wall, left by a previous inmate of that cell: "I will act the way I am treated, so help me God." Jones recalls, "Suddenly a chilling fear of — and for — society engulfs me as I remember the poignant pencil message scrawled on the wall," in cell thirty-eight.

As Hannah Arendt observed, "The practice of violence, like all action, changes the world, but the most probable change is to a more violent world."

Real nonviolence, by contrast, rarely has a backlash, because if it's real nonviolence it does not operate by coercion. It operates by persuasion, often a kind of deep persuasion that moves people below the conscious level. "Compelling reason to be free," or as Gandhi puts it elsewhere, "moving the heart," is qualitatively different from merely forcing others by some form of punishment or sanction. Since the opponent has changed willingly, he or she is not looking for an opportunity to get back at you. When Satyagraha works it doesn't just change one party's position, it changes the *relationship* between parties. Once they have seen the situation from our point of view, those who once were our opponents move closer to us in spirit. This is integrative power. It is apparently no mean force, for Karen's courage did something that the entire government of Colombia was unable or unwilling to do. That's a lot of power! Something wakes up in a Karen Ridd or a Gandhi — or you and me — and that something is going to change people. It is not something learned with our intellect (though the intellect can later help us understand it) but heart-knowledge. And one of its characteristics is that it communicates itself on the same "gut level" to onlookers.

> [Martin Luther] King started from the essentially religious
> persuasion that in each human being, black or white, whether
> deputy sheriff or manual laborer or governor, there exists,
> however tenuously, a certain natural identification with every

other human being; that, in the overarching design of the universe which ultimately connects us all together, we tend to feel that what happens to our fellow human beings in some way also happens to us, so that no man can continue to debase or abuse another human being without eventually feeling in himself at least some dull answering hurt and stir of shame. Therefore, in the catharsis of a live confrontation with wrong, when an oppressor's violence is met with a forgiving love, he can be vitally touched, and even, at least momentarily, reborn as a human being, while the society witnessing such a confrontation will be quickened in conscience toward compassion and justice.

Revisiting Science and History

We have now begun to see some of the rather deep implications of the educational model as the approach of choice for reducing — who knows, perhaps some day eliminating — violence. It is in this model that one can most easily grasp the key fact that nonviolence is fundamentally a kind of *force*. Gandhi, among others, would use that kind of language from his earliest period.

Power is of two kinds. One is obtained by fear of punishment, and the other by acts of love. Power based on love is a thousand times more effective and permanent than the one derived from fear of punishment.

Or again,

Sanctions are of two kinds: one, physical force, and two, soul force — Satyagraha. Physical force is nothing compared to the power of truth.

Today science itself is learning to speak another language. The mind-boggling discoveries of "new physics" are widely felt to hold deeper significance for what we think the world is than any conceptual breakthrough in recorded history, and the implications for areas beyond the physical world (for one of the major breakthroughs has been to breach that barrier between the material and other worlds) are intriguing but far from understood. As this new language has slowly made its way from the minds of physicists to the world at large, it has given us a new and promising vocabulary to describe the nature and the effectiveness of nonviolence, which was rather difficult to account for in the "hard" language of Newtonian objects. The noted criminologist Harold Pepinsky is one who has taken advantage of the new, more powerful vocabulary. (Where he says "responsiveness" I would say nonviolence.)

> Violence and responsiveness operate by the same principles at
> all levels, from the interpersonal to the international. Every
> human being . . . is at once the subject and the object of both
> violent and responsive energy. Crosscurrents of violence and
> responsiveness run constantly in all of us, and help to
> account for perversity and unanticipated behavior at any
> given level.

Whatever kind of power or forces we are speaking about here, we human beings experience them as a deep choice which is really supremely simple — and here Pepinsky uses more conventional language. "From moment to moment, it is a profoundly religious choice whether to commit to violence or to democracy."

Whether we use the scientific or the religious vocabulary, Pepinsky's insight brings out a perplexity: why is it that we generally remain so unaware of nonviolence? If it is a moment-to-moment reality, should we not be talking about it cogently and often? Should it not be common fare in history and science, among other venues?

I'm not sure I have an answer to that question. Sometimes we are
better at perceiving what are *not* moment-to-moment realities, just as it
was hard to see the Milky Way because we're part of it. The ancient
Greeks, that most inquisitive people, discussed how to wage war and manage slaves at great length, but they never discussed war or slavery as such,
or for that matter economics, or the position of women. Whatever may
be the reason that the history of nonviolence is just beginning to be
written and that its theory is just beginning to be devised, it was a galling
frustration for Gandhi from the earliest years. He knew by the time he
wrote his classic 1909 manifesto, *Hind Swaraj* or *Indian Home Rule,* that
what he was up against was more than an empire; it was nothing less than
what we would call today an outworn, inadequate paradigm. "History"
as we knew it was constitutionally unable to help.

> The fact that there are so many men still alive in the world
> shows that it is based not on the force of arms but on the
> force of truth or love. . . . Little quarrels of millions of
> families in their daily lives disappear before the exercise of
> this force. Hundreds of nations live in peace. History does
> not and cannot take note of this fact. History is really a
> record of the interruption of the even working of the force
> of love or the soul. . . . History, then, is a record of the
> interruptions of the course of nature. Soul-force, being
> natural, is not noted in history.

Those are very sobering words, which anyone who has tried to get
the press to cover a nonviolent event can verify. I would like to mention
another example like that of the unreported teenagers doing volunteer
service to their communities. During the 'sixties a day-long student demonstration at Columbia was disrupted for exactly one minute by a fracas
of some sort, very possibly caused by outsiders and even *provocateurs.* That
evening on the network news exactly one minute was dedicated to report-

ing on the students' demonstration. Guess which one? 1909-1969 — nothing changed. The press was still doing this, albeit with a slight budge of difference, in Seattle in 1999. How many people died, I wonder, while the learning curve lay there, flat as a Kansas prairie?

Yes, news media sometimes suppress stories of corruption in high places; that is the political dimension. In the cultural dimension, they virtually *always* suppress stories about nonviolence. I wonder whether the latter suppression, which is more unconscious, isn't hurting us more in the long run.

In any case, the cultural dimension is a paradigm that embraces all aspects of human knowledge, and for a long time now it's been embracing them with only one arm. Some years ago, when I was serving as a dean at Berkeley I got a call from a graduate student who was looking for some leads on aggression among primates. No scientist myself, I was already known around campus for my strange interest in violence and aggression and this student had been sent my way by a behavioral scientist at the University. There was something odd about our conversation, and I was shocked when I realized what it was: he had not the foggiest idea that the theory of innate aggression was controversial. He just assumed — his mentors led him to assume — that our primate cousins behave with raw aggression, competition and win/lose struggle, period, though as Gandhi observed, if nature was set up to work that way it would not have lasted very long. Now we have de Waal:

> I speak from years of frustration with the literature on human behavior. . . . Except for reports on preschool children and an occasional anthropological account, I am unaware of data in this area. . . . I recently asked a world-renowned American psychologist, who specializes in human aggression, what he knew about reconciliation. Not only did he have no information on the subject, but he looked at me as if the word were new to him.

Traces of the Future

A few years after the execution of Jesus, in 39 C.E. to be exact, the emperor Caligula conceived the insane idea of having a statue of himself as incarnate Zeus installed in the great Temple in Jerusalem. To Caligula, for whom excesses in the pursuit of egotism were no vice, this must have seemed a wonderful idea; but for once it was going to blow up in the imperial face. As his Syrian legate, Petronius, advanced on Jerusalem to carry out the disastrous order, people of all kinds and stations began flooding into the capital — men, women and children — collecting together in their alarm from cities, villages and farms from the whole area west of Galilee. They came without weapons in their hands, some of them came holding emblems of allegiance to the empire; but they told Petronius in no certain terms that this sacrilege could not be allowed. Petronius, of course, threatened to unleash his troops on them. They replied that they were perfectly willing to die rather than see such an outrage to their religion.

Petronius, no particular friend of the Jews, was nonetheless at a loss how to handle this unarmed resistance. Unable to persuade them, and loath to massacre them wholesale (something that legates had done enthusiastically with more conventional uprisings), he backed down and took the risk of writing to Rome to make some excuses for stalling the emperor's less-than-brilliant scheme. Caligula, true to form, immediately sent orders for Petronius' execution. But at this point fate intervened. Caligula was assassinated, which saved Petronius, and, for now, the Jewish religion in its homeland.

This successful Satyagraha, however much it took Petronius unawares, was not an isolated occurrence. Apparently there was something in Jewish culture at that period that brought out this kind of response by masses of people even though the "normal" kind of resistance, violent resistance, was not ruled out and would finally prevail, with disastrous results. John Crossan finds no less than seven popular uprisings of this very different type between 4 and 65 C.E., and reports that "all . . . were nonviolent, all had very specific objectives, and four out of the seven achieved those objectives without loss of life."

Now that's history. If nonviolence is a law, as we have been suggesting, it should have left traces all over the historical record. And we find — now that the bias toward violence is beginning to relax — that it did. Its history, more forgotten, more overlooked even than the history of women's experience (with which it is in several ways interconnected), is beginning to be recovered. I am thinking not only of historians of nonviolence such as Peter Brock, Thomas Weber and Staughton and Alice Lynd, but of mainstream historians like John Crossan, who are beginning to show greater sensitivity to the role played by organized nonviolence in the stream of human events. This is an encouraging development. My whole object is to elevate nonviolence from that tiny, specialized field and show that it is the concern not of activists, not of the downtrodden, but of everyone. It is the heritage not of a few rare scholars but all of us. It is something absolutely everyone can use, and if we want not just to reduce a particular type of crime or protect some particular victims but get *violence* out of our path, it is probably the only thing we can use.

If we put the Temple Statue Satyagraha alongside the much smaller action of Karen Ridd (smaller in terms of how many people were involved), we see that the same driving force lay behind them, and we can understand why many have not hesitated to call that force love — meaning not the affect, the emotion that we usually call love, but a self-sacrificing devotion such as Karen had for her friend and her cause, which was so strong that it overcame her fear for her own life, just as the Jewish masses' intense love for their religion and culture caused them to put their own lives without hesitation at the mercy of the Roman swords. And this force, for which love seems to be the best term available, is always there in human consciousness, though often the surface of events, particularly in times of pessimism like our own, does a good job of concealing it.

So nonviolence is law, not luck. Satyagraha is not hit-or-miss. There are undoubtedly, as Pepinsky says, elements of "perversity" and surprise outcomes when we're dealing with something so subtle as a "living force." That does not mean that we can't learn more about that force and begin using it more systematically. Because a computer goes down, for reasons known only to itself, that doesn't mean there is no such thing as electromagnetic energy or that we'll never succeed in putting it to work. Even though we can't always predict exactly how a nonviolent intervention will turn out on the visible surface of things, we can still deal with nonviolence exactly as we would a force of nature. In fact, nonviolence *is* a force of nature — only it happens to be a force of human nature, which is the trickiest kind. We human beings are, as science writer Louise Young puts it, "complex, volatile and impressionable." But that does not mean that no laws govern our behavior. Or that only negative ones do.

> The message that comes down to us from Easter Island is the way violence breeds more violence. Acts of cruelty become progressively easier to commit when they are reinforced by example and supported by tradition. On the other hand, acts of kindness and compassion can be reinforced in a civilized society. Human nature is complex, volatile, and impressionable. Capable of both good and evil, it can be influenced by life experiences. An education in violence uncovers the beast in the human nature.

And an education in *non*violence? We have the pleasure of exploring that right now.

3 No Power to Describe: The Nonviolent Moment As Peak Experience

Either I don't give in to my rage, which means
going crazy . . . or I give in to it, which means I
go to jail.
— Franklin Smith, American teenager

When my spiritual teacher was still living in India, on the Nilgiri Hills, he had a friend who was very much like himself: a compassionate, sensitive nature with strong feelings about justice and fairness. One morning the two of them were walking through the bazaar and came upon a villager with a caged bear. The cage was so small that the poor beast could hardly turn around; it seemed to Sri Easwaran and his friend to be crying out for help with its eyes. They walked off without speaking. Later that day, Easwaran went to call on his friend and found him trembling with anger. "I'm going to take my gun to the bazaar," he burst out. "I'm going to set that bear free, and shoot anyone who tries to stop me. "

"Wait a minute," Easwaran put in hastily. "Hold on just a bit. Let me see what I can do."

First he went around to the owner to try to reason with him. It turned out the man, a simple villager, was from his own state of Kerala, so it wasn't hard to broach the subject after chatting a while in their native language. "Look here, don't you think that creature is suffering in such a small cage?"

"Do you think I like to keep him penned up like that?" he explained. "But what can I do? A new cage would cost me more than a month's earnings."

"Would you be willing to use a decent cage if I could get one built for you?"

"Of course."

Next stop: the local carpenter. By luck, he turned out to be a Kerala man also. Easwaran explained the situation and then came to the point. "You give me your rock-bottom price for a new cage."

"Brother, I have a family to feed; but for you . . ."

Then back to his angry friend. "Suppose we could get a better cage built for so-and-so many rupees and the owner agreed to use it, would you put up the money?"

"Gladly. . . . But that owner will never agree."

"He's already agreed."

Sri Easwaran was as angry as his friend at the sight of the dumb animal's suffering. That's important to realize; but equally important is the key difference in approach. The one saw a path to a solution, and quickly took it, while the other was hung up between the choices with which we're all too familiar, the dilemma that teenager Franklin Smith calls "living a crazy man or dying a sane one." And so he fumed, while Sri Easwaran set about writing a happy ending for the bear, for his friend, the carpenter, the owner — and doubtless himself.

Only a minor event, if you want to look at it that way, but you could also look at it as a parable. How many crises does our government face every year to which it reacts with either violence or capitulation, either imposing sanctions, as with Iraq, or fuming helplessly, as with Bosnia, East Timor or Tibet?

It is all rather reminiscent of the two kinds of student — or rather two kinds of training given to students — in the Davitz experiment. The nonviolent are not people who don't feel anger. On the contrary, they can often prize anger (at least, the kind of anger Sri Easwaran and his friend felt) because first of all that capacity to feel for others, which sometimes means getting angry over what is happening to them, is one of the things that makes us fully human. Second, and more important, that kind of anger is potentially the emotive power to correct the situation. For, in the light of the Davitz experiment, we would not say that Sri Easwaran did what he did in spite of his anger; he did it *with* his anger. By not giving in to his angry impulse to do something to that bear owner but instead looking for a constructive way to help the bear *and* its owner, he unconsciously converted the energy he was feeling as anger into constructive effort. Emotions are power. By themselves, however, they are not necessarily wisdom. Wisdom was for him to choose, which he did. In that choice, blocking one path, he opened the other.

This impromptu "shuttle diplomacy" was actually a fairly obvious solution, when you think about it. The trouble is that when we get angry, most of us can't think about it. Just when we're motivated to do something, we lose sight of the obvious thing to do. As an old proverb has it, "Anger is a wind that blows out the lamp of the mind" — unless our mind is alert enough to set its sails for a better course.

If one still thinks this was a small event, we can think back to one which had exactly the same dynamic, but changed the course of history. I am thinking of the anger Gandhi experienced that fateful night of May 31, 1893, when he was thrown off the train at Pietermaritzburg a week after his arrival in South Africa. This was no minor irritation; according to his own testimony, Gandhiji was furious. That, along with the fact that Gandhi is more than usually articulate about his inner experiences, is what makes this event (among millions of similar insults we human beings endure at one another's hands) such an important window into the dynamics of nonviolent conversion. The first clue as to how he finally succeeded, after a night of bitter reflection, to see the creative way out is that he didn't take the insult personally. He saw in it the whole tragedy of man's inhumanity to man, the whole outrage of racism. Not, "They can't do this to me," but, "How can we do this to one another?" The second clue is the state of his faith in human nature. Already at that period he believed that people could not stay blind to the truth forever. He did not yet know how to wake them up; he just knew they could not want to stay forever asleep. That is how he was able to find the third way between running home to India and suing the railroad company.

Imagine the old-fashioned locomotive carrying this "coolie barrister" from Durban up the mountains to Pretoria, standing at the station in Pietermaritzburg with a good head of steam. You could shovel in more coal and bottle up all that power and pretend it wasn't there until finally it exploded, or you could open the valves and scald everyone on the platform — but surely you would want to use it to drive the train. This is what Gandhiji was going through with all the emotional power built up in him by the accumulated insults he had met since his arrival at the Durban pier. He chose neither to "pocket the insult," as he says, nor to lash out at the immediate source of the pain. He launched what was to become the greatest experiment in social change in the modern world.

Within a few years of this event, Gandhi was working fifteen hours a day, seven days a week at a pace that would frighten even an advanced workaholic. Two secretaries could not keep up with his correspondence, any more than they could keep up with his breathtaking "walks" when he scampered off down the road each evening like a sandpiper. On a lecture tour in Gujarat taking him to two, sometimes three villages a day, he had to remind those arranging his punishing itinerary that he was only mortal. He kept this pace up for over fifty years, taking breaks only when conveniently detained in "his Majesty's prison." What untold damage that energy would have wrought if it had been stifled inside him, as it was in millions of other Indians groaning silently under the heel of an increasingly destructive colonization, or vented as raw violence, as was dangerously close to happening with many of them.

Peak Experience

The escape from violence is often experienced as a kind of strange joy. You pay a price, often a heavy one, but the sudden discovery of the creative path out of the dilemma between fear and anger, capitulation and attack, comes with a great feeling of release. It has been called, as in Buddhism, the "middle way," but the best expression for it comes from someone who experienced it under extreme duress, Andrew Young, who uses the words of an old spiritual, "The Way Out of No Way."

An episode that beautifully illustrates this way occurred during a march for voter's rights in Birmingham in 1964. The marchers, mostly black, were converging on City Hall when they suddenly found their way blocked by a phalanx of police and firemen. They hadn't prepared for this eventuality, and not knowing what else to do, they knelt down to pray. One of those marchers reports what happened next:

> [After a while, we] became "spiritually intoxicated," as another leader described it. . . . This was sensed by the police and fire-men and it began to have an effect on them. . . . I don't know what happened to me. I got up from my knees and said to the cops: 'We're not turning back. We haven't done anything wrong. All we want is our freedom. How do you feel doing these things?' The Negroes started advancing and Bull Connor [the notorious segregationist police commissioner] shouted: "Turn on the water!" But the firemen did not respond. Again he gave the order and nothing happened. Some observers claim they saw the firemen crying. Whatever happened, the Negroes went through the lines.

Political power, we hear, grows out of the barrel of a gun; but in this case the police had all the guns, while the marchers, it would seem, had all the power.

Whether we call it "integrative power" or say this was an "act of love," the experiences of Joan Black in her ER and the marchers confronted with cold authority in Birmingham, different as those experiences are, give a sense of how potent a force is involved here and how many ways it can manifest itself. What happened in Birmingham would seem to be as strong as mob violence, only somehow its reverse. What is the source of this power?

In both cases, the source is an intense fear reaction, *which was not acted on*. It was acted *out*, you could say, the way Sri Easwaran did not act on his angry thoughts but channeled them into creative action. The marchers could have given up and gone home, or they could have attacked the police and firemen. But they didn't want to just react, like automata. They were on a higher plane just then. Shortly before, one of their leaders had said, "We're going to win our freedom, and as we do it we're going to set our white brothers free." They breathed the heady air of freedom, and walked on.

And the firemen whose hands were frozen on the nozzles of their hoses? In them, as Gandhi would put it, their dormant reason was "compelled to be free." A confrontation like this, where feelings are intense on both sides and one of them precipitates an unexpected, successful outcome by a clear and clarifying act of courage, is what one scholar calls the "nonviolent moment." From the point of view of the nonviolent actor, we can call it a peak experience. A peak experience is one in which we are thrown back onto deeper resources by an emotional challenge.

One of the participants in the 1960 sit-ins at cafeterias in the South who was beaten by a racist mob can add for us some very clear insight into the psychology of such an experience. "You feel the pain," he said, "but you don't become bitter, you don't become hostile. . . . You sort of lose yourself. . . . You become involved in the circumstances of others." There is nothing supernatural about being able to carry out this kind of struggle, and there certainly is no guarantee that suffering will not come our way. But like a mountain climber pushing forward into the thin, bitter air of an icy peak, or a ballet dancer pushing her or his body beyond limits, there is such a thing as rising above pain. In the 1996 Olympics Kerri Strug gave her coach "one more jump," landing on a badly sprained ankle, and the whole world winced watching her face twitch at her otherwise perfect landing. There is this difference: the nonviolent actor is deliberately seeking to manifest the pain that others are trying not to see. So in his or her case, the pain is not just something to put up with along the way; it's part of the point.

The fact is, even if you don't stick your neck out in today's world, pain happens. It's very important to remember that when people say nonviolence is risky, that people get attacked when minding their own business and not even dreaming of changing the world, and there is a nonviolent way to respond to that kind of pain as well, as the following story illustrates.

One day in 1992 an eighty-year-old woman was mugged and badly hurt in New York City. Eileen Egan, however, was not your typical mugging victim. She was a lifetime peace activist, a coworker of Dorothy Day and Mother Teresa, who naturally saw things a little differently than most people. A good writer, she was also able to articulate her vision, for example, in a pithy interview in *Parade* magazine two years after the attack, called "I Refuse To Live In Fear." Egan is another insightful spokesperson for the kind of experience we're talking about, and its long-term results. Without using the word "nonviolence," she managed to describe precisely what makes this principle work, and in everyday language we can all follow. She started from the assumption, she tells us, that the worst result of the attack was not her broken hip and ribs but the potential "brokenness" of her fellow-feeling toward the man who attacked her. Like the effect of television violence, the effect of real violence will, if we let it, spread into our feelings toward all our relationships. Egan was extremely concerned not to let that happen. Instead of letting herself get vindictive, then, she tried to make friends with her attacker, staying in touch with him as he wended his way through the prison system, and she describes how it helped her avoid the "posttraumatic stress" that might have followed such a brutal attack. Note that so far *he* doesn't seem much affected by her generosity; but that doesn't prevent her from benefiting from it. She explains,

> I've forgotten about the attack completely. I used to get
> nervous when somebody came up behind me, but that's gone
> now. There are so many more important things to worry
> about in the world.

But wasn't she angry? Of course, but she had something to *do* with her anger, so it left no scars. Remember nurse Black?: "I saw a sick person and had to take care of her." We saw this early on in the case of Karen Ridd, and we'll continue to see it behind every example of real nonviolence we meet. One of the things, then, that accompanies the peak experience, maybe that makes it possible, is a higher vision. In the nonviolent person's outlook even an attacker is a person. He or she will not dehumanize another human, even one who has dehumanized himself.

And that vision has another aspect. Practically all the rescuers who risked their lives to help Jews and other refugees during the Holocaust felt "that what an individual did, or failed to do, mattered;" that "they could influence events . . . [and so] what they did, or failed to do, mattered a great deal." Along with the vision that we are all human together, each of us equally real, there is a sense that human action and your own emotional struggle to act well is very meaningful; you're deeply aware that your efforts have an impact on the world. As Egan says, "If somebody has chosen a life of violence and doesn't get the result he expected from his victim [i.e., fear and anger], it may help him to see life differently." Kindness begets kindness, visions communicate, mood affects mood. Advertisers exploit our impressionability all the time — why can't we? As of 1992, Egan had not seen much of an answering mood from her former assailant. Not a problem. Perhaps he was touched, but not ready to let on. In any case *she* certainly reaped benefits from her attitude, benefits that a professional counselor would be thrilled to impart.

Berta Passweg was a Jewish refugee who had escaped to Egypt. One day, a friend in Alexandria said, "Berta, you should pray for Hitler." Seeing Berta's shock she explained, "Not that he succeeds with his evil intentions, but that God changes his mind." When Berta was finally able to do this, she found that "I don't think it had any effect on Hitler, but it had an effect on me. . . . All hate and bitterness against the Germans had just vanished and I could meet and talk with them without resentment."

For Berta Passweg and Eileen Egan, unlike Joan Black or Karen Ridd, the violence had already happened. In the former cases we are talking about healing, not preventing, violence — healing and not letting it spread. We are also talking about an individual rather than a group, compared to the Freedom Riders or the Birmingham marchers. These would seem to be incidentals that don't affect the basic principle or the way the peak experience feels and works: either way, purpose overrides pain.

I mentioned that we can see the same dynamic in groups and in individuals. Yet it is important to start with the individual, rather than the big march or the strike, even though most people associate nonviolence with group actions. Actors can, of course, get swept up in a wave of group enthusiasm, but the real source of nonviolent power is still coming from within them, and neither they nor we should lose sight of that. Groups don't have emotions, only individuals do.

The founding moment of Satyagraha, in my view, is the famous oath taken in the Empire Jewish Theater of Johannesburg on September 11, 1906, when a packed audience of Indians swore not to obey laws that were about to be passed depriving them of their basic human dignity. Gandhiji's explanation of the oath's meaning for each one in that vast crowd sheds light on the roots of its power in the individual.

It is quite unlikely, but even if everyone else flinched leaving
me alone to face the music, I am confident that I would never
violate my pledge.

He asked each one of them to "search their hearts" and take the
pledge only if it were really a matter between himself and God, notwithstanding what anyone else or the group as a whole would do. In other
words, though the oath-taking was to be done *en masse* it was not a mass
action; it was a summation of individual actions. That was to remain its
sustaining power.

Eighty years later, Cardinal Jaime Sin would say this about the huge
"people power" uprising in the Philippines that dislodged Ferdinand
Marcos.

It was amazing. It was two million independent decisions.
Each one said, in his heart, 'I will do this,' and they went out.

Since violence and nonviolence come about subtly, long before they
are seen in outward action, it should not be too surprising if certain traits
of character or norms of a whole culture are causing violence without
our being aware of it. Our modern culture has quite a few of these, and
one of them is the way "we've started to understand every human encounter as a symbolic clash of group interests," as writer Louis Menand
points out. "Violence can be talked about in the abstract, but violence,
like sex, never occurs in the abstract. . . . Groups are essentially imaginary.
Souls are real, and they can be saved, or lost, only one at a time."

There is a certain dehumanization inherent in the temptation to see
people as a group — be it a corporation, a state, a race, even a gender —
instead of seeing them as individuals. In nonviolence, at any rate, you
never do this. How could you? For "soul-force" you need souls. In a
group act of soul-force numbers can be handy, but they're never essential.
"In Satyagraha it is never the numbers that count," Gandhiji said. "Strength

of numbers is the delight of the timid. The valiant of spirit glory in fighting alone."

Developing Nonviolence: Making the Moment Last

A few years before Karen Ridd's team got to Guatemala, Sue Severin, a Marin County, California health educator, found herself so frustrated and angry over the terror imposed on Nicaraguan villagers by the Reagan-era policy of "low-intensity conflict" that she set aside her career and volunteered for a highly dangerous project: to join a faith-based citizens group going down to document terrorist activity along the Honduran border. It was an effective way of converting her anger to useful action and, like many nonviolent projects, it led further than she anticipated. It was on this mission that Sue and the other North American team members stumbled onto the power of *nonviolent interposition,* or more specifically the technique that is now called *protective accompaniment.* Wherever they went, particularly during their longish stay in the formerly besieged village of Jalapa, there were no Contra attacks. So on their return to the States, Sue and others decided they had no choice but to go back and offer the protection of their presence to the people among whom they had lived, and to do it in as many areas as possible. Naturally, this was a frightening prospect, and she was as frightened as anyone while sitting in her comfortable, safe home in Marin County reading about what "the Contra" was doing in those remote jungle villages. But, as Dutch child rescuer Cornelia Knottnerus also found, "The best antidote to fear is action." Strangely enough, while Sue and the others were actually in Nicaragua, fear was never a problem.

> While I was there I never felt fear. I think the main reason
> was, I was there out of choice. . . . I found — much to my
> surprise — that I became very calm in danger. I'm a Quaker
> and don't go very much with "God" language, but the only

way I can explain it is, I felt I was in the hands of God: not safe — that I wouldn't be hurt — but that I was where I was supposed to be, doing what I was supposed to be doing. And this can be addictive. Maybe that's why we kept going back.

We began this chapter with a story that illustrates the conversion of anger. By this time we've seen that fear, too, can become fuel for the fire of unsentimental, active love when one chooses the nonviolence response.

Severin's reminiscence offers a number of other insights. She clarifies something about the feeling of empowerment, almost of invincibility, that sometimes comes over nonviolent actors and enables them to face and often overcome danger with preternatural courage — the Birmingham marchers' "spiritual intoxication." As she points out, it is not a naive feeling of invulnerability, as though they were temporarily teenagers again. It is something both subtler and more realistic: what empowers you is the conviction that what you are going through is meaningful. In Severin's words, this is what you are "supposed to be doing," and these words are echoed by Marge Argelyan from Chicago, who did very similar work in Hebron in 1996. "This experience had the most integrity of any work I've done." They were echoed by Solange Muller, daughter of the Assistant Secretary General of the UN, at a meeting in New York. "When you find work like that, you never go back."

In times like ours, when life has become meaningless for so many, it's not hard to understand how the taste of nonviolent struggle can be "addictive." Just listen to testimonies from the women and men who risked their lives to save Jewish and other victims of the Holocaust.

Professor and Mrs. Ege played a prominent role in the highly successful Danish rescue operation. Mrs. Ege: "We helped the Jews because it meant that for once in your life you were doing something worthwhile. . . . I think that the Danes should be equally grateful to the Jews for giving them an opportunity to do something decent and meaningful." A trapeze artist, Speedy Larking, said it with less restraint: "I feel — hang it — I feel like throwing myself down on the road and saying, 'Thank you!'" But it is a physician, Dr. Strandbygaard, who really takes our breath away. "Isn't this strange? . . . It's almost like experiencing again the overwhelming love of one's youth."

Heady stuff. These intense, fulfilling moments, we have said so far, come from the inner struggle to control our "biological" response of fight or flight. Such a struggle can lead to a peak experience that often has its effect on our opponents. It *always* has effects, like those we've just been hearing about, on the doer — on ourselves. Next chapter we'll focus on the obvious question: how and with what degree of reliability can we expect our opponent to "get it"? But it's not quite time yet to leave the world of the actor's own inner experience.

In the grip of nonviolence, people experience more intensely. Life feels more "real." It is like the strange feeling of Yeats' Irish airman, who has no earthly reason to be risking his life fighting for the British.

> Nor law, nor duty bade me fight,
> Nor public men, nor cheering crowds,
> A lonely impulse of delight
> Drove to this tumult in the clouds;
> I balanced all, brought all to mind,
> The years to come seemed waste of breath,
> A waste of breath the years behind
> In balance with this life, this death.

It is like that experience, of course, but rather different. In war you are risking your life to kill others; in nonviolence you're risking your life (if necessary) so that no one else will be killed — ultimately so that no one will ever have to face death again at the hands of their fellow humans. Nonviolence is what William James was looking for: the moral equivalent of war.

In one's own nonviolent moment a flash of spiritual light momen-

tarily rends the darkness of the prevailing image of ourselves as a separate, competitive, neo-Darwinian animal who knows nothing but threat
force. This leads us to a very important question: How can we keep that
light switched on? If nonviolence is "addictive," how do you feed the
habit?

Psychiatrist M. Scott Peck gives a good description of just this process.

> I do not know what creates a mystical experience. I know that
> fatigue can loosen 'ego boundaries.' I also know that I am
> now *able to do voluntarily what happened to me then involuntarily*: to
> see, whenever I remember and choose to do so, that all my
> enemies are my relatives and that all of us play roles for each
> other in the order of things.

One time or another, I think we've all had glimpses of a peak experience. Though it happened over thirty years ago, I vividly remember one
afternoon in Berkeley when I was playing basketball with five other guys
in Live Oak Park. All of a sudden — maybe one of us had just sunk a
really pretty shot — the three of us, my teammates and myself, were in a
rally. We were invincible. It was magic; every pass connected, every shot
sank. It was more like a ballet than three guys playing ball. Then it ended.
The spell — or whatever it was — broke. We went back to being our
bumbling selves, and I don't even think we won the game. An actor, an
athlete, a dancer, even a professor has peak moments when suddenly they
"get it," or "it clicks." The difference is that a professional actor or athlete
or whatever learns how to reenter that state on demand, so that with
enough training he or she can make it happen whenever it's needed. There
is nothing particularly mysterious about this, even though the "learning"
that's involved has to be more than just at the conscious level. The training of a "career satyagrahi," who will need to keep certain "natural" reactions under control when he or she is at that lunch counter — or of

someone who wants to stay alive some day in a dark alley — is very similar. You learn to be calmly alert under any stress.

The fact is that neither Joan Black nor the Birmingham marchers nor Karen Ridd nor Sue Severin nor Eileen Egan were totally unprepared for their nonviolent moment. Joan Black was on duty in an emergency room. Her medical training and her setting predisposed her to see a distraught person as a person — someone who needed help. Karen Ridd and Sue Severin were carrying out a nonviolent mission for which they had had a modest amount of training. The Birmingham marchers were in the midst of a long drawn-out nonviolent struggle, in which they had perhaps some training and certainly the rare benefit of inspired leadership.

This was also the case with Jawaharlal Nehru. Like thousands of his countrymen, the future Prime Minister of free India was drawn to the Mahatma's nonviolence, but there was more to it than just getting the idea, as he discovered when he was caught in a *lathi* charge by mounted police during a peaceful demonstration in Lucknow in 1928. (A *lathi*, or *lathee*, is a metal-tipped bamboo staff that Indian and British police used liberally in those days.)

> And then began a beating of us, and battering with lathees
> and long batons both by the mounted and the foot police. It
> was a tremendous hammering, and the clearness of vision
> that I had had the evening before left me. All I knew was that
> I had to stay where I was and must not yield or go back. I felt
> half blinded with the blows, and sometimes a dull anger
> seized me and a desire to hit out. I thought how easy it
> would be to pull down the police officer in front of me from
> his horse and to mount up myself, but long training and
> discipline held, and I did not raise a hand, except to protect
> my face from a blow.

Training: Outer Work

What was that long training and discipline? This was one of the most misunderstood aspects of Gandhi's leadership. When he asked his close coworkers to live simply, identify themselves with the poorest in the land, make their own cloth — even observe certain dietary rules — he was not laying down moral precepts in our sense of the word. He was actually training them to be a little "spiritually intoxicated" all the time. He knew nonviolence doesn't just happen when the chemistry of the situation is right. He would have applauded the words of the Buddhist leader Thich Nhat Hanh.

> If you wait until the time of crisis, it will be too late. . . .
> Even if you know that nonviolence is better than violence, if
> your understanding is only intellectual and not in your whole
> being, you will not act nonviolently. The fear and anger will
> prevent you. . . .

If you know in your whole being that "your enemies are your relatives," you can have a spectacular effect on those around you. One of my friends, David Hartsough, who is white, was sitting in with a small group of civil-rights activists at a segregated lunch counter in Virginia in the early 'sixties. They had been sitting there without getting service for close to two days, and being harassed almost without letup by an increasingly angry crowd. As neither the sitters nor the proprietors backed down, tension increased. Suddenly David was jerked back off his stool and spun around by a man who hissed at him, "You got one minute to get out of here, n . . . lover, or I'm running this through your heart." David, who had had his eyes closed, repeating the twenty-third Psalm up on his stool, stopped staring at the huge bowie knife held at his chest and slowly looked back up into the man's face, to meet "the worst look of hate I have ever seen in my life." The thought that came to him was, "Well, at least I've got a minute," and he heard himself saying to the man, "Well, brother, you do what you feel you have to; and I'm going to try to love you all the same." For a few frozen seconds there seemed to be no reaction; then the hand on the knife started shaking. After a few more long seconds it dropped. The man turned and walked out of the lunchroom, surreptitiously wiping a tear from his cheek.

Not all nonviolent moments are this harrowing. This one shows, though, what a difference you can make when you see life differently *and* practice what you see, so that your love of nonviolence starts putting down roots below the mere intellectual conviction and starts to occupy "your whole being." David is a committed Quaker, as were his parents. They practiced acting out their peace convictions as their life-style, thereby reinforcing their conviction that there is "that of God" in everyone. And he had undergone a fair amount of special training, as far as one can ever be trained to respond creatively to such an emergency. Like policemen, even soldiers, he had learned through belief and practice that when someone opposite you is upset, *you* don't have to be.

These, then, are the ingredients for developing nonviolent responses so that they become part of our personality: a deep conviction about the unity of life, the inspiration of real nonviolent leadership, practice in real, or failing that, in "role-playing" situations, and finally — Gandhi's special legacy — a life lived by nonviolent principles. One would be really lucky to have all of these — leadership is especially hard to come by in today's world — but with some combination anyone could deepen her or his innate capacity to become an effective "actor of love."

Because this capacity is an innate response, there's no reason to fear that we're repressing anything when we set out to develop it. On the contrary, when we find "the way out of no way" between anger and fear we are disinhibiting a natural capacity we all possess but of which most of us are not aware. Most of us don't try to develop it, for the simple reason that most of us have ceased to believe it exists. But that is due to our cultural conditioning. I think in fact that it's violence that's artificial;

it's violence that is a mechanical "solution" that cheats us of an opportunity to grow — as individuals, by mastering an important part of our mind; as a people, by working out a real solution to what divides us. A nonviolent response originates, always, in the struggle to master emotional forces inside ourselves. And my guess is that this very struggle is what feels so meaningful and makes the nonviolent peak experience "addictive." Conflict is an opportunity, because negative emotions are an opportunity, for conversion.

A teenager gave perfect expression to this recently after he had had a loaded gun held to his head by someone who robbed his backpack. His first reaction was pretty knee-jerk: "I should have been packing." A moment later he realized that having a gun would hardly have made him more secure in that situation. Finally, on really mature reflection, he realized that if he had had one, "I'd have gripped the handle instead of coming to grips with my fear." Speaking for a small group of American volunteers in Hebron, where they were trying to stand between Israeli bulldozers and Palestinian homes and orchards, Randy Bond said, "We were a small group of ordinary people doing some rather extraordinary things in a hurting part of our world. We had to stretch ourselves and our capabilities to do these things, that's the only way we grow."

Isn't growing what we're supposed to be doing with our life?

Training: Inner Work

Emperor Ashoka ruled most of northern India from around 269-232 B.C.E., and we will meet with him again, because he ruled as so very few in human history have done: by nonviolence. His rock edicts, a number of which are still to be read all over India, tell us how his guiding principle was not aggression but the moral order, or *dhamma* (Sanskrit *dharma*), which among other things meant the renunciation of wars of expansion, tolerance toward all religions, protection of the helpless, even hospitals for animals. The mute rocks speak in a voice that can "resonate in our ears across two millennia or more, evoking a liberal vision with an incredibly contemporary ring." This is Edict Forty:

> People can be induced to advance in the Dhamma by only
> two means, namely moral prescriptions and meditation. Of
> the two, moral prescriptions are the lesser, meditation the
> greater. The moral prescriptions I have promulgated include
> rules making certain animals inviolable, and I have estab-
> lished other rules as well. But even in the case of abstention
> from injuring and killing living creatures, it is by meditation
> that people have made the greatest progress in the Dhamma.

"Meditation" may be the only word in the English language with a less agreed-on meaning than "nonviolence;" and as we see from the close connection Ashoka draws, that may not be a coincidence.

The classical definition of meditation is provided by a famous text thought to be roughly contemporary with the Buddha, the *Yoga Sutras,* which begins, "Meditation is the obstruction of thought waves in the mind." (Sutra I.2, my translation) By "thought waves" (*citta-vrtti*) Patañjali, the otherwise unknown sage who composed this text, includes any men- tal event — a feeling, an image, a desire — not just a linguistic thought. It could be, for example, a wave of anger or fear, and that shows us imme- diately the connection of meditation with nonviolence, and why Ashoka felt meditation was better than rules and regulations, even moral regula- tions, for creating a nonviolent regime.

Getting the mind under control: that's a tall order! Meister Eckhart puts it beautifully.

> This needs prodigiously hard work. . . . A man must be
> closeted within himself where his mind is safe from images
> of outside things. . . . Second, inventions of the mind itself:
> ideas, spontaneous notions or images . . . he must give no

quarter to on pain of scattering himself and being sold into multiplicity.

Patañjali's definition of "yoga" (meditation, in this case) comes from his collection of sutras, or aphorisms. Such texts were meant as scientific manuals, if you will, consisting of bare formulas meant to be expounded by a competent authority. So in practical terms, a few things have to be added to his aphoristic expression to show us how actually to do this, especially in the modern period. First, as Eckhart says, meditation is not a state you slip into but a discipline you work at. Clearly, one has to have a tool to do this "prodigiously hard work." In my case, that has meant that I practice at regular times every day, under the guidance of a good teacher, and I do it by concentrating with all the willpower I can muster, minute by minute, on an inspirational passage that I've previously memorized to keep spontaneous thought-waves from arising.

To describe it this way, meditation may seem like a dreary exercise, hardly the thing to make heroes and heroines out of anyone; but that would be because we know so little about the capacities of the mind. "So far as we know," writes neuroscientist Robert Livingston, "the usefulness of cognitive processes such as consciousness, perception, judgment, and volition have not begun to meet any limits." Our first examples in this book were of individuals or groups of individuals who were thrown into a deep state of concentration by an emergency, like Joan Black or my friend David Hartsough at that lunch counter. We are talking here about learning to reach deeper states of concentration even without an emergency. Once when Gandhiji visited the ashram (spiritual community) of a well-known sage in South India, the sage remarked to his students after he left, "Today we have been blessed by the presence of a real yogi." They asked him how he knew that, and he said,

When you look at him you can see that he is absorbed in yoga, for whenever he looks at something he pays all his attention. He never glances at anything else. Many other leaders came with him, but they were looking everywhere, as if they had five or six pairs of eyes."

So let us not overlook this humble-seeming capacity: one-pointed attention is the psychological key to nonviolence. And to illustrate its power, and at the same time its accessibility to non-mahatmas, let me borrow a description of a peak state of performance from a more familiar, not to say unlikely source:

> Despite his off-field manner, which is often ordinary, even prosaic, Montana is special because when he faces danger, he is completely concentrated. What we don't know is how he does it. . . . Sometimes things happen in slow motion for Joe at the most crucial time. The world slows down and things get big and he feels as if he has total control. He was in that world when he threw the winning pass to John Taylor [in the crucial game of the 1989 season, against the Cincinnati Bengals]. Montana simply went about playing quarterback as if the 49ers were ahead and there were still two quarters to go. "It happened sort of in slow motion," Montana admitted. He had dropped back to pass and suddenly everything slowed down and became totally clear. Joe saw two defenders go after Roger Craig and he saw Taylor break into the clear and he threw his pass. Then he lost sight of the ball, heard the screams of the fans and the world returned to normal speed.

Strange as it might sound, this is a precise description (minus the stuff about pass receivers and fans) of a state of consciousness that Indian sages called *dharana*, or "firmly held attention." They taught that dharana was the first of the three stages — attention, meditation, and complete absorption in the Supreme Reality — in the long journey to complete fulfillment of meditation, which is to say, of human potential. In this first stage, dharana, our attention is often on something outside (like whether Craig or Taylor is in the clear); the second stage, meditation proper, is the systematic control of the activity within our mind (remember the two areas of control Eckhart talks about); and the third stage, or *samadhi*, is — well, hard to describe.

There is nothing particularly Eastern or Indian about the capacity for meditation. It was more systematically and continuously cultivated in India than any other civilization, to my knowledge, but it was hardly unknown to others. Some of the "heaviest" meditators in the world, like Meister Eckhart or Teresa of Avila, sprang up in the West. Nor has its discovery, or periodic rediscovery, always happened in the context of a religion. This is a remarkable insight of William James about education, which he made in his *Principles of Psychology*:

> The faculty of voluntarily bringing back a wandering attention over and over again, is the very root of judgment, character and will. No one is *compos sui* if he have it not. An education which would improve this faculty would be the education *par excellence*. But it is easier to define this ideal than to give practical directions for bringing it about.

I doubt James was consciously aware that he was paraphrasing one of the names for meditation in ancient India, which is *brahmavidya*, or "supreme education." Yet his description of bringing back a wandering attention "over and over again" is precisely what meditation is. It is indeed difficult to find practical directions for bringing this about. In both civilizations, this legacy, once cherished, has all but disappeared behind the glitter of materialism But materialism can never keep its hold on us indefinitely — witness the way interest in and knowledge about meditation has soared since Swami Vivekananda's sensational introduction of

India's spiritual heritage at the Parliament of Religions in Chicago in 1893 (the very year, interestingly enough, that Gandhiji went to meet his destiny in South Africa).

Today many people are familiar with William James not as the author of the above remark, but from his classic essay, the *Moral Equivalent of War*. That he had both interests is hardly a coincidence. "War begins in the minds of men," after all. The Bhagavad Gita, the beloved Indian scripture that so deeply influenced Gandhiji, not only confirms this insight but gives us a clear sense *why* the untrained mind spawns violence — and what to do about it. This teaching is dramatized in a famous interchange between the hero, Arjuna, who represents you and me, and his friend and charioteer, Sri Krishna, who happens to be God. There's nothing wrong with the mind that training won't cure, Krishna tells Arjuna. One must simply learn to "still the thought waves in the mind," in accordance with the ancient wisdom. Arjuna laments in language we can all appreciate, "But Krishna, the mind is so shaky and agitates so violently — you may as well ask me to control the wind." And Krishna's answer is, "I agree, but it will come under our sovereignty — with a little detachment, and constant practice."

The moral equivalent of war is the internal one, the "war within." In that "war" — the individual's struggle to pacify her or his mind — no one gets hurt, and however much we succeed, that much of our innate, powerful capacities for nonviolence come into play. It has always been much harder to recognize this war than the wars we wage outside. Today we are enjoying a growth industry in behavioral training to reduce violence; you will find versions of it in classrooms, in prisons, in workshops for peacemakers and in corporations. It's a good first step. Practicing nonviolence ourselves is another. And meditating is the next. For those who care — and dare — to undertake it, meditation is the deep training that the Dalai Lama recently called "internal disarmament," which enables us to intervene right where violence starts, at the very root of hostile thoughts. There is no question that whichever way you go, whether

it's working on your behavior or through the direct and most difficult
regime of meditation, or both, the mind is subtle and resists correction.
That is its nature; this is not easy for anyone. But through training, as the
Gita says, it is doable, and as we make progress in this line one of the
rewarding results is that nonviolence can become second nature. That is a
"two-edged" reward: training pacifies the mind — and a mind of peace
cannot but project a harmonic force into the world around us. That effect on others is what we can turn to next, but this has been a pretty dense
introduction and could do with some summarization.

Wrapping Up

Nonviolence begins in inner struggle — specifically, the struggle to
keep negative forces such as anger, fear and greed from having sway over
us. It's a struggle that has immense spiritual benefits for the individual
and leads to an exhilarating sense of purpose that is very often lacking in
modern life. A Dutch couple named Vos was among several who took in
Jewish children during the Nazi occupation, putting themselves and their
own children at considerable risk. The inevitable day came when Mrs.
Vos's mother came to visit, and was understandably upset to find refugees
there in the house, endangering her grandchildren. Her daughter explained:

> We find it more important for our children to have parents
> who have done what they felt they had to do — even if it
> costs them their lives. It will be better for them — even if we
> don't make it. They will know we did what we felt we had to
> do. This is better than if we first think of our own safety.

And she agreed.

This rising to heroism by perfectly ordinary people, this empowerment, can also be achieved outside such acute crises, especially, but even

sometimes without, meditation or other kinds of training. One hears as much constantly from former gang-members or trouble-making students in the many programs dotted around the nation's schools and neighborhoods where someone has bothered to reach out to them with an alternative. They often discover they've always had the skills to be a mediator, for example, but no one showed them how to use them, and when someone does they feel an exhilarating sense of self-worth, like "hidden gold mines."

While the feelings of fear and anger that come over every one of us from time to time are natural, it is also natural for us to want to master them. The dilemma of violence, whether felt in the mind of a Franklin Smith or acted out by a nation that can see only a choice between doing nothing or doing harm, is itself some indication that the "natural" reaction of fight or flight is not all nature has in store for us. The existence of a "way out of no way" and the deep sense of emotional reward people have felt on following that way would seem to say that this is a path, if not *the* path, nature had in mind all along.

When we speak of nonviolence as a peak experience precipitated by certain conditions, though, we are just beginning. It is like discovering that some bread mold in a petri dish has inhibited bacteria, or that some new kind of energy coming out of a Crooke's tube has printed the picture of a key on a nearby photographic plate: the work of getting this force into useable form then has to follow. Peaks have valleys. The occasions for potential nonviolent moments, can be totally unexpected (like Eileen Egan's mugging), or a calculated risk (as at Birmingham), or pretty much staged (as at the Dharasana salt pans). But they're still *occasions*. What we want is integrative power to become sustained and habitual — as, after all, the practices of threat force have been allowed to become.

So we went on to talk about the two levels of training: behavior (and we'll have more to say about the role of culture at this level) and then the mind itself, where the seeds of behavior lie.

Gandhi was the one person in the modern world who most conspicuously made this training a way of life, fine-tuned by relentless scientific experiments. While much has been written about his shrewdness and the results, positive and negative, of his great campaigns, the inner dimensions of his struggle and its results have been relatively passed over. They are, of course, more difficult to document. When he went into the Round Table Conference for the "day in court" that he had worked toward for thirty years, on September 15, 1931, he had nothing but a few notes to speak from, and had told Ronald Duncan as they rode to the meeting, "How do I know what I am going to say? I'm not there yet." His impromptu speech is said to have been a masterpiece. (The authorities didn't allow it to be recorded.) How do we explain this uncanny ability of his? Where did he get his boundless energy, his ability to go on in the face of disasters that would have floored any of us, carrying his titanic pace into his seventies? How on earth did he divest himself of so much of his personal desire, and "unnecessary" possessions? And fear? And there are other mysteries. The father of a friend of mine happened to be in India in the forties, a time of high tension, and was asked to carry an important message to Gandhi. I asked him, what was his main impression of the Mahatma as a person. He said, without hesitation, "Health." He had never seen such ebullient good health, even though, from a medical point of view, some of the numbers on Gandhi's blood pressure were in the danger zone at that desperate time.

While Gandhiji is best known for his resistance to the industrial life-style through simplicity and the "reduction of wants" — shock treatment for modern economies — he was also constantly advocating a deeper resistance to the culture that produced that life-style, the culture of consumption, external achievement and conquest. Though he rarely used the word meditation itself (it had become so unknown even in India that to mention it would bring on clouds of misconception) his enthusiastic practice and recommendation of allied techniques like prayer and the repetition of a mantram (a name of God) thread through his teaching from the earliest period. Yet even if he had never said a word about these disciplines, we could surmise that he had practiced them to perfection just from his life and its achievements, neither of which could be explained otherwise than by the assumption that this is a man whose mind was utterly at peace. His life was his message, and the message was, here I am, the consummate activist, but the first field of action is my own heart and mind. Clearly, he belonged to those who return to the Inward Way that humanity forgets age after age.

His own testimony on how the conversion of anger affected him personally is a fitting wrap-up to this discussion of the source of nonviolence. It reveals, I think, one of the most important secrets of his life.

> It is not that I am incapable of anger, for instance, but I succeed on almost all occasions to keep my feelings under control. Whatever may be the result, there is always in me conscious struggle for following the law of non-violence deliberately and ceaselessly. Such a struggle leaves one stronger for it. The more I work at this law, the more I feel the delight in my life, the delight in the scheme of the universe. It gives me a peace and a meaning of the mysteries of nature that I have no power to describe.

4 "Work" Versus Work

> Remember, violence works; big violence works
> better. No revolution ever got off the ground
> without massive violence.
> — Tom Metzger, White Aryan Resistance

> People try nonviolence for a week, and when it
> doesn't "work" they go back to violence, which
> hasn't worked for centuries.
> — Theodore Roszak

Nonviolence may give us a deep sense of purpose that's missing in our modern life, it may be a healthy way out of the "fight or flight" response to danger, but if it doesn't work, we may as well quit right now. Theodore Roszak jogs us into realizing, however, that whether nonviolence works or not — whether anything works or not — may be a little less simple than first appears.

In this chapter we want to do two things: the first and most important is to understand what it really means to say something has "worked," in other words to get from the simplistic to a realistic sense of action and consequences. The second is almost as important: to enlarge our field of vision concerning the various forms of nonviolent action. Building on the events we've already considered, it will be more and more obvious that nonviolence is much more than a form of protest. After these two recalibrations, we will be able to see past what Gandhiji once called our "inane" conception of nonviolence to appreciate more realistically "the greatest force mankind has been endowed with."

But first, let's turn the tables on our friends the cynics and ask, how well does *violence* work?

Sociologists Robert Jewett and John Lawrence analyzed American thinking about violence in an instructive book in the 1970s called *The American Monomyth*. The two writers studied popular entertainment and advertising, looking for what they called a "monomyth" about violence, and they found it summed up in one figure who epitomized the heroes of popular culture at that time: Superman. Superman stories, they found, uniformly propagate three beliefs about how violence works — how it preserves law and order and protects the innocent:

(1) Violence is never misused. Superman is incorruptibly good, effectively omniscient, always on the right side.

(2) Violence doesn't really hurt; it's "clean." When Superman swoops down in front of a car full of fleeing crooks and stops it dead, the crooks tumble out chastened but not wounded. Maybe one of them has a bandage on his forehead, but there is no pain, no suffering — and of course there is no "collateral damage." No bystanders are accidentally hit, even in a high-speed car chase.

And above all,

(3) Violence never rebounds. Superman is invulnerable (except for the occasional Cryptonite-induced dizzy spell), so even if the criminals wanted to, they could never hurt him back. But they don't want to. They are always successfully neutralized. Putting them in jail is the happy ending of the story. We never hear about what happens to them in jail — for example, that they learn more violent techniques in prison and come out to seek revenge on the community.

Wow.

Incredibly enough, these were then — and other versions of it still are now — the narratives that shaped our way of thinking about violence. We keep thinking that with one more clean weapon, one more restraining device, one more prison, the police will be able to get an edge on crime and restore our security. But that thinking is as unrealistic as the comics on which it is, perhaps, partially based.

In the real world, violence does, at least sometimes to be sure, achieve its immediate purpose. There is no question of that. In Santa Rosa, California recently, a man who had been terrorizing elderly people in a certain neighborhood entered one home too many. The owner got out his gun and turned the tables on this wretch, who is now safely behind bars. Or take a very different example: in 1991 the "international community" bombed Iraq until dictator Saddam Hussein was forced to pull the remains of his shattered army out of Kuwait — and off our oil supply. Violence *can* get things done: this is true; but is this all there is to it — does this cause-effect arc really exhaust the dynamics of violence?

Because the media present and re-present this one side of the story, we plain do not notice that a raft of other things, some of them much more important in the long run, ripple out as the "event cone" of violence widens more and more. We do not notice that most of the homeowners who go get their guns are overcome or even killed by their much more professional intruders, just as many of the people who pull out a gun or a knife in some kind of quarrel end up the victims of "victim-precipitated homicides." We rarely think about the number of guns stolen from homes or the number of children who use them on their friends. Above all, we do not notice that every time an act of violence "works" — and let's repeat, some of them do — there's trouble somewhere down the road.

If we knew where to look, we would see the trouble every time. Does the criminal who is "safely" behind bars plan to go better armed next time? Does the dramatic story in the paper send other homeowners out to get guns, which four out of five times end up hurting someone in the family instead (that's solid fact)? If you count up all the accidental deaths and other mishaps that result from keeping a gun at home, they are almost *forty times* more common than the scenario where an intruder is scared off. And finally, does the violent solution, despite its satisfying "conclusion," which is really only a step toward many other conclusions, ratchet up the level of violence in the community as a whole? We usually don't even ask these questions, yet they are the ones that determine which way we're really headed: toward safety or toward death, chaos or community.

During the Gulf conflict more bombs fell on Iraq than were dropped in all of World War II. This incredible punishment "worked": Saddam Hussein did indeed withdraw what was left of his forces from Kuwait. Yes, but what else happened? About 100,000 people died; billions of dollars worth of oil was burned in the open air or poured into the waters of the Gulf, creating an unparalleled ecological disaster. It has been estimated that the war cost Iraq alone $77 billion. And now for the really bad part. Over 200,000 Iraqi children died either during the bombing raids or in the aftermath, when infant deaths in Iraq during the first eight months after the attacks rose 300%. Then they went on dying, the children, and by the time of this writing they are still dying because of economic sanctions kept in place to force the unrepentant dictator into line — for evidently all that bombing did not cause President Hussein to have a change of heart, only to harden it. In order to thwart the Iraqi ruler's intentions by violence, we have brought about the greatest humanitarian crisis — some, like former Attorney General Ramsey Clark, would say the greatest crime against humanity — since World War II. That consequence cannot be brushed aside. It is not irrelevant to our destiny.

Let us pause here to ask, in the name of what kind of logic have we inflicted this appalling suffering, year after year, on this people and these children? Dictators by definition do not care about the well-being of their subjects. So by hurting their subjects . . . ? In fact it has been pointed out often enough that our sanctions weakened the Iraqi people to the point where they could no longer resist their harsh leader even if they wanted to. We did his job for him.

We could have predicted both these results, if only we understood the dynamics of violence. We would then have realized that in terms of the *type* of force applied, harsh sanctions are only quantitatively different from bombing. We would have realized that we ultimately strengthened the ruler of Iraq's hand, not because we wanted to, but because we used the same kind of force he does. He relies on violence. We didn't come up with an alternative.

When President Bush launched Operation Desert Storm with the ringing words, "The liberation of Kuwait has begun," he wanted us to think of the liberation of Europe from Hitler's armies. (The official line had been all along that Iraq was bent on, and somehow capable of, world conquest.) He might have been a little more careful about his historical precedent. The massive air attacks ordered by the Allied leaders who met at Casablanca in January, 1943 were an experiment that was designed to achieve the destruction and dislocation of the German military and the undermining of the morale of the German people sufficiently to undermine their capacity for armed resistance. Since the Germans who remained alive did give up, it is easy to convince ourselves that the bombing had the desired effect. Yet, as the great pacifist writer Vera Brittain pointed out early in the game,

> The 'experiment' has demonstrated, so far, that mass bombing does not induce revolt or break morale. Victims are stunned, exhausted, apathetic, absorbed in the immediate tasks of finding food and shelter. But as they recover who can doubt that there will be, among the majority at any rate, the desire for revenge and a hardening process, even if, for a time, it may be subdued by fear?

According to many studies done after the war, and after other wars, her prediction was quite correct. Particularly interesting is the bombing of civilian targets in the North-West Frontier Province of India by the British in 1930, which we'll have occasion to return to. "500 tons of bombs were dropped over the Pathans, but their spirits remained uncrushed. The number of Red Shirts increased from a couple of hundreds to 80,000."

So the unwonted results of the massive bombing of Iraq were not incidental, or unpredictable. They were the results of very general and predictable rules: in principle bombing people does not lead to unmixed good results. In principle violence does not lead only to good results, even if it leads to some results that one side considers good. Violence is, in principle and ineradicably, a destructive force. In May, 2000 *Newsweek* published a previously-suppressed NATO report making it clear that instead of crippling the Serbian military the year before (only fourteen tanks were destroyed, for example, not 120 as earlier claimed) it had terrorized the civilian population by bombing generating plants, bridges and other infrastructure of daily life.

As Professor Pepinsky says, human beings are embedded in "crosscurrents of violence and responsiveness" and we are always, at every moment, influencing our surroundings by our "profoundly religious choice between violence and democracy." For all we know, there were still other eddies and crosscurrents released by our choice of violence in the Gulf: the demoralization of the Iraqi people, a "deep hatred" among the Iraqi youth for us, spasms of violence unleashed against the Kurds of the north and Shiites of the south — and we must think also of the wider world. Shortly after the Gulf war, Serbs and Croats unleashed unparalleled violence against their Muslim neighbors. Was that a coincidence? Or may they not have picked up a resonance from the brutality visited on the Iraqi people by the American and European states acting under UN auspices? The heartless bombing, the massacre of Iraqi soldiers trying to flee Kuwait, the brutal entombment of others in their trenches (not to mention the continuing sacrifice of the children) were all examples of Muslims not being treated as human beings. Was the bombing of the World Trade Tower in New York by Islamic fundamentalists a few years after the Gulf conflict also a coincidence, or the attack on the U.S.S. Cole?

The Gulf conflict had another, extremely bad result that is not controversial, once you give it a moment's thought: every time we use violence to solve a problem we send the signal that violence is the way to solve problems. In the present case, it is hard to ignore the desensitization of the CNN-watching American public for whom the war was turned into a video game. In the world of violence, as we've seen, nothing is more dangerous than trivialization, than losing our human sensitivity. This is why the task in nonviolence, by contrast, is often to awaken sleeping consciences by making people aware of the pain they're causing — making them feel it empathetically.

That task is becoming ever more difficult. Since the Gulf debacle, the U.S. military has increasingly been using video games to train personnel. They claim that they're doing this because video games have become as realistic as real combat; but I claim that consciously or unconsciously they are doing it *to make combat seem as realistic as video games.* Which is to say, not real at all. Unconsciously they are training their personnel not just to use weapons — that's secondary. What has always been the more difficult trick in military training is getting soldiers not to feel what they're doing when they use their weapons on live targets. "Once I met a Vietnam veteran on an airplane," Henri Nouwen writes.

> He told me that he had seen so many people killed on
> television that it had been hard for him to believe that those
> whom *he* killed would not stand up again in the next movie.

No wonder Simone Weil says, "War is unreality itself."

I won't dwell on this here because it's been so graphically laid before the public now by the books of Lieutenant Colonel Dave Grossman; but the point to remember is that whenever we prepare minds for war we unprepare them for life, and that hurts all of us. This is a severe hidden cost of the war system — and by extension, of all violence.

Earlier, I used the handy image from physics of an "event cone." This is how physicists describe the fact that even the tiniest event — say, the emission of a gamma ray from a decaying particle — ramifies forward into the future, changing events and altering seemingly unrelated possibilities at a great remove in time and space. In its event cone, the working of violence begins to look a lot less "surgical." It too can create a "butterfly effect" of cascading disorder. So our intuition that violence is a disruptive, not a constructive, force begins to look a lot more plausible.

In his classic study, *Man, the State and War*, Kenneth Waltz, who is by no means pro-war, tries to show that however deplorable war and violence are in general, they sometimes preserve "order." You would certainly think so. Ironically, though, he cites the bloody suppression of the last Moro rebellion in the Philippines as an example. (This caught my attention: my grandfather served in the unit that brought in the famous Philippine resistance fighter, Emilio Aguinaldo, in 1901.) The war may have been an ugly business, was Professor Waltz's point in 1964, but it paved the way for a "stable regime" for that country — under Ferdinand Marcos! The "stable" Marcos regime collapsed unceremoniously in February of 1986; and its successors had trouble with the Moros for ten more years. In Professor Roszak's happy terminology, the war "worked" but it didn't work. It didn't have successful long-term results. Gandhi frequently said, "Violent revolution will bring violent *swaraj* (regime)." Not maybe, not sometimes: he meant it as a law. Sometimes it may take a long time for these unhappy results to mature, and then we have to have good eyes to see the connection, but it's there.

The principle, to repeat, resides in the very nature of violence, not just in war. The majority of Americans believe that the death penalty deters homicide; but in one of the few reliable studies on the actual results of capital punishment it was found that introducing the death penalty actually seems to *increase* homicides, by about two percent. The title of the study is, "Deterrence or Brutalization." The state destroys a human life to "send a message" to would-be murderers; but in reality it's sending not one but two, somewhat contradictory messages. On the conscious level its message is mainly about retribution, about warning; but on a deeper level it is unfortunately more about the expendability of human life — and the impossibility of bringing a violent person back into the community. Evidently, the deeper message, as usual, is slightly more effective.

Or more than slightly. As Sr. Helen Prejean points out, Texas executes more people than any other state, "Yet its murder rate remains one of the highest in the country." New York, which does not have the death penalty, reduced its crime rate dramatically in the first four months of 1992, largely by expansion in other, more preventive areas of crime control. These other areas are, incidentally, ones that a state can afford to institute when it is not spending $2.3 million on every capital case.

The more closely we look, the more it begins to seem that our instinctive reliance on violence for security is misplaced. Violence is always a slippery way to go, with as many bad repercussions as good ones. That feeling in us which tells us that violence works is not based on facts, and I suspect the reason we don't look at those facts too closely is simple. If the facts say that violence doesn't protect us very well *but we don't know what does*, those facts are disturbing. The rules of cognitive dissonance take over, and facts bow out. A teen I quoted earlier, the one who had his backpack robbed at gunpoint said, "I'll never get caught slipping again. The next guy who tries to run up on me is getting blasted." Then he came to his senses — part way — and corrected himself. "I'm glad I didn't have anything that day. I would have killed that fool." Really? With a loaded handgun pointed at your temple? Would you not rather have become, like the Sonoma County woman who carried guns for protection until she got killed reaching for one, yet another case of victim-precipitated homicide?

... And It Even "Works"

Anyone who does what I do becomes by turns frustrated, despairing and amused at the certitude with which people tell us that nonviolence doesn't work. If nonviolent volunteers tried to interpose themselves between hostile forces in former Yugoslavia, one person told me, they would just be wiped out — martyrs. "They'd all be machine-gunned," said another with equal certainty. Yet at the time they made these statements (at a meeting of the U.S. Institute of Peace in Washington in the spring of 1993), only one person had been killed and three wounded in the whole history of nonviolent interposition, a history going back to the early part of the century and involving tens of thousands of not overly trained volunteers. In Haiti, in ten or so months of accompanying threatened people, seventy volunteers from a consortium of peace groups defied the ruthless paramilitary, FRAPH, without taking a single casualty. As I write this, not one volunteer (knock wood) has ever been killed in one and a half decades of doing the kind of high-profile, sometimes quite confrontational work of Karen Ridd and Sue Severin in Central America, nor has anyone being accompanied by them. (How many heavily-armed soldiers and guerrillas have been killed in that period!) Once, after my talk about the Indian freedom struggle some years ago at a local college, a student challenged me, "What about the tens of thousands who got killed?" When I asked him what he was talking about he started spinning out scenes of atrocious massacres he had seen somewhere. It turned out that he had seen them only in his imagination. Outside of the massacre in 1919 at Jalianwalla Bagh in the Punjab, and what happened in Peshawar in the thirties (which this student could not possibly have known about) almost no satyagrahis were killed in the thirty-two years of intense struggle Gandhiji conducted in India. Fewer were killed in six years of civil disobedience in Georgia than in six nights of rioting in Detroit.

"Acts of love" that arise in a peak state of self-control *do* work, beyond the psychological work they do within ourselves. They work, generally speaking, on three levels. (1) They persuade people to change in the ways that we want — often. (2) Contrary to all expectations, they don't get you killed nearly as often as violence does. Otherwise expressed, nonviolence is dangerous, but not nearly as dangerous as violence. (3) And finally, they work on the much deeper level that is precisely where violence fails most reliably. Every time someone uses real nonviolence things get better, the system moves forward toward stable peace, whether or not the actor achieves his or her immediate goal. For the rest of this chapter we'll be exploring these claims as we try to fill out our picture of what nonviolence looks like in the "real world" of politics and history. So let's open the file.

Down to Cases

I want to begin, despite some misgivings, with an event of high drama. Misgivings because I know how easy it is to get entranced by a spectacular climax and miss the years of preparation that went into it, which is to miss the essential ground that a nonviolent moment springs from. A friend of mine who was quite the ballet dancer in his earlier life tells me that Margot Fonteyn was once gushed over by some admiring fans. Ms. Fonteyn said, "You see all this 'effortless' grace, this 'spontaneous' beauty. Little do you realize the hours of sheer torture that went into it." I don't want us to miss the years of careful training, but let's start, nonetheless, at the climax of the freedom struggle in India on May 21,

1930, when more than 2,000 unarmed volunteers walked up to the gate of the Dharasana salt factory in Gujarat and were beaten to the ground by guards whose vehemence went on without relenting throughout the day. This event, brilliantly reenacted by Sir Richard Attenborough in the film *Gandhi*, was the climax of the Salt Satyagraha and, in large part, of the freedom struggle itself. When he saw wave after wave of unarmed volunteers, in regular bands of twenty-five, walking into a hail of beatings without even lifting an arm to protect themselves, American correspondent Webb Miller wired, "In eighteen years of reporting in twenty-two countries I have never witnessed such harrowing scenes." Yet on they came, walking deliberately into the blows, taking only a short break during the afternoon heat, with their crude first-aid station patching up the fallen and splinting their broken bones.

Now the fact is that not only this "raid," but also the entire Salt Satyagraha campaign, were, technically, utter failures. Outside of a few minor concessions wrested from the government in the existing salt laws, nothing seemed to change. Yet now we know that this bloody climax made India's freedom inevitable, because it showed what the Satyagraha volunteers were made of, and what the oppressive system of government that the British had imposed on India was made of. When freedom came sixteen years later, the agony of the 320 hospitalized marchers, and the two who died, had born its fruit.

If Gandhi noticed the delicate irony, that the campaign that did the greatest work didn't "work" at all, it would not have fazed him. It illustrates perfectly his formula for successful action, which comes straight from the Bhagavad Gita: use the right means in a just cause and leave the results in the hands of God. In another idiom, if you put good energy into a situation, good results have to follow, somewhere.

Anyone who works for nonviolence has seen this phenomenon, though usually on a smaller scale. Before all-out war broke out in Kosovo, in March, 1998, a group I work with sent six observers to the region to give moral support and some nonviolence training to ethnically Albanian students demonstrating against their already harsh mistreatment by the Serbian regime. I happened to be coming back from Denver the day after they reached Prishtina, and by mere chance I ran into our board president waiting for the same plane back to San Francisco. Steve greeted me with some alarm, "Have you heard the news? David [our executive director] is arrested. They're all in jail." We sat reading the details on my laptop. We had failed. The whole group was arrested on a minor technicality and sentenced to ten days in a Serbian jail, followed by expulsion. What we did not know was that the American attache was at their hearing, and events had already taken a course of their own. Within hours pictures of the six Americans, with their shaved heads, started appearing on world news services. By the time we reached San Francisco the press was on full alert. Our friends were released the next morning and back in Washington soon afterward giving press conferences and visiting senators. Camera crews were knocking down the door to our tiny office a day later — and Kosovo was world news. In the event, there was no big turnaround. The "international community" (I always put that in quotes, because it isn't much of a community.) completely failed to stand up to President Slobodan Milosevic and left the Kosovars to their fate until matters got much worse and they could see their way clear to using bombs (which made matters *much* worse). But you have to be realistic — and humble. We were a handful of unknown locals ten thousand miles away, operating on a shoestring, and yet we succeeded beyond our wildest dreams in bringing an egregious situation to world attention.

I sometimes think that the reason we can't easily understand nonviolence is that the reality of the thing is so enormous that we're like ants crawling over a colossal Gulliver. No one, not even Gandhi, could grasp the whole thing at once. One has to sketch in the picture of how it works from various angles, like that popular form of Hindu worship called *arati* where you take lighted camphor or an oil lamp in your right hand and move it in slow circles around the head and neck of the god you're worshipping, be it Ganesha or the Divine Mother, or whomever. You are garlanding him or her with light. When this is done in the *sanctum sanctorum* of a temple, or the worship room deep inside a non-electrified home, the shifting shadows as you illuminate the divine image from every angle give a distinct impression of movement. Ganesha comes alive.

To illuminate the worshipful picture of peace, we, too, have to move reverently around her, seeing her beauty from every angle. That's why I made bold to put one of my own small experiences side by side with the mighty "experiment with truth" at Dharasana. Both illustrate, even in their disparity, how deeper forces seem to take over and conduct nonviolent efforts to good, but not always foreseen, conclusions. Now I share with you four examples of nonviolence (and a few extras I couldn't resist) that are as different from each other as can be — spaced pretty evenly around the wide circle of the possible. With some imagination, peace can come alive for us at the center.

I. The Rosenstraße Prison Demonstration

"It never would have worked against the Nazis." This routine objection has to be taken seriously, because what people really mean by it is, since nonviolence wouldn't have worked against the Nazis — i.e., since it's too weak to work against powerful opposition — we have to keep violence around to fall back on. But if we do this, nonviolence *cannot* work. Nonviolence plus violence, nonviolence with violence held in reserve, is no nonviolence at all. That makes the objection, if it were true, serious indeed.

There are several things wrong with it, however. One is, how can something not work when it hasn't been tried? With a very few exceptions, one of which we're about to consider, the only weapons people knew to use against Nazism were either passivity, which was a disaster; or violence, which, as we're beginning to learn today, was a flawed success. The objection is based on sheer speculation. And worse than that, it's false.

In Berlin, in 1943, on a gray weekend at the end of February, police and Gestapo swept through the cold streets and arrested the remaining Jews, mostly men, who had been left more or less at large because they were Jews "of Aryan kin," i.e. married to non-Jewish wives.

There was little resistance to the unannounced roundup, as may well be imagined. The arrestees were brought to a large, recently converted building on the Rosenstraße, a few blocks from a major Gestapo headquarters, without incident. Only two weeks earlier, in Munich, the student-led "White Rose" conspiracy had been betrayed to the Gestapo and virtually all its youthful members were on their way to the guillotine. However, in Berlin the "Jewish Radio," as the still remaining Jews' informal phone network was called, was buzzing, and within hours the wives and, in some cases, mothers of the arrested men learned where they had been taken. What then took place was like nothing that had ever happened under Nazi rule. By the following morning, from every part of the city, "as though in answer to a call — as though prearranged," the women converged on the Rosenstraße detention center, demanding the release of their loved ones. All day they defied repeated orders to leave. As their numbers swelled to more than six thousand, the prisoners themselves took courage and began clamoring through the barred windows to be released. It was an acutely embarrassing display. Gestapo headquarters, as mentioned, was but a few blocks away. One or two machine guns could have swept the street clear of these troublemakers — if there were nothing in the world but threat force.

For many years this episode provided an answer to the inevitable "it never would have worked," because in fact the demonstrations worked. They created an impossible dilemma for the regime, and within a few days the Gestapo, not the women, blinked. By Sunday the men were free.

Some of them had been already deported to concentration camps. They were told never to talk about what they had seen there, and hastily put on trains to Berlin, so hastily that some of them couldn't get back their own clothes.

Until recently I thought, like everyone else who knew about the episode, even most Germans, that the "Aryan-related" sons and husbands were no doubt quietly rearrested later in twos and threes, and this time there was no one to save them. So the demonstration had a spectacular but not a lasting success. It "worked," but it did not work. It did not have much lasting effect on the whole system. Or so we thought.

Finally, in 1996, a full-length study appeared, *Resistance of the Heart* by Nathan Stoltzfus, documenting what actually happened, not only in Berlin but in Paris and other cities that also had the *Mischling* ("mixed-breed") problem and where the local headquarters were watching anxiously for guidelines from the German capital. The book is full of fascinating details about the insanity of Nazi logic, and the contradictions of violence — for example, that the Führer himself refused to make a decision. He whose "fanatical will," he once boasted, had "rescued the German nation," was paralyzed. Nonviolence paralyzed him. The big surprise Stoltzfus turned up, however, is that virtually everyone snatched back from the jaws of death by their loved ones out in front of number 1-2 Rosenstraße survived the war. As did their colleagues in Paris and other capitals under Nazi control. In other words, tens of thousands of people were rescued by this impromptu demonstration by untrained women, women who had been living for more than a decade under a regime of authoritarian terror the like of which the modern world had rarely seen. Nonviolence was almost never tried against the Nazis, but when it was, it scored a resounding victory.

The very success of the demonstrations raises a somewhat embarrassing question: why did they stop? Why did no one see the vulnerability of the fascist armor this episode revealed? As Stoltzfus points out, probably one reason the episode has been so well ignored lies in this implication, that if one demonstration worked, others might have done more. And imagine if they had started sooner . . . ?

Rather than conclude that the event was passed over in silence because we are embarrassed by its very success, I prefer the charitable, and more practical view that we blind-sided it not so much out of moral cowardice as cultural ignorance. You just don't see what's coming at you from another paradigm, even if it's right before your eyes.

The resistance at the Rosenstraße detention center did not noticeably slow the Nazi juggernaut all by itself. Would we have expected it to? It's unlikely that more than a handful of those involved even knew the name of the force that they were wielding, much less how to build on it. As a full-fledged insurrection it was too little, too late — as if the women had had any such intention. Still, the events of that dramatic weekend reveal a solid nonviolent principle: through a courageous act of self sacrifice, the demonstrators brought about a momentary rehumanization of the Jewish prisoners — their loved ones — in the hardened hearts of the Gestapo. It was not only somewhat awkward to massacre in broad daylight such a large crowd of German women. The demonstrators gave a salutary yank on their captor's ideological blinders.

But they were, needless to say, totally untrained for such resistance. The chances are that few of them were aware of what was really going on in India or would have dreamed they could apply it in their own circumstances. Some of them may have been there when the Führer deigned to appear briefly with a most un-Gandhian Indian freedom fighter, Subhas Chandra Bose, whose way of resisting the British was to join the Axis forces. Thus, without leadership or a sense of how to proceed, they were naturally not able to capitalize on their discovery. Their spontaneous demonstration therefore "worked," i.e. it accomplished the desired result right there at hand; apparently it did not do much work (without quote marks) to change the system, because whatever the peak of courage reached by the demonstrators on that occasion, they had no idea how to turn it into a movement, either by bringing about a more enduring conversion within themselves or some kind of outward organization. For that reason, we can assume, it had no noticeable long-term effect. That is not the case with the next event I would like to consider.

2. The Saint of Auschwitz

At Auschwitz, one day during the summer of 1941, a Polish prisoner from Block Fourteen managed to escape. The routine punishment for such an event was to take the entire block, several hundred men who were hanging onto life by a thread, and force them to stand at attention until the escapee was hunted down. If he were not found, ten others would be culled out and left to die in "the Bunker," a bare underground cell, without food or water. It was considered the worst thing that could happen to you at Auschwitz. Guards and prisoners alike strained to catch the occasional sounds from the soldiers and dogs searching the surrounding swamp. Hours went by. Gestapo Commandant Fritsch paced back and forth in front of them like a pendulum of doom. The miserable daily soup ration was brought out, but Fritsch ordered it poured down the drain before the eyes of the starving men. Finally, toward evening, the search was declared a failure. One after another, ten men were pulled out of formation to pay with their life for one man's desperate escape. "Long live Poland!" shouted one; another, a father, broke down and wept, "My poor wife, my poor children. Good-bye, good-bye!"

Then, once more, an unheard of thing happened. A prisoner stepped calmly out of line and started walking toward the Commandant. For some reason, no one shot him. Commandant Fritsch instinctively pulled out his pistol, but only shouted, "Who is this Polish *Schwein*?" Word shot around: it was Father Kolbe of Niepokalanów. For the last two years, Father Maximilian Mary Kolbe had been a living symbol of human endurance and dignity for the whole camp. Now he walked up to Commandant Fritsch and calmly said to him, in good German, "I have a request." When he recovered from the shock, Fritsch barked "Well, what do you want," and Kolbe quietly said, "I would like permission to die in place of one of these men." A priest was almost as low as a Jew in the grotesque ideology of the Nazis, and Fritsch scornfully granted the request, totally misunderstanding its power. The husband and father who had wept, Sergeant Franciszek Gajowniczek, would live. After eight brutal days, Father Kolbe was put to death with an injection of gasoline. (Franciszek Gajowniczek died recently at the age of ninety-three in his home city of Brzeg, having testified at the Papal institution of Kolbe as a Martyr of the Church.)

We'd be justified to call this act the climax of Father Kolbe's spiritual career. What was the effect of his final, unpremeditated sacrifice? What good did it do? This is the testimony of an eyewitness, George Bielecki:

> It was an enormous shock to the whole camp. We became aware someone unknown among us in this spiritual night . . . was raising the standard of love on high. Someone unknown, like everyone else . . . went to a horrible death for the sake of someone not even related to him. Therefore it is not true, we cried, that humanity is cast down and trampled in the mud. . . . Thousands of prisoners were convinced the true world continued to exist and that our torturers would not be able to destroy it. . . . To say that Father Kolbe died for one of us or that person's family is too great a simplification. His death was the salvation of thousands.

The "salvation of thousands" here is not metaphorical. For you and me, a mood swing up or down is not a matter of life or death; but to a prisoner at Auschwitz that is exactly what it was. As every doctor knows, when a person is critically ill the will to live can make the difference between life and death, and in the death camps everyone was critically ill. A prisoner who lost his or her will to go on visibly collapsed and was generally dead within two weeks. It's quite possible that thousands, not just Sergeant Gajowniczek, who would otherwise have died in that man-made hell, got the courage to live on, in some cases long enough to see the day of liberation.

So it seems that nonviolence did work against the Nazis; not to save Father Kolbe's life, of course, (which wasn't his purpose), and not *only* to save the life of one other person (which was), but to release a forbidden ingredient — hope — into the nightmare of dehumanization in which the Nazis had tried to entangle the minds of millions.

This was done by a single man with no external resources whatever; yet in a sense it was even more effective than the Rosenstraße demonstration that was carried out by six thousand citizens who were technically free. It is the degree of the sacrifice, not the number of the sacrificers, that gives a nonviolent act its power. Consider what Father Kolbe was up against. Hitler's stated ambition, "to prepare a generation of young people devoid of a conscience, imperious, relentless and cruel," had succeeded with many like the guards at Auschwitz, some of whom had been systematically dehumanized since they were children. But Father Kolbe had been systematically training himself since *he* was young. At Auschwitz itself he had endured extreme abuse without succumbing to hatred; he had intense faith that there was a supreme, compassionate reality behind all appearances, which in his case was Mary, Mother of God, and this reality was present even in his oppressors though they were entirely unaware of it. He thus was literally a match for them. His humanity was, to use a phrase of Gandhi's, "mathematically proportionate" to their inhumanity.

Once you know what to look for, the underlying forces that determine the outcome of a nonviolent act are not too difficult to discern.

Perhaps if we knew this science somewhat better, we would be able to assess such cases still more accurately, or even predict their outcomes. One thing is certain: nonviolence *did* work against the Nazis. It worked when it was tried, it worked proportionally to the dehumanization trying to hold it in check. It will always work against oppressors — provided you've trained yourself as well as they have.

It should be clear now why Theodore Roszak put the word "work" in quotes when he wrote that people say nonviolence doesn't "work." It's extremely important to be clear about what we mean when we ask whether any act did or did not "work." If we mean, did it do just what we wanted, visibly, immediately, then indeed nonviolence sometimes doesn't "work." It did not, for example, save Father Kolbe's life. But if we mean, did it have a long-term positive effect on the whole system, perhaps one that the actor didn't foresee, then we get a very different answer. In these terms we can make a central proposition about nonviolent versus violent effectiveness that's key to understanding the whole subject:

Nonviolence sometimes "works" and always works,
while
violence sometimes "works," but never works.

Sometimes one hears a common variation on "It never would have worked against the Nazis," namely, "It sure didn't work against the Nazis!" People who say this are assuming that the millions who went to their deaths in the Holocaust were being "nonviolent." As we've seen before, it's extremely important to be clear about the difference between passivity and nonviolence. Was Father Kolbe "passive" when he stepped forward to die for another human being, thus setting the Nazi lie on its ear? Outside of the isolated, little-known events like the two we've just considered, active nonviolence was rarely tried against the Nazis or anyone else in the Western hemisphere. The Munich students of the White Rose conspiracy, for example, issued leaflets calling for "passive resistance;"

but they had little notion what passive resistance was, not to mention the subtle but important difference between it and active nonviolence. No, it was passivity that was tried against the Nazis. Harsh as it may sound to say this, when one is passive in the face of such aggression, passive out of fear, one is going along with the violence, obeying its logic. This is not to condemn anyone caught in such a trap; to say that someone was passive out of ignorance of an alternative is not to say he or she was morally wrong, which in any case is language I seldom use. It is not to condemn those caught in such a tragedy; it's to understand our choices so that people will not be caught in them again.

The trap that sprang shut on the "Aryan-related" Jews of Berlin on February 27, 1943 was the result of an evil that had gone on practically unopposed for two decades; and the power that forced apart the jaws of that trap long enough to let some victims escape must have been, at least for that moment, just as strong. What gave these women — leaderless, unorganized, untrained and probably unaware that what they were doing has a name — strength enough to face down the Gestapo? It was love for their husbands and sons. Perhaps we can think of the bond between husband and wife, and mother and son — the force of love that holds together the "nuclear family" — the way we think of the "strong force" that holds together the nucleus of an atom: sometimes it shows its strength only when pulled apart.

These considerations bring us to an important element in nonviolent science that is often forgotten by those who object that it "never would have worked" against a very violent opponent. It makes a lot of difference that Nazism went practically unopposed for so long.

I have found it useful to think of the way violence feeds itself, the escalation of conflict, as a steep curve (see figure on next page) where time is plotted against intensity — intensity measured not by the number of weapons but the degree of dehumanization, the single most telling parameter of hostility. The important thing to bear in mind is that nonviolence, like violence, also comes in degrees. In both cases time turns up

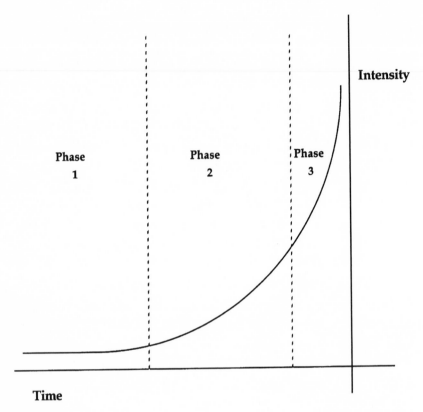

Intensity

Phase
1

Phase
2

Phase
3

Time

The escalation of conflict

a rheostat and progressively more energy, violent or nonviolent, is activated. Therefore, when a conflict has been allowed to go on and on before
you finally intervene, the degree of nonviolence you need has to "escalate" accordingly. The longer you wait, the more soul-force you need to
apply.

For practical purposes, we can say that conflicts escalate in three
stages. In the first stage, on the low "foothill" of the curve, conflicts can
be successfully handled by the arts of conflict resolution. There is a wors-
ening dispute, perhaps, but the parties to it (either directly or through a
mediator) can still work things out by representing grievances and nego-

tiating them; give and take is still possible. But a time comes when it is not. As anger increases, "hearing" shuts down. Then a different level of force has to be invoked. Gandhiji defined this psychological boundary very well, speaking as usual from his own experience:

> Things of fundamental importance to the people are not secured by reason alone but have to be purchased with their suffering. . . . If you want something really important to be done you must not merely satisfy the reason, you must move the heart also.

We have now crossed the border, in other words, into stage two, the zone of Satyagraha. In this land the "law of suffering" which Gandhiji discovered in South Africa applies, because we need to reach the other party at a deeper level than reason. One party has to "give when it hurts" and reawaken the seriously alienated opponent by voluntarily taking on that very hurt, not trying to avoid it — the hurt, or at least the risk of being hurt. The women at the Rosenstraße detention center showed that sometimes just risking pain, which involves the mastery of one's fear, can be extremely effective.

Father Kolbe carried the same principle to the extreme degree. Here the dehumanization had become so intense, the power relationship so unequal, the time for acting so short, that he had to lay down his life to make it work. He illustrates how to apply nonviolence at the really steep section of the curve, stage three, when there's nothing for it but the final sacrifice. Again the power comes, as Gandhi often stated, from the satyagrahi's being *willing* to die. Whether or not he or she will actually die depends on various external circumstances, but he or she is not bluffing. When Gandhi fasted unto death, it was not a ploy. He made the supreme renunciation and put his life on the block, leaving his opponents to respond as they would. (In his case they always yielded, but sometimes at the eleventh hour.)

I find that this graph, aside from its general usefulness, settles "would never have worked" objections very well, for almost without exception, those who make it are thinking of an extreme situation in which we have to imagine ourselves suddenly invoking nonviolence very late in the game — for example, when an entire nation has gone on dehumanizing its consciousness without let or hindrance for decades. Naturally, this stacks the cards! We the "international community" were helpless in Yugoslavia because we stood around doing nothing while Mr. Milosevic used his state-controlled media to drive his nationalist Serbs into a frenzy of hatred. Nonviolence in Germany would have been much less costly in 1918, or 1920 — as in fact it was, during the Kapp Putsch — or 1932. Nonetheless, that there is a way for nonviolence to work even late in the game is what the Rosenstraße women and Father Kolbe begin to show us. *How* nonviolence would work against the Nazis depends on when you imagine it might have been applied and by whom; *whether* it would work is not in question. Assurances to the contrary notwithstanding, it would work — in fact, it did.

Some years ago — but his judgment still applies — the well-known activist and scholar, David Dellinger, who titled his autobiography *From Yale to Jail*, deemed that we understand nonviolence about as well as we understood electricity in the days of Marconi and Edison. This strikes me as an apt comparison. Marconi and Edison knew they were dealing with a natural force, and that it must have a great untapped potential, but little else. Gradually they figured out the manner of this force (despite its mysterious nature; to this day no one really knows what electricity *is*) and started learning how to use it without getting hurt. Which is exactly what we're talking about.

Comparing, for example, the Rosenstraße demonstration with the episode of the Birmingham marchers we can further refine our sense of what makes a nonviolent interaction tick. The Berlin women had one powerful thing going for them: the "nuclear power" roused by the extreme threat to their loved ones. This was not there to sweep aside the fear in the Birmingham marchers, but several things *were* there to enhance the nonviolent power of their impromptu action. They were being proactive, for one thing. It was they themselves who were on the march, not passively overtaken by surprise events. They did have the advantage of inspired leadership. And most importantly, they had gone through a certain amount of preparation. More: they were a community of faith, and were able to draw inspiration and ideas and wisdom from the Indian freedom struggle with which, we now know, they had fairly extensive contacts. All these things helped them rise beautifully to the unexpected opportunity for their nonviolent moment, even though they may not have been thrown back on their deepest resources quite as much as the women of Berlin, whose sheer desperation we may well imagine. The modest training — and impressive leadership — of the Birmingham marchers also enabled them to do the critical thing the Berlin wives could not do: follow up. This may be the most important difference in terms of a major, systemic effect on the future. Like many spontaneous non-violent episodes, Birmingham succeeded. Unlike many others it was part of a movement that also, in large part, succeeded, and that against a resistance comparable to Nazism in its ideological vehemence.

3. Holy Experiments

The events we have described at Berlin, Birmingham and Dharasana share a similar structure, and they are the kind of events most people associate with the word "nonviolence": a protest movement by an oppressed group resisting abusive authority. Even here, on familiar turf, we found many myths and misconceptions that needed chipping away before we could appreciate how even rudimentary nonviolence can be surprisingly effective against determined and serious opposition, that is, against people with a very dehumanizing outlook whose bullying has gone unchecked for a long time.

Now we can push off into less familiar territory, or if you will, widen the lens. Nonviolence can't be only a weapon of the oppressed, any more than electricity can only appear as great flashes from the sky, or gravity only work on falling apples. We have tended not to look for nonviolence anywhere else, because we think that the powerful don't need nonviolence while the weak have no other recourse. By now we should begin to suspect both these assumptions.

Nonviolence can, of course, come "from below," but it can also be offered from the high seats of power. Colonial America can boast one of the best-known examples. Almost a century before the Revolution, in March, 1681, King Charles II gave William Penn governorship of the vast territory that today bears his name. Unlike most colonists, Penn crossed the Atlantic with a double mandate. Empowered by his King to administer a colony, he also came with the blessings of his spiritual mentor, who was one of the greatest dissenters of British history and one of the most effective promoters of radical nonviolence ever in the West: George Fox, founder of the Society of Friends. Penn used his mind-boggling opportunity to carry out what history now calls the "Holy Experiment" — seventy years of governance by nonviolent principles.

Even before leaving England, Penn wrote a now-famous letter to his new subjects, the Delaware Indians, which witnesses to a tolerance far ahead of its time. He said, in part:

> I am very sensible of the unkindness and injustice that hath been too much exercised toward you by the people of these parts of the world . . . but . . . I have great love and regard toward you, and I desire to win and gain your love and friendship, by a kind, just and peaceable life.

Penn actually carried this out to a remarkable degree. In all ways that were possible, given the growing inequality of the situation, he tried to prevent the indigenous peoples' exploitation by Europeans. "The result was to be an unparalleled record of some seventy years of almost completely unbroken peaceful association" between them. From our own perspective, perhaps Penn should have refused to rule over the native peoples at all. That is easy to say nearly three hundred years after the fact, and perhaps *perfect* nonviolence would have said it then; but life doesn't become perfect all at once. The beginnings of nonviolence in the colony made a relative paradise for the indigenous and the conquering peoples compared to the bloody shambles of a relationship that obtained elsewhere, and whose legacy we have still not overcome.

In the Holy Experiment, nonviolence (needless to say, still an unknown word at that time) was no rebellion against established authority; it *was* the established authority. Nor was it spontaneous, accidental or *ad hoc* as so many nonviolent episodes still are today. It "trickled down" from the mind of George Fox, the originator of Quaker theology and social teaching. America has been home to many utopian experiments, but not to many utopian *regimes,* especially regimes that furnish a model — if we would only use it — for governing on a national scale. The colony experienced problems of every kind, including friction with the crown, but despite them the house that nonviolence built on early Quaker lines showed that nonviolence could work in every department from defense to criminal justice. It also showed that a regime based on this principle of order is robust. The Experiment endured until the vision faded and the Quaker party lost its mandate at the ballot box. It was not overwhelmed either by the world around it or by the power of the crown above it, both of which were based on depressingly conventional principles. For seventy years it housed under one judicial roof a diverse collection of colonists from many parts of Europe and several religions who lived in a relatively high state of harmony under the "Great Law" their governor had set up in 1682. This Law was in many ways more humane than the crime bill of 1991. Capital crimes were reduced from two hundred to exactly two — treason and murder — a tremendous step forward for its time, which we are now reversing. The Great Law even abolished war — on December 7, 1682. (Why not celebrate *that*, instead of Pearl Harbor?) The Quaker regime produced both internal and external kinds of security: the colony remained an island of peace when storms swept over surrounding territories, traumatizing the relations of the red and white races down to our own time.

In this way, despite its problems, the seventy-year Quaker regime "laid the foundations for what became some of the . . . guiding principles of an entire nation." America as a whole owes something to the Holy Experiment, which was based squarely upon ideals and principles which we would recognize today as nonviolence, and tried to carry those principles out in social policy, criminal justice, religious toleration — even national defense.

As Gandhi would later declare, "Nonviolence that merely offers civil resistance to the authorities and goes no further scarcely deserves the name." Under his leadership, it went much further indeed, and in terms of power relationships it went in three directions. While the Indian satyagrahis were resisting the Raj, they were also, even primarily, trying to be nonviolent towards the Muslim community that shared the British yoke with them, and towards the "scheduled castes" who were beneath them in the ancient Hindu social hierarchy. If their anti-British resistance was from below, in terms of political space, they were also nonviolently working sideways on the communal question and downwards toward the former untouchables, renamed by Gandhiji *harijans* or "Children of God." He came to feel very early on that these two relationships were, if anything, more important than nonviolence towards their rulers, that relationships of truth with their equals and with their social "inferiors" — with the underclass they themselves had created — were an essential prerequisite to loosening the British hold. Nonviolence was the rule of life, not the rule of only one kind of relationship.

Gandhi himself never showed the slightest inclination to take public office, but there was a long tradition in India of the ideal ruler who would hold sway over his or her subjects by integrative instead of threat power, and that ideal came close to being a reality in at least one famous case we've already discussed, when emperor Ashoka, whom H. G. Wells called the greatest emperor in history, built his rule on Buddhist principles in North Central India. Ashoka had ascended the throne of his father's sizable kingdom probably in 269 B.C.E. When he had exercised power for about eight years he won a famous victory; but instead of rejoicing, he records that the horror of war was borne in on him by the scenes of death and suffering. That vision turned an ordinary conquest into a personal crisis of self-conquest that was to change history. Here's how the emperor describes it in his own words:

When the King, Priyadarsi [Ashoka], Beloved of the Gods, had been consecrated eight years, Kalinga was conquered. 150,000 people were taken captive, 100,000 were killed, and many more died. Just after the taking of Kalinga the Beloved of the Gods began to follow Righteousness [Dharma; i.e. he adopted Buddhism], to love Righteousness, to give instruction in Righteousness. When an unconquered country is conquered, people are killed, they die, or are made captive. That the Beloved of the Gods finds very pitiful and grievous. . . . Today, if a hundredth or a thousandth part of those who suffered in Kalinga were to be killed, to die, or be taken captive, it would be very grievous to the Beloved of the Gods. If anyone does him wrong it will be forgiven as far as it can be forgiven. The Beloved of the Gods even reasons with the forest tribes in his empire, and seeks to reform them. But the Beloved of the Gods is not only compassionate, he is powerful, and he tells them to repent, lest they be slain. For the Beloved of the Gods desires

safety, self-control, justice and happiness for all beings. The
Beloved of the Gods considers that the greatest of all victories
is the victory of Righteousness.

Ashoka reigned from 273 B.C.E. until he died of natural causes in
232, having considerably enlarged the already great territories handed
down from his famous grandfather, Chandragupta Maurya. As this edict
makes clear, he had no intention of abdicating the responsibility of securing his realm; indeed, he enlarged it, but he was never again to practice
violence as an instrument of conquest. He showed that one in power
could be pragmatic and yet compassionate; he showed, if you will, not
only that compassion comes from strength — it begets strength. William
Penn was a major contributor, through an important essay, to the tradition of "perpetual peace" thinking in Europe, but Ashoka's influence
went even further, for it was he who spread Buddhism to much of South
East Asia.

It is interesting to compare these two real experiments with the fate
of a utopian regime in Aldous Huxley's novel, *Island,* which so captured
the imagination of the 'sixties. Its psychedelic version of mysticism and
its escapist picture of a free life spoke to that generation's hungers; but in
one important respect it perpetuated, unconsciously, the very worldview
we were trying to escape. The novel ends with doom hanging over the
island paradise, which is about to be overwhelmed by a neighboring state.
The outside world is jealous of the island. That's realistic enough. And
because the islanders are unagressive they have no defense. That isn't.
Neither the Holy Experiments of Emperor Ashoka nor of William Penn
was defenseless against outside pressures. Neither is contemporary Costa
Rica — one of twelve national states without a defense force, and one of
the very few which does not rely on a defense arrangement with any other
state — or other smaller and lesser-known regimes that have renounced
the protection of violence in some way or degree.

In fact, we can check the validity of Huxley's imaginary finale in

another way. At dawn one day, the Gaviotans who provided us with the
opening image of this book were getting ready to go to work when they
found themselves "visited" by an armed unit of the *Fuerzas Armadas
Revolucionarias de Colombia.* The uniformed brigade tried to explain to the
utopians the need for armed struggle. "There is no neutral ground in
Colombia," the *commandante* argued. "You're either with us or against us."
But the Gaviotans replied, "We're with people, not politics." The guerillas left them in peace. They had been ordered not to hurt *los gavioteros*
because the latter's experiment was so valuable. Small scale, the episode
shows again that when it comes to the power of nonviolence, even Huxley's
imagination did not go far enough. It allows us to discern that yes, nonviolence doesn't "work" — in novels; but its alleged defenselessness is
not borne out by the logic of science or the facts of history. With nonviolence you can protect the good as well as disrupt the schemes of the
tyrannical.

4. Springtime in Prague

In the late spring of 1968, the Soviet high command became alarmed
by the "dangerous" liberalizations of party secretary Aleksander Dubcek
that were threatening to create a different kind of communism in Czechoslovakia. Their response to "socialism with a human face" was to order
massive Warsaw Pact armies into the country. Soviet military experts predicted it would take four days to bring Czechoslovakia to heel, and by
military criteria they were right. But those are not the only criteria on
which the real world runs. Lacking a military means of defending themselves, the Czechs came up with a rough-and-ready civilian resistance that
was non-violent in character. They could not keep the Soviets out, but
they could and did refuse to obey curfew orders, using that time to stroll
about in the streets and plant flowers in soldiers' rifles or engage them in
heated discussions. They turned street signs around and watched armored
columns rumble off aimlessly into the countryside; in one such episode,

an entire Polish army was fooled into circling back to the Polish border. (A friend of mine was in a Prague bookstore when a Russian tank pulled up outside. One of the soldiers came in and patiently waited his turn at the cash register, then asked for a map of the city which he politely paid for in Czech money.) They published alternative media to replace banned papers and radio stations, with Czech police often delivering outlawed newspapers in their squad cars. They defended not their territory, but their institutions, and they did this not with weapons but with a characteristic Czech blend of humor, courage and solidarity. As far as possible, life went on as if the occupation forces were simply not there.

Remember, they were not dealing with the dispirited Russian Army which was to bog down in Afghanistan and Chechnya; they were dealing with half a million determined troops, under orders to put down what they were told, and many must have believed, was a full-fledged counter-revolution. And for eight full months, from August 20, 1968 to April 17, 1969, these armies were frustrated by untrained citizens who kept on fraternizing with them as people while determinedly non-cooperating with them as invaders. As a KGB agent ten years later confided, after a few drinks, to Gene Sharp of the Center for Nonviolent Sanctions at Harvard, "My boy, it was a complete disaster!"

Later, when the ghastly Soviet empire collapsed from inside taking most of world communism down with it, jubilant Western analysts (for whom there had been almost nothing real outside the Cold War) would call it the "end of history." What are we going to learn from all this history, then? Should not the spontaneous Soviet collapse have prompted a sobering reflection that we could have dealt with the communist menace in a different mode, without that expense of human life, that mortgaging of the hope of half the world, not to mention the psychological trauma endured by all of us when all life on earth hung at risk? Prague Spring, as it came to be known, showed the innate weakness of such an oppressive system, and the glimmer of a way to exploit that weakness. It is one of the best-known examples of spontaneous nonviolence in Europe, but like all examples of nonviolence anywhere, scarcely known to any but a small band of prophetic enthusiasts.

In the eight months that it took for Moscow to reassert control over Czechoslovakia, whole armies had to be rotated out of the country and replaced with troops who had not been "corrupted" by contact with the civilians. Resistance sputtered on even after their leaders were coerced into accepting a shadow compromise. Most of the new recruits were brought in from remote parts of the Soviet empire and could not understand a Slavic language. An armed resistance that held off such an overwhelming force for eight months would have passed into folklore — a new Thermopylae, which we remember after two thousand years. But in 1968 there wasn't even a name for the type of resistance the Czech civilians were carrying out, and so we were left with the great irony of Prague Spring — that because an untrained people achieved this resistance for eight months without shedding a drop of blood the world hardly noticed anything was happening.

Now, however, we do have a name for this kind of resistance, thanks in large part to Gene Sharp's pioneering work. What the Czechs did is now known as Civilian-Based Defense (CBD). CBD is one of two main forms in which nonviolence has emerged as an alternative to war, and we'll give both a thorough review later, in chapter seven. We should note, for now, two principles of CBD by which a determined and reasonably united people can withstand an invasion, as in Prague, or an internal takeover such as the failed Kapp Putch in Weimar Germany in 1920, or even resist within the context of an occupation, like the Norwegian schoolteachers' strike which prevented the Nazification of the Norwegian school system. One is: a people who will not submit cannot be ruled. They can be killed, but they cannot be ruled. The other is: if a people can steadfastly discriminate between a group of people and their agenda — between the sinners and the sin — resolutely resisting the latter while as resolutely acknowledging the humanity of the former, they develop an almost irresistible counterforce.

Did the Prague resistance "work?" Perhaps not. It did not save the Czech liberalization. And yet, I would say, it "worked" extremely well, considering that it bought the country eight exhilarating months, even though it was an impromptu reaction by people who had no training and no real leadership for this kind of social action, most of whom probably could not have told you what it's called, not to mention how to apply its principles with flexibility and appropriateness. It "worked" well enough to allow us to think that it might have finally prevailed, had the Czechs been determined to go on until the peace was won, had they understood what they had stumbled upon.

And did Prague Spring work (no quote marks)? Let me draw on the testimony of an eyewitness, my late friend Petra Kelly:

> During the summer of 1968, when nonviolent citizens in Prague were resisting the occupying Soviet forces, my grand- mother and I were there in a hotel near Wenceslaus Square, under house arrest. Even after Dubcek and his close associ- ates were arrested, the people remained steadfast in their resistance. Eventually . . . the Soviets were able to reassert their authority and delay the reforms of the Prague Spring by twenty-one years. But through their sacrifice and suffering, the people of Czechoslovakia . . . later did indeed succeed in their "Velvet Revolution." These events demonstrate the power of nonviolent social defense.

The power, in other words, to change things for the better, to solve unforeseen problems down the road — and sometimes those at hand as well. Prague Spring did not last long. But then, neither did the mighty empire that seemed to win that unequal struggle.

Say It With Flowers?

The stories of many Holocaust rescuers have been coming to light in recent years — fortunately, since a few of the rescuers are still alive. Oskar Schindler, who is not, was made world-famous by the novel and Stephen Spielberg's film about his "list"; but in peace circles one of the best known stories unfolded in the village of Le Chambon sur Lignon in the Haute-Loire, not far from Marseille, which is to say, in Vichy territory. It was also Huguenot territory, where a Protestant minority had endured persecutions in centuries past. When the occupation came to Le Chambon, Pastor André Trocmé and his wife Magda inspired their whole parish to set up an underground escape route that went on spiriting refugees out of the country, under the noses of the Vichy government and the nearby Tatar Legion of the SS, throughout the war. If our four sets of examples show that nonviolence can work against bitter opposition, or from the political top, or against whole states — if this begins to give us some sense, in other words, of the variety and range of its applications — then the resistance at Le Chambon will enable us to disengage something fundamental about their inner consistency.

The resistance of the Chambonnais is one of the very few cases that is not one of leaderless, "amateur" effort. Trocmé had come to his convictions early and knew of Gandhi through the Fellowship of Reconciliation (FOR), a venerable peace organization begun by two Quakers, a German and an Englishman, who found themselves on a railway platform at the outbreak of World War I and swore never to let the enmity of their countries come between them or stop their common thirst for peace. Thus FOR has today one of the longest track records of an existing peace group, and one of the best foundations in nonviolent principles. Outside of the Danish underground's rescue of that country's entire Jewish population, the resistance at Le Chambon was the largest such operation in Europe, and has been relatively well known to a general public since ethicist Phillip Hallie wrote his study, *Lest Innocent Blood be Shed*. One interesting question is, how did an operation of that size escape the attention of the Germans?

And the interesting answer is, it didn't. Many years after the events of 1942-45, Hallie found out that the Commandant of the region, Major Schmehling, had known what *les responsables* of Le Chambon were up to the whole time, but he was so moved by the villagers' courage that he actually defied the SS to protect them. "I am a good Catholic, you understand, and I can grasp these things," he explained to the Trocmés twenty years later. At the time, the Chambonnais had no idea that Schmehling was protecting them at such risk to himself. If it had not been for Hallie's research, neither would we. Imagine how many things of this sort we *never* find out — how many such stories are hidden in history, a science which until recently was not concerned to look for them.

Le Chambon is an example of nonviolence that both "worked" and worked; it saved thousands of people (i.e., it "worked against the Nazis") and it created an enduring light in the midst of vast darkness. It was Schmehling, who had been impressed by the sincerity of one of the Chambonnais in his trial testimony, who explained to SS leader, Colonel Metzger, "This kind of resistance has nothing to do with violence, nothing to do with anything we can destroy with violence."

The Chambonnais carried on their work for three years, daily sticking by their choice to risk death rather than abandon the responsibility they had accepted. Therefore, in addition to Trocmé's astute leadership, they had the advantage of passing through the crucible of sustained experience. One result of this was that they moved past the stage that's reached by most of the events we consider nonviolence or peace activity in the world — the stage of symbolic resistance. Things began at Le Chambon the way they begin very commonly when the urge to resist awakens — as symbolic defiance; but they did not stop there. "The saluting of flags, the ringing of bells, the giving of oaths dissolved as important issues for the Chambonnais. . . . What was left was the one *activity* that made Le Chambon a village of refuge: the saving of innocent lives." This important point is so often misunderstood that it must be stressed: in nonviolence, you don't say it with symbols. When Sir Richard Attenborough's film brought the phenomenon of Gandhi to public attention, one startled journalist, I recall, said that *Gandhi* was about "the mystery of a man just sitting, holding a flower." I have seen, I believe, every still photograph and every foot of film of Gandhi that's in public domain. He never holds a flower in any one of them. He has a staff, a spinning wheel, a microphone, but never a flower. The man used tools, not symbols.

It is important for us to realize that because someone wears a ribbon or has marched from point A to point B with a placard, they have not been nonviolent. Not yet. And therefore if their demonstration doesn't "work" (or work, needless to say), we have no right to say that nonviolence failed. There hasn't *been* any nonviolence until there has been personal struggle or sacrifice, followed by outer work — both things that are, in their respective ways, quite concrete. They are not requests or signs, they are acts. They may be symbols *also*, but first and foremost they are real.

But surely Gandhi led those protest marches in South Africa and India? Yes, but look at those famous marches a little closer. The first, now known as "The Great March," was launched in South Africa on November 6, 1913 when Gandhi found himself in charge of several thousand striking mine workers and their families. It was first of all a deliberate act of civil disobedience undertaken by the miners-turned-satyagrahis from Newcastle in Natal province, who entered the Transvaal to court arrest. It was, in other words, an illegal act; Indians who did not live there were not allowed to enter the Transvaal. It was not about going from point A to point B to show you cared about something. These mine workers had lived on company property; when they walked off the job they lost their homes, and there was nothing for it but to march to the Transvaal where Gandhiji would try to accommodate them at his ashram. Thus the march was not a mere symbol; they were not merely voting with their feet. They were going somewhere they had to go — and defying the law in the process.

Now recall the most famous march of all, the one that launched the climactic Salt Satyagraha of 1930, when Gandhiji and seventy-eight ashram volunteers undertook a two-hundred mile "pilgrimage" to the seacoast town of Dandi to take illegal salt from the ocean in defiance of the Government monopoly. Along the way, some 70,000 people fell in with the civilly disobedient "pilgrims." You may know the scene from Attenborough's film: what you see is real people going down to a real sea to get real salt that had been unjustly withheld from them for the purpose of rank exploitation, and once again they were breaking an unjust law to do it. What could be more basic, more concrete, than salt? If anything, it was the absurd monopoly over salt-taking that was smoke-and-mirrors, a construct which millions had taken for real until Gandhiji's brilliant gesture broke the illusion. Of course, Gandhi could have taken a train — but then how would he have brought with him those tens of thousands. Call it theater, if you will, but not symbol.

Let's look again at the Gandhian definition of power I cited in chapter two, and mark the precise language:

> Of power there are two kinds. One is obtained by the *fear* of punishment and the other by *acts* of love.

I emphasize the difference between *fear*, on the one hand, and *acts*, which again points up the greater concreteness of nonviolence over violence. Symbols can play a role in the initial stage of a movement; they can encourage people to stand up and be counted, to show solidarity. But once they're all there and counted, what will the people *do*? If they keep on waving flags and marching from point A to point B, they will be going against the spirit and the deepest reality of nonviolence. You could almost say, at that point symbols perpetuate the very thing the actors should be trying to dispel: the belief that only threat force has real power, and thus nonviolence is merely an appeal to the other's sentiment, not, as Gandhi insisted, an awakening of his awareness. This contradiction may be why, in practice, many symbols backfire in nonviolent action — for example the "Goddess of Liberty" put up by the students and other protesters at Tienanmen Square, which infuriated but did nothing to incapacitate, much less dissuade the authorities.

Threat power, on the other hand, does not come from punishment, in Gandhi's instinctive word choice. It comes from the victim's "fear of punishment." No fear, no power. It has even been argued, I think cogently, that the scariest "what if" scenario of this century — "What if Hitler had gotten the bomb?" — is really not as compelling as it may sound. OK, what if he had used atomic bombs on one or two cities *and what if we then said,* "Do your worst: we will not give in"? Would he want to rule over a radioactive wasteland? In actual legal and political experience, threat is a much less reliable way of getting people to comply than it seems. We have to react to the threat as it was intended or it won't work. Tyrants rule by fear much more than by the actual power they have to inflict harm. To repeat, if you have no fear you cannot be deterred. This is why Gandhi says that love (Satyagraha) "compels reason to be free" while punishment only works on those who emotionally cooperate by fearing it. The Nobel-prize winning biologist, Albert Szent-Gyeorgyi, brought this out very well in an appreciative summary of Gandhi's historical significance (like most people, he used the word "force" for what we would call "threat force"):

Between the two world wars, at the heyday of Colonialism, force reigned supreme. It had a suggestive power, and it was natural for the weaker to lie down before the stronger.

Then came Gandhi, chasing out of his country, almost

single-handed, the greatest military power on earth. He
taught the world that there are higher things than force,
higher even than life itself; he proved that force had lost its
suggestive power.

Violence can hurt you but it can't make you change your mind or
even your behavior. Only fear of violence can do that. On the other hand,
people who have used nonviolence successfully, at any stage of conflict,
have inevitably found that they need something more than symbols.

The Washington-based Search for Common Ground is one of the
most successful international conflict-resolving organizations in the world,
to my knowledge. They began by simply trying to get people who may be
bitterly opposed, who think they have no common basis of agreement —
for example "pro-choice" and "pro-life" people — to identify some common ground to build on. John Marks, the President of Search, has found
that, "While dialogue is important, in our view, it should lead to something concrete. We want opponents . . . to work together on shared problems" like cleaning up religious sites by ethnic Slavs and Albanians. "Working together on shared problems" is precisely the formula discovered by
psychologists who found themselves with an artificial conflict in a summer camp, and then found that only by having the two parties work
together to fix the truck or get the well working could they be brought
back together. Symbolic events such as seeing movies or eating ice cream
together didn't do it.

If nonviolence had no inherent power, then signs and ribbons and
statues would be about the most effective thing you could do — but
then, if nonviolence had no inherent power there would be no reason to
write a book about it.

Social Warming

For all the ugliness of his message, white supremacist Tom Metzger makes an unarguable point in our headnote: violence comes in degrees. There's such a thing as "big, massive" violence, and it "works"; the bomb that destroyed the Federal Building in Oklahoma City on April 15, 1995 had more impact than a lone protester railing against the government from a soap box. This would be a trivial observation were it not for the fact that the corollary, which we have been trying to demonstrate, is somehow less obvious to us: nonviolence, too, comes in degrees. Any amount of love you launch in any situation will do work; but if you want it to "work," i.e., to have a specific effect then and there, then it has to wield *enough* love to outweigh the hate that's operating in that situation. The hate set loose at Auschwitz was extreme; therefore the tremendous power of a supreme sacrifice, such as Father Kolbe made, was required to counter it when the moment came for him to act decisively against it.

Gandhi said that the success of their efforts in the last Free India campaign in 1942 was "mathematically proportionate" to the purity of their nonviolence. I believe he meant it literally, and I for one believe that it was — it is always — literally true. If we had some idea how to measure the forces I'm here calling love and hate, we would probably see that there were no accidents or surprises in the long process that ultimately gave India her political independence. We know how deep, how second-nature in people and how institutionalized in society was the distortion of race relations when Rosa Louise McCauley Parks refused to give up her seat on a Montgomery bus on December 1, 1955. In the years that followed, much of that dehumanization was exposed and released, the institutions it had built dismantled. *How* much, could we measure it, is the sum total of the force set in motion by her training at the well-known Highlander Folk School, by her courage, by Martin Luther King, Jr.'s genius and by the power of sacrifice and the sustained work that he inspired in so many.

The weather is notoriously unpredictable. But something about it, as we know to our cost, is only too predictable: if we keep pouring fluorocarbons into the atmosphere, if we keep on burning up forests and fossil fuel, we will heat up the planet. Global warming is a man-made phenomenon we have never before experienced. Because of global warming, small perturbations in the atmosphere that are themselves perfectly normal and unavoidable can cascade into terrifically destructive storms. When and where these will occur we cannot predict, but we can predict that they *will* occur, more and more, if we continue heating up our planet. There will be other effects of global warming, too. We can safely predict only one thing about the changes wrought by such an unnatural development: they will not be good.

It is just this way with violence. We cannot predict *who* will lose it and walk into which high school with what kind of weapon, but we know sure as anything that as generation after generation watches more violent television and movies, and plays more dehumanizing video games, there will be more suffering from violence. Here is the judgment of the American Psychological Association's Commission on Violence and Youth in 1993, which was echoed over the next few years by the U.S. Surgeon General, the American Medical Association, the National Institute of Mental Health, and virtually all of the country's most prestigious health organizations: "There is absolutely no doubt that higher levels of viewing violence on television are correlated with increased acceptance of aggressive attitudes and increased aggressive behavior."

If the media had a conscious policy of incapacitating us from doing anything about violence, they could not be doing better, for they try to direct all our attention to the part of violence that we cannot predict, namely who will "lose it" when. If we are to be a free, responsible people we shall have to put at least ninety percent of that attention back on the basic fact we can predict: violence begets violence. And on its converse: nonviolence begets nonviolence.

Nonviolence is a science if there ever was one, but it cannot make predictions as neatly as mechanics or electricity, for Satyagraha is what Gandhi called "a living force," not a physical one. In this science we cannot avoid the mystery of free will and the subtlety of the human mind. Those "crosscurrents of violence and responsiveness" Pepinsky refers to as running constantly in all of us help to account for episodes of violent behavior, but cannot predict them exactly. They do not put a formula in our hands that would let us say, "If we get thirty hours less violent programming per week there will be three thousand fewer homicides per year." How and when violence will break out is going to remain a mystery. It would take some sort of "chaos theory" to gain exactitude in predicting how a person or a mob will react. Sometimes you're nice to people and they nonetheless blow up at you. That is life.

But there is one thing about violence/nonviolence that is very simple and very predictable, and again it may be the only basic thing we have to know about it: that somewhere, somehow, violence will always hurt, while somewhere, somehow, nonviolence will always heal. To ring a slight change on the formula we arrived at earlier, *violence sometimes "works" but it never works, nonviolence sometimes "works" and never fails to work* to make human life somewhere somewhat better.

So nonviolence is, like the weather, at once mysterious and predictable. Gandhi once said, "Nonviolence is not the inanity it has been taken for down the ages." Sigh. My peace studies colleague, Professor Gordon Fellman, has accurately described the way nonviolence is portrayed in, for example, *High Noon* — a far more influential piece of art than Huxley's *Island*. In this iconic film we see a leading lady with scruples about killing, but this "nonviolence" of hers is portrayed as "undeveloped, a simplistic, weak alternative with no program, no imagination, and no real integrity." As soon as we see that nonviolence is not a kind of outcry but a kind of power, strong in its own right, and then that it can be offered by anyone towards anyone, whether one is in a concentration camp or a president's suite, we begin to break out of the "inane" limitation of nonviolence to a mere tactic that may possibly "work" if your opponent is nice.

That having been said, we have broached a daring proposition that we'll develop more fully later on: that when you have sufficient knowledge of how nonviolence works and can think of the appropriate way to mobilize it, it could even be used to make obsolete the scourge of war.

And yet we have just begun. Despite the variety of the fields in which we've so far traced nonviolence in action, we have looked at only one aspect of what Gandhi called this "matchless weapon." It has two. Once we realize that nonviolence is a primary reality, not a non-something, we begin to realize that its classic expression may not be in the protest mode at all, real *or* symbolic. It is true that Gandhiji once called himself a "professional resister," when he was asked his profession in a British-run court; but out of court he gave a rather different account of his life's work. "My real politics is constructive work." Nonviolence is not only a method of struggle against wrongs (as Penn and Ashoka demonstrate) but also — indeed primarily — a force that builds things right in the first place. For most of us, who are not protesters, this takes nonviolence off the shelf and puts it right into our own hands as an entirely new tool that we can use every day to design the future we and our children get to live in; and to this intriguing prospect we can now turn.

5 A Way Out of Hell

How much more delightful! to an undebauched
mind is the task of making improvements on the
earth, than all the vain glory that can be acquired
from ravaging it.
— George Washington

Put the lover of justice to shame with your
compassion.
— St. Isaac of Syria

Mubarak Awad has been a guest speaker in my
nonviolence class as often as I can get him. A
big, gentle man, an extremely engaging and
sincere speaker with a keen sense of nonviolence, his vivid, Arabic-in-
flected English always adds a note of authenticity when we discuss one
of the world's most important non-violent uprisings, the first Palestinian
intifada (literally, "shaking off," or "shaking up"). Mubarak, after all,
founded the Palestinian Center for the Study of Nonviolence, which I
suspect had a lot to do with that movement. The Israeli Government
certainly thought so. His most dramatic visit was undoubtedly in 1990,
when he came in fresh from his expulsion from Palestine. Along with the
glow of martyrdom, Mubarak had real inside information to share with
us. My students already knew enough not to accept uncritically the media image of the intifada as a violent, even a terrorist uprising; but what
we didn't know was what it was like to be there "on the ground," facing

riot-armed Israeli soldiers. Mubarak, a trained psychologist, was the ideal person to share that with us.

The intifada began in 1987 when it became clear that the terrorism and guerilla tactics of the Palestinian exiles had not worked and it was up to the Palestinians actually living under Israeli occupation to do something about their destiny. What they did was resist with Gandhian techniques of selective boycott, shutdowns, and the like (mostly learned from Gene Sharp *via* Mubarak) plus some indigenous ideas of their own with a dash of highly confrontational stone-throwing — a mix I have for simplification called "non-dash-violent," i.e. refraining from serious violence against your opponent without trying to love him or her out of the opponent category. (A mix that, as in the present case, can often slide into full-blown violence — but neither I nor my students saw that coming yet.) This put the Palestinian youth, in particular, under a lot of pressure. Because so many adults were being arrested, teens were forced to take up responsibilities and face dangers — beatings, imprisonment, death — that most of us don't have to cope with even as adults. This, of course, impressed my students greatly. But what surprised Mubarak, and all of us, was that when the intifada got under way, the youth of the occupied territories stopped taking drugs. Drug and alcohol abuse, until then a serious problem, virtually disappeared.

We asked him to go on. In the Gaza strip and Israel proper you had the same class of youth, ethnically and economically, as in the occupied territories, he explained; but these young people had no way to participate in the uprising. Sure enough, there was no such change in this "control" group. Where there was no intifada, drugs and alcohol continued their destructive course.

You may be wondering at this point what I'm leading up to. Am I saying that the way to get rid of the drug problem is a nonviolent revolution?

Of course not. What I'm saying is much more outrageous: as far as

I can see, we can get rid of *all* problems with a nonviolent revolution. Not just drugs; not even just crime itself — just about everything but death and taxes. How can I make this extravagant claim? If we start from the streets of Ramallah and Beit Sahour we can thread our way to the answer.

Addicted to Meaning

By coincidence, shortly after Mubarak told us about all this, the papers carried a surprising report about substance abusers in the United States. Three researchers, working quite independently of each other, all found to their surprise that the conventional wisdom about who takes drugs in America is wrong. The typical drug abuser in America is not a black male, not strapped by poverty in a ghetto; all three scientists had turned up a totally different profile:

> The same person who gets ahead in the workforce and is
> more of a risk taker, is more daring, [and more] susceptible
> to drugs. . . . [They have] a far more active life-style, are
> much more engaged in political campaigns, are much bigger
> users of information.

They are, in short, the most upwardly mobile people in American society, the "cutting edge."

None of the three scientists could explain why being more capable than average made you more, rather than less, vulnerable to drug abuse. One said it's because of "some hidden factor," another wondered whether "there's something in the basic personality" of the higher achievers, without proposing what it might be. The third scientist was at least on to something: these people are "high sensation seekers," he observed. Accordingly, he prescribed a program of terrific sensations for them: sky diving, bungee-cord jumping and disco dancing, with MTV-style jumps from one thing to the next and heavy metal music. This sensation blitz indeed helped them stay off drugs — better than bumper stickers that "just say no." But this approach only begs the question: what made these talented, energetic young people think that they could find happiness in sensations in the first place?

I want to propose to you that these active, intelligent people are not really looking for more sensations. They *think* they are, because that's what the mass media condition all of us to think. What they are really looking for is some meaning in life.

> The Cooperative Institutional Research Program recently surveyed the brightest young people in the United States. It found them overwhelmingly materialistic [with] an unprecedented concern with money, power and status. The biggest declines involved altruistic interests and social concerns.

These are clear signs of people without a sense of purpose.

The Americans and Palestinians who got out of drugs in such different ways — a high sensation program, on the one hand, and a largely non-violent revolution on the other — had both gotten into drugs for similar reasons. Despite the striking contrast in their outward circumstances, both had succumbed to hopelessness about their life. The Palestinian youth faced a stark future where every chance to grow was blocked by a contemptuous, domineering oppressor. The North Americans were facing a life of temporary, external satisfactions they already knew to be hollow from personal experience. They were rich, but in a way they were very poor. They were what Mother Teresa called "the spiritually poorest of the poor" because they could not see their way to a life of service and meaning.

So they were both looking for a purpose in life, and I'm afraid the purpose of life is not bouncing on the end of a bungee cord. I would safely bet that after a while the swooping sensation in the belly, the rush of being a human yo-yo to jarring music will wear thin, and the sensation-seekers may even find themselves going back to the needle. Materialism and sensationalism are part of the problem, not the solution — and it's a much bigger problem than that facing this group in particular. It's everyone's problem. If we had the whole country bouncing on bungee cords, would it solve crime, homelessness and despair? In Roszakian language, high sensations may "work" (for some), but they don't work.

Here is where the intifada of 1987-1992 was different. It didn't just give young Palestinians something to do, it gave them something *meaning-ful* to do. True, bungee cords and the intifada both give you danger and excitement, but nonviolent resistance gives you danger, a sense of risk, for an overriding purpose; in the other case danger, namely thrills, *is* the only purpose. I can't help recalling here the words of Sue Severin, the Marin County health professional who went down to Nicaragua with Witness for Peace. .

> The only way I can explain it is, I felt I was in the hands of God: not safe — that I wouldn't be hurt — but that I was where I was supposed to be, doing what I was supposed to be doing. And this can be addictive. Maybe that's why we kept going back.

Almost uncanny, that Severin should use the word "addictive" in this connection; but that is how powerful meaningful work can be — strong enough to overcome chemical dependency. Recently *Youth Outlook* (*YO*, a San-Francisco based youth newpaper) interviewed a young addict in San Francisco who gave a heartbreaking explanation of why he takes heroin. "I want quiet peace to inject my soul with forever." He was looking for peace. Who is not? He looked for it in drugs because he was conditioned — and today who is not conditioned — to think that what we need comes from outside us. Peace is something you inject; security, health, are things you buy. Yet, for whatever reason, some of us begin to suspect that what we're looking for *isn't* outside us, it's the inner peace that can lift us even out of potent addictions, the peace that comes when we've found a convincing purpose for our life.

Is my outrageous claim starting to make some sense?

Criminal Injustice

Over the years, I have seen hundreds and hundreds of young people working on projects that are similar in spirit to the intifada uprising, if not as dangerous. This has been one of the great privileges of my life. Some months prior to the NATO bombing of Ex-Yugoslavia I served as moderator for a Berkeley "teach-in" on the sufferings of ethnic Albanians of Kosovo. On the panel were two young people who had just come back from two days in a Serbian jail. They spoke with quiet passion. They spoke from the deep security of having found something to do about their concern and suffering for the world. They spoke cogently, without anger (though some Serb nationalists in the audience were charging the atmosphere with plenty). They spoke with love. I remember thinking how I would want all my students — in fact, I would want every person alive — to have such a sense of quiet fulfillment in their life.

What I'm not saying is, let the kids do peace work; it's good for them and it may keep them off drugs. I'm saying that these young people have stumbled onto something — a principle. It is a principle we too can apply in our own way, individually, and then corporately. To illustrate that, I want to enlarge our focus to a problem that is arguably the biggest we now face as a society, perhaps as a civilization.

At the present time, roughly one half the juvenile detention and incarceration in America is for drug-related crimes. The amount Americans pay for illegal drugs is staggering — officials noted with naive satisfaction that it came *down* to $57.3 billion in 1995. In response, we throw on another $17.9 billion to wage a "war" on mind-altering drugs that is failing. On that point scores of analysts who have studied the hapless war in detail all agree. Under these circumstance, we cannot afford *not* to follow up the implications of the cases like those we've just been considering, cases of "spontaneous remission" of drug abuse in America and Israel-Palestine. They seem to open up the suggestion of an entirely different approach, one that is not a war on drugs, not a war on crime — odd as it may sound, not a war at all.

Drug abuse, like violence, could be looked at through various lenses, or models, as we've already seen. In most of the West we have chosen, rightly or wrongly, to look at it as a crime. There are other possibilities, but all right, let's take this as an opportunity to look at the whole question of crime. The war on drugs is part of our war on crime in general, and that larger war is doing just as badly. "Let us begin with a fundamental realization," writes criminologist Richard Quinney at the head of an important book called *Criminology as Peacemaking.*

> No amount of thinking and no amount of public policy
> have brought us any closer to understanding and solving the
> problem of crime. The more we have reacted to crime, the
> further we have removed ourselves from any understanding
> and any reduction of the problem.

In a word — the word of Ruth Morris, in her landmark book *Penal Abolition* — our criminal justice system itself, not just the war on drugs, is "an expensive, unjust, immoral failure."

This double failure — the rise in crime and violence and the nation's inability to do more than contain them, if that — has brought our civilization to a defining moment. In April, 1967, when we were in the grip of the Vietnam War, Martin Luther King, Jr. made the prophetic observation that for every nation there comes a time when it faces a defining moral crisis. "Though we might prefer it otherwise," he said in his famous speech at the Riverside Church in New York, "we *must* choose in this crucial moment of human history." We did not rise to that challenge of Martin Luther King, Jr.'s, we did not find an honorable end to the war; but in my opinion we did not altogether sink below the possibility of redemption. Rather, as always seems to happen when such problems are not resolved, we have lurched on into another crisis, or perhaps the same one in a different guise.

> This is a watershed moment in California's history, a moment when we can take a path toward becoming a healthier society, or when we can consign every penny of future funding toward a failed system of human warehouses.

Note how similar this language of Vincent Schiraldi, former director of San Francisco's Center on Juvenile and Criminal Justice, is to that of former Attorney General Ramsey Clark, in a recent fund-raising letter.

> Our country is confronted with a stunning moral crisis. We have placed 1,366 people on death row. And we are adding more every week. . . . In the immediate future we may begin killing two hundred people per year. Only three countries, South Africa, China and Iran, execute nearly as many.

Shortly after Ramsey Clark made this statement, South Africa dropped out. The new, antiapartheid regime under Nelson Mandela abolished the death penalty along with racist ideology. That leaves us and China now leading the industrial world in penal severity, as we are in crime. (The number killed by guns in the United States each year are on another order of magnitude from that of any other industrialized nation.) In recent years the World Court has twice appealed to the United States to postpone or commute a sentence of death, to no avail. That's a hard statement to have to make about the world's oldest democracy — that we're leading the world backwards into punitive violence.

But crime is a crisis that has opportunity to it as well as dangers. To see the opportunity amid these many negatives we have to look at things in a different light.

Crime and betterment

To refocus, let me share with you this story, or most of it, as it came streaming into my computer one day back in 1992.

```
Reference: Latin America
Title: ENVIRONMENT: OUTLAW POACHERS BECOME
NATURE RESERVE GUARDIANS
an inter press service feature
by roberto herrscher


buenos aires, nov (ips) — in an argentine nature
reserve, poachers who once hunted endangered spe-
cies have been converted into the conscientious
guardians of the animals they once stalked.

the remarkable conversion took place in the ibera
nature reserve, in corrientes province, 700 kilome-
ters north of argentina's capital.

In 1987, pedro perea munoz took over the director-
ship of the ibera reserve. munoz met two poachers,
"mingo" cabrera and ramon cardoso, who had lived in
the reserve for as long as they could remember.

their life was difficult. carbrera and cardoso
lived deep in the swamps of ibera and survived by
fishing and hunting. from time to time they would
travel to the small village of pellegrini, on the
```

southern border of the reserve, to sell carpincho, deer and alligator hides. instead of adopting an antagonistic attitude, munoz understood that these men knew ibera better than anyone and that hunting was their only means of survival.

"they couldn't believe it when i offered them a job. now they are the most dedicated and conscientious guards (at ibera)," munoz told ips. . . .

"to understand nature, one must be peaceful. these men were born with this. they were hunters by necessity, and now, as guides and guardians, there is no one better. by just looking into the eyes of people entering the reserve, they know who the poachers are," munoz said. . . .

amongst the clear crystal wetlands of ibera live the last 700 members of a rare south american swamp deer — a large mammal, whose hooves end in toes united by membranes. ibera's residents also include the aguara guazu, a small wolf in danger of extinction. a variety of rodents, lizards, alligators and multicolored birds complete the population of this unique and delicate ecosystem. cabrerea and cardoso are just two of six guards in the reserve, but they are the favoured guides for researchers, photographers, and members of ecological expeditions.

"now that we understand the importance of the reserve, we see that, without realizing it, we were spending our whole lives preparing for this," cabrera said.

** End of text from cdp:goodnews **

This event turns our expectations wonderfully upside down. Cabrera and Cardoso were technically "criminals," and warden Muñoz certainly could have treated them as such. Yet what a lost opportunity that would have been! Instead, he did the exact opposite. Instead of looking on the two men as the *cause* of the problem he turned to them for the *solution*. They solved it; and notice two other results. (1) The whole affair changed from a conflict to a classic "win-win" configuration in which everyone gained. Muñoz got the job done; Cabrera and Cardoso changed from outlaws to employees, harmers to helpers. Everybody won — even the animals. (2) Cabrera and Cardoso got something out of this experience of profound, permanent benefit which we're starting to recognize as a signature of nonviolent activities, namely a sense of meaning. "We were spending our whole lives preparing for this."

Muñoz is not the only person ever to have such an outlandish idea about crime and "criminals." About the same time as this breakthrough, two American schoolteachers came up with the idea, again quite independently, of taking young offenders who were in detention and putting them in charge of some severely handicapped youth. Sharon Roberts was one of the teachers. As she admitted, she was asking a lot of the Los Angeles school board: to let her "put the most dangerous people in L.A. in charge of the most vulnerable." The paradox worked brilliantly. Again, both the disabled youth and the offenders "won." "I was used to being a thug on the street," says Alfred, age 16, member of the Cripps, on probation for being accomplice to a shooting, "but now when my home boys come around . . . I tell them I have other things to do." Things like taking a disabled girl named Star to class, while he earns high school credits and work experience:

> This shows I can do something. It's the first time I've felt like
> that. I feel more kindhearted and stuff than I thought.

Note how in Alfred's mind now being helpful is the only thing that counts as "doing something." He has already come a long way from the prevailing paradigm attitude that to "do something" you have to help *yourself* (not to mention hurt someone else). But the big winners were you and me — society as a whole. Young detainees who would have caused worse trouble down the line, almost without exception, were given a way out of this desperate spiral by the only method that can ever do that. They found good in themselves.

In ancient Rome there was a saying, *Curruptio optimum pessima*, "The corruption of the best people is the worst kind." We might flip this around and say, *Redemptio pessimum optima*, "The reinstatement of the worst people makes them the best." This is not too paradoxical; after all, as we saw in the case of the high-achievers who got into drugs, it's often the most capable people with the highest expectations who get the most frustrated with modern life. They feel most keenly the lurking emptiness in the modern definition of achievement, and at the same time they have those great capacities which they turn to nonconstructive ends. In the worst troublemakers lies, often, the most creative potential. The trick is knowing that it's there, then having the courage to reach for it.

A good example is the peer mediation programs catching on in many schools. Teachers and administrators have been thrilled to find that not only do the programs "chill" a lot of the violence in school yards and classrooms, but a peculiar pattern emerges all across the country. The biggest troublemakers turn out to be the best mediators. How odd.

After his "conversion," one of those mediators told a friend of mine that to be a mediator you have to "check your ego at the door." You're not just in it for yourself, is what he meant. You have to put your own feelings aside. Then he added, still more significantly, "I've always had the skills to be a mediator, but I didn't use them before because I had no one to show me how." Nor is he that special; everybody has this capacity so very few learn to use. "We're all like hidden gold mines."

His statement is a like a textbook of conflict resolution condensed into three sentences. (1) You have to "check your ego at the door," get a little above your own personal feelings. Some kind of spiritual sacrifice, large or small, is the basis of any action that can result in peace. (2) All it would take for most people to get their hands on this skill is a little training. (3) And finally, given such training, we discover a "gold mine" in every one of us. If we don't find a way to mine our inner resources it causes the greatest trouble for us and society; when we do we can find ourselves becoming the most creative peacemakers. Whether they start out as poachers in an Argentine game preserve or youth offenders in Los Angeles, the most difficult people are often the ones most capable of helping us create loving community if we would help them out of their difficulty.

So what the Associated Press writer called the "remarkable conversion" of Cabrera and Cardoso is no more remarkable than the intifada youth who stopped taking drugs, or the "most dangerous" of Los Angeles who discovering the satisfaction of taking care of another, helpless human being. In all three cases the "worst" had gotten that way because they saw no way to use the good which lay — often quite unsuspected — within them. All that would have been lost if the prevailing approaches to crime had been adopted.

Cunning as serpents

This fact, of course, does not mean that we should immediately put offenders in charge of the disabled, endangered species and peacemaking. Let us be idealistic, yes, but not naive. Quite a few "troublemakers" might rise to the occasion; but some would not. Writer Norman Mailer discovered this to his cost. Mailer was, quite understandably, repelled by the hypocrisy of labelling people as "criminals" when we ourselves create the conditions that foster crime; so as a kind of personal protest he used his influence to get a particular violent offender released from jail and into his custody. Once free, the man promptly murdered someone. Mailer realized with added shock that he had more than once left his eighteen-year-old daughter alone with his unstable guest.

In a way, Mailer's well-meant mistake was more than just a question of naivete. It was also very typical of something we do when we become aware of something very wrong and react impatiently: we reverse the wrong instead of solving it. In his eagerness to get rid of the "victimizer" label society had put on this man, Mailer swapped it for a "victimized" label. This person had been made bad by society, so it wasn't his fault, therefore he was innocent, therefore he was "good." Reversing labels doesn't get us closer to reality. What we really want to do is get *rid* of labels. That's the only way we can see each other as people. When a label comes between people like one of those gels they use on theater lights, it is the beginning of violence. Sliding that gel out of the way is rehumanization. In the world of criminal (in)justice, rehumanization is being able to look at people realistically, and seeing how they became lawbreakers. Then we will understand what to do with them *and* — so much more importantly — what to do so that others do not go through the same process.

Mailer's first impulse was absolutely correct. As Ruth Morris says, "Let's be clear that the dangerous few [in prisons] are used by all those who want to keep the other ninety nine percent in our present expensive, unjust, immoral system." This is the logic by which a handful of militants can be held up by those who want to discredit a whole struggle. (All ethnic Albanians, even grandmothers, were labelled "terrorists" by the Serbian regime.) Mailer was only applying a well-known principle of nonviolence, that noncooperation with evil must never shade over into animosity toward evildoers — not even into labelling them as such. It may seem like a small thing — "criminal" is just a word, after all — but with that word goes the whole dehumanization response, and in the case of criminal justice that means the whole system Ruth Morris speaks of with such stinging accuracy. Gandhi was against using the word altogether.

The word criminal should be erased from our vocabulary; or else we are all criminals.

But then, Gandhi, the perfect Christian, felt that "man is not capable of knowing the absolute truth and, therefore, not competent to punish" in the first place. We want to stay away from such dangerous radicals, of course. Let's stick with some reliable professionals, like Dr. Arnold Trebacher, criminology professor and head of Washington's Drug Policy Foundation. Speaking from his own professional experience, Trebacher says, "The English and Dutch have taught me . . . that you can disapprove of drug use, but you don't have to hate users." But this was Gandhi's point. If you don't want to hate them, we have to stop labelling them. And Dr. Trebacher is only echoing one of the most important principles in Satyagraha — and Christianity. The definition of a Christian, Augustine said a millennium and a half ago, is "We hate the sin but not the sinner."

Today this ancient creed is surfacing in the vexed area of criminal justice, providing the underpinning of a new outlook, called *restorative* as opposed to *retributive* justice. Let's give Harold Pepinsky the space to spell this out.

> In decades of sampling millennia of literature across traditions, and everyday attempts in any facet of life's attempts to become more socially secure and safer, I see everyone applying one of just two social control systems: peacemaking, or what I call 'warmaking.' In the context of governmental efforts to control domestic social disorder, Ruth Morris calls 'warmaking' 'the retributive justice system.' . . . When one chooses to make war on a social problem rather than to make peace with it, one adopts this system of thought: The first order of business is to identify and assess blame against those personally responsible for the danger and insecurity we face; these are our enemies. Next we try to isolate them and subdue them — stamping out the enemy's will to fight. The

process entails passing judgment on enemies and punishing them (i.e., taking power away from them by locking them in cells).

If you decide to regard threatening social disorder in the *peacemaking* social control system, blame gets in the way of cleaning up the social mess and restoring antagonists' capacity to get along safely together, as in being able to turn your back without fear on someone who has attacked you. While the preeminent task of the warmaker is to be the biggest, baddest combatant you can be, the preeminent task of the peacemaker is to *weave combatants, weakest victims first, back into a social fabric of mutual trust, mutual safety, mutual security.*

This "new" way of thinking (as we'll see later, it was widely practiced among indigenous societies) is not only a sentiment but has a pragmatic principle behind it. Jeremy Bentham said somewhere, "Sanguinary laws have a tendency to render men cruel, either by fear, by imitation, or by revenge," while laws dictated by mildness humanize the manners of a nation and the spirit of government. What laws, what practices are beginning to tap the power of "mildness" in and around today's grim prisons?

Points of Programmatic Light

One of the most successful restorative justice projects in the U.S. was started in 1975 at Greenhaven State Prison in New York. Significantly, it was started not by scholars or social workers; it was initiated by prisoners themselves. Calling themselves the Think Tank (an intentional pun, I assume), they contacted a local Quaker group to help them find nonviolent alternatives to prison life and what it was doing to them. What emerged from that collaboration quickly spread to fifteen states and

Canada and is now widely known as the Alternatives to Violence Project (AVP). What is AVP? Essentially, it is a set of workshops designed to allow men to unlearn aggression in a rehumanizing environment. The theory is simple, and it's becoming familiar:

> Social learning theorists have demonstrated that aggression and violence are learned behaviors. They can, therefore, within biological and genetic limitations, be altered by utilizing social learning principles such as [role] modeling. . . . Research has demonstrated that utilizing positive responses which are incompatible with the act of violence (e.g., smiling; state of muscle relaxation; open, clear, direct communication; active listening; the development of trust, etc.) renders the likelihood of aggression and/or violence much more improbable than do negative sanctions such as punishment, shame or guilt.

We might want to query those "biological and genetic limitations" (was Gandhi another species?), but we can certainly accept, indeed applaud the "basic premise of AVP, as explained at the beginning of every workshop . . . that human beings don't have to be violent with each other, that human violence is not a given, even in prison." Teaching nonviolent techniques, therefore, "can . . . greatly profit assaultive people." For example, teaching them (or us) verbal skills reduces the need to react to a provocation with violence. (As Winston Churchill once said, "It is better to jaw, jaw, jaw than to war, war, war.") More than this, being more articulate helps them preserve their integrity and self-esteem in embarrassing situations. "This sense of worth," Lila Rucker reminds us, "is tied to our sense of connectedness to other human beings."

That is basic to the nonviolence worldview; we are not talking only about getting some assaultive people back in line with "normalcy," but getting them over some of the spiritual isolation accepted as normal today. When they can channel some of their considerable assertiveness into social competence, reorienting their drives from "power over" somebody to "power with," they are making the kind of constructive change that even "non-assaultive" types need to learn.

As Rucker says, "It can bring tingles of excitement if we allow ourselves to conjure up images of transforming *correctional* centers into *healing* centers." Frankly, I agree. I confess, I feel tingles of excitement about programs like AVP. Imagine if we could convert the entire criminal justice system from warehousing and punishment to restoration and social healing. And this happens, often, when forward-looking reformers combine indigenous practices with their innovations, as we'll touch upon in this book's epilogue. But . . .

In India there is a story about a villager who is out gathering firewood near his village and meets a holy man. The sage tells him about a forest of sandalwood trees deeper into the forest, and the villager is enchanted to find them, and enjoy not only their purifying fragrance but some income. However, when he goes back to thank the holy man, the latter tells him, "Don't stop there. If you go further on you find a copper mine." The villager is thrilled, but — not being Indian, I will make the delightfully long story short — the holy man tells him "don't stop there" until he comes to a silver mine, a gold mine, and finally a diamond mine.

If we could somehow convert the entire judicial system to healing projects like AVP, it would help immensely, because those projects arise from right principles. "Criminals" are human beings with full human potential, who have become alienated. If crime is alienation (a kind of violence) it cannot be healed by vindictive punishment (another kind of violence). The real cure must come from something which is *not* a kind of violence and does not further alienate. Instead of telling offenders, "Hey, get outta here!" as one colorful prison activist puts it, restorative programs say, "Hey, get back in here!" It is indeed mind-boggling to imagine what it would be like to convert our whole criminal justice machinery from punishing to healing.

Yet it would be dishonest and probably ineffectual to stop there. For think of how much damage has already been done by the time someone lands in prison. Ray Schonholtz, founder of San Francisco Community Boards, once told me, echoing the insight of Deborah Prothrow-Stith, "Our entire justice industry is after the fact, like our entire health industry. It's all after the fact." Even programs that heal instead of punishing are after the fact. "Don't stop there," the sage would tell us; go deeper into the forest. Go further back down the chain of causality; go deep, go into our value system and find the changes that will prevent crime, violence and alienation from happening in the first place. The real awakening that comes from hearing "conversion" stories like Cabrera and Cardoso, like the innumerable high school troublemakers who become the best mediators, like the young offenders in Los Angeles, or the thousands who have been through AVP and related programs, the challenge they imply is not to heal the wounds of alienation once it's happened but to change the alienating conditions of this world so people like them — like all of us — can live fulfilling lives.

Is there not a certain hypocrisy in doing anything else? After all, what is a "criminal?" Let me remind you of something we discovered about one of the most bruising conflicts of the twentieth century: "Why are they killing one another? . . . People here [in the Balkans] have always believed, and still believe, what they see and hear on television." Well, frankly, "criminals" are people who believe what they see and hear on television: that people are separate, that life is a fight, that happiness is outside us, that we are all doomed to compete against each other for limited material goods.

This, is of course, a more subliminal message than the unsubtle hate propaganda of state television from Belgrade. It is more subliminal — and therefore more effective. And it has not been going on for a mere five years, but at least forty (to speak of television in particular). In a culture that puts out messages like these from every radio and television tower all day long for over forty years — messages whose underlying philosophy is the very stuff of violence — it is hypocrisy to do nothing but punish those who succumb to that message in a way that's illegal. And it is folly to think that when you've caught those individuals you will gain security. "I will act the way I am treated, so help me God"; this is handwriting on the wall for all of us if we keep setting loose the demons of alienation and then looking for what Ruth Morris calls the "pseudo-security" of locking "criminals" out of sight. Real security has an entirely different face.

> The retributive justice system, with its established hierarchi-
> cal rituals, robed judges, armed police and locked cells, offers
> quite literally a concrete substitute for the deeper security we
> have lost. More tragic still, we take this quick fix, and it
> appeases our inner hunger just enough that we fail to seek
> true security in the caring community, where we can be
> certain of love and support no matter what happens. We can
> never lock up the last offender . . . but we can create the kind
> of community where we know that, whatever the future
> holds, we will be surrounded by love and support.

The Cultural is the Political

So let's "go further," as the wise man in the forest would say. We can use nonviolence to solve the problem of crime, but we need to start before the cell doors close on some of us. To go further in this case means to go three steps up the chain of causation and see where and how we can intervene at those earlier stages:

First: We need *restorative justice* for arrestees, particularly if they are young. AVP and Sharon Roberts are pioneers, showing us what we need for the whole system. This is not a terribly radical suggestion; it is new to the public (I first saw the term "restorative justice" in the papers in June,

1998), but it is no wild or particularly new idea to social scientists. To quote Ruth Morris one last time, "When university programs become training grounds for orthodox guards, prison administrators, and lawyers and police who grind out our retributive and destructive system they . . . are out of touch with the literature of serious research that documents over and over the inherent inability of a revenge system to accomplish any positive social purpose." Restorative justice is step number one, for cases where we've already failed.

Second: we need much more support for programs that can head off criminal behavior — again, especially for young people. In almost every American city police and volunteer organizations try to give youth something better to do than run around in gangs. They organize basketball games, create places for them to spend time, and best of all get in and spend time with them. One of the biggest hurts in society today is the loss of trust between old and young; it probably rivals the lack of communication between the genders in its destructive effects on human culture. "Big brother" or "big sister" programs are a way to overcome a part of this, but again, they are no substitute for families. Nothing is. A solid, loving family does crime prevention in the true sense of the word. Barred windows and metal detectors are prevention in the most cynical sense of the word. (They may "work" but they do bad work.) Youth programs are in between.

But why speak of only programs in this middle zone, when we have a highly developed network of programs stretching back over centuries: our schools. By now most of us are becoming aware that the prison budget is draining money from the school system — absurdly, since it's been proven time and again that schooling is the second most potent way, after the family itself, of keeping people from committing crime. Still, at the start of the 'nineties, to cite one instance, expenditures for K-12 and higher education nationwide increased a little over eight percent apiece; correction expenditures for youth and adults increased eighteen percent (and in the ensuing decade educational outlays sometimes went *down* while prison walls went up).

Wilbert Rideau is an articulate writer who killed a bank guard at age nineteen and has been paying for that mistake in Louisiana State Penitentiary since 1962. He has no stake in pretending that the prison system reduces violence and can be pretty blunt. Tough anticrime measures are, quite frankly, a "crock," he says. "People don't want solutions to crime, they only want to feel good." He has a point. Four-fifths of the prisoners in the long-term facility at Angola State Prison are high school dropouts like himself. Instead of getting tough on them after the damage is already done, "I'd like to see more efforts aimed at really improving people," he says. "Crime is a social problem, and education is the only real deterrent. . . . Put your money there." A Greek proverb wraps this up succinctly:

οταν ανοιγει μια σχολη, κλεινει μια φυλαχη.
'When a school opens, a prison closes.'

Or to put it into billboard rhetoric, "Open a school, close a prison." Education is very rehumanizing. It has even worked, in some bold experiments, *after* criminalization. In Massachusetts a young woman who had served several "normal," i.e. punitive, sentences for other crimes was then "sentenced" to taking a literature class. Her comment was, "It's the first time anybody ever gave me a chance."

Should we convert the whole criminal justice system to an educational system? You know, we could do a lot worse. Should we bring back the money that's been diverted from schools to the correctional system? We could do a lot worse. But we must also do much more.

Third: We must patiently, resolutely, take apart the culture of violence our material civilization has given rise to and replace it part after part, institution by institution with a culture of peace, basing that new culture on the long overdue "revolution of values" Martin Luther King, Jr. called for in a famous sermon two weeks after his New York declaration against the war.

While it is true that education is the antidote to violence, it is not true that education means nothing more than getting youth to stay in schools. How can it, when today they are bringing violence into school with them in the form of 100,000 guns every day? In this country, which now has more shopping malls than high schools, if we were to go ahead and restore the money to schools that's been drained away by the prison system, that would not solve the problem by itself, because children would be sitting in those spacious, well-kept-up, air-conditioned schools learning almost nothing but how to make money. The greatest enemy of education is not a lack of funds, though that hurts; it's a lack of purpose. Lack of funds is only a symptom of the present culture of materialism. It is this same culture that also makes us think it's safer to build prisons than schools — and creates the atmosphere in which young people feel they have to have guns with them in school.

Education is enduring a two-edged attack which more government funding — and I agree it's needed — does not fully address. On the one hand, children get to school so indoctrinated by what they've seen on television that there's little room left for teachers to operate. The mass media are basically practicing education without a licence. On the other, the general public and — I hate to say this — educators themselves have lost sight of the purpose of education. They have come to feel that education means only one thing: getting ready for a job. A very education-friendly candidate for superintendent of education in California recently dared to suggest that "we need to integrate visual and performing arts into the curriculum" from kindergarten up. I was ready to dash out to the ballot box; but then she added, "This is important . . . because of the requirements of the new economy." Not the eternal requirements of a sense of purpose, beauty, meaning. Oh, well.

So even those who advocate education as an antidote to crime must realize that putting people through schools so they can get jobs is not education. Indeed, defining education as such is, in fact, part of the problem. As we learned about the typical drug user in America, our culture seems to call certain life-styles a "success" which are actually resounding failures in terms of saving people from frustration and emptiness. Actual human needs can be strikingly different.

> Man [or woman] cannot flourish if his entire world consists only of objects that he can see, hear, touch, taste or smell. Instinctively, whether he be a New Guinea tribesman or a Wall Street tycoon, a human being tends to feel that life on this earth must be subject to some sort of higher purpose.

Recently this observation was echoed by another high-level health authority:

> A few years ago the Department of Health, Education and Welfare in Massachusetts published a study, since replicated in France, in which scientists and statisticians looked once again at the risk factors for heart disease. They found that the number one predictor of fatal heart attacks, initially described as job dissatisfaction, was more precisely pinned down as lack of meaning or purpose in life.

At the beginning of this book I suggested that meaning and purpose, namely their absence, explain the suicides of teens in South Boston. But it is not just teens. In South Africa, when apartheid finally fell, some of the whites who had clung to that system to give meaning to their lives felt the bottom dropping out from under them. In one or two cases, whole Afrikaner families committed suicide because they felt "that there is no way forward. . . . There is no future for whites in this country." One authority said of the "Heaven's Gate" cult suicide in San Diego in 1997 that the cult members fit a "typical pattern" of people who "sought a consuming purpose" for their life. Typical of whom? According to the medical evidence just cited, every single one of us seeks a consuming purpose for our life. When the predominant cultural message is that we are separate, physical objects bent on consumption, that purpose is going to be hard to find.

I was for a while involved in a program that taught meditation to people who had been diagnosed HIV positive. We were prepared to discover, and we did, that meditation and the allied disciplines protected them from some of the worst effects of their anxiety, including some of its effects on their already weakened immune system. What surprised us, though, was the number of people who told us, "If I could get back my health at the cost of giving up everything I've learned here, I wouldn't do it."

So the full, deep solution to the crime epidemic, the solution that works *before* people do damage to themselves and others, is restorative not just for some who have fallen through the cracks, but for the culture itself. Yes, we need many more restorative programs in jails. Yes, we need to rebuild schools and let them teach young people how to live. But we also need to develop a culture that facilitates, rather than discourages, "man's search for meaning."

The scientist I am quoting with that last phrase is Viktor Frankl. Frankl, trained as a neurosurgeon in his native Vienna, passed two-and-a-half years of his life in the living hell of Auschwitz and survived to write his bestselling book, *Man's Search for Meaning,* directly out of that devastating — yet for him strangely triumphant — experience. From the abyss of violence he rose to ask the deepest question of our existence: what is the meaning of life? What are we supposed to be doing here?

Even to ask that question had some restorative value; but Frankl went further. He saw that real meaning cannot be concocted. It has to be *discovered*. "I think the meaning of our existence is not invented by ourselves but rather detected." Thus while even a *sense* of meaning is therapeutic (even if you get it from bungee-cord jumping), we all have to get connected in some way to some purpose higher than ourselves and beyond ourselves. Ninety-one-year-old Leona, who spends her spare time using her expert sewing skills for others, says it so well. "I figure if you can't help somebody, what's the use of living?"

Frankl's insight (on which his "third school of psychotherapy" is based) is that we can't simply make up something meaningful to do; we *have* something meaningful to do. The real search is to find out what it is. Everything I've been saying in this book is meant to shed light on that search, for I believe it's possible to define what is meaningful for us who live in this crisis of history. The task is to create loving community, and the way to understand and address that task is through nonviolence. Whoever we are, we have some way to do this. This is the work that will give our lives purpose, individually and together. The most beautiful expression of this task that I know of comes from a letter Einstein wrote when he was seventy. It is no surprise that this little paragraph is becoming so well known.

> A human being is a part of the whole, called by us the
> "universe," a part limited in time and space. He experiences
> his thoughts and feelings as something separate from the rest
> — a kind of optical delusion of his consciousness. This
> delusion is a kind of prison for us, restricting us to our
> personal decisions and to affection for a few persons nearest
> us. Our task must be to free ourselves from this prison by
> widening our circle of compassion to embrace all living
> creatures and the whole of nature in its beauty.

The task that Einstein speaks of is not for this age only; it is the human task for all time, part of the human condition. But that task presents itself right now with critical urgency, when loving community and "the whole of nature" are being so seriously torn apart by the forces of greed and alienation. In the case of the crime problem, we are expelling people from society and locking them up in warehouses, not to mention expelling them altogether from the community of the living with the barbaric death penalty, not realizing that it is we ourselves who remain in prison — the prison of our ill-will, our fear and anger which seals ourselves off from them. We shall escape from our prison of delusion when we let them out of their prison of concrete and iron.

Toward the end of 1997, the still-living laureates of the Nobel Prize for peace made a joint plea for changing human consciousness in the coming millennium. They named their call the "International Decade for a Culture of Peace and Non-Violence for the World's Children." Humanity is slowly beginning to learn that nonviolence is a creative force that contains within itself the principle of creative order. It alone seems to be a way to deal with conflict that contains the energy of peace in its very process. Nonviolence (and as far as I can see, only nonviolence) does this by elevating rather than depressing the human image. It alone leads to long-term, deep changes in the social system which will eventually result in the desired goals of loving community within the given society and stable peace with others — in a word, loving community all round. We can now add what may be the most important characteristic: nonviolence provides people with a high, inspiring goal — a task that can be implemented in endless ways to fit each individual's capacities, be it as small as turning off your television set or as large as de-institutionalizing war.

History has not yet given us an example of a full-scale, nonviolent revolution that rebuilt a culture from the ground up. Even India's freedom struggle, by far the biggest and the purest, went out of control toward the end. But it has given us enough hints that we can see how such a thing might be possible. The way the intifada youth turned off drugs, for example, was part of the character of the first intifada as a whole. Because their schools were constantly being shut down by Israeli authorities, Palestinian teachers set up clandestine schools in the basements of their homes or the backs of stores. Because commercial links between Palestinians and Israelis were disrupted, some the result of deliberate acts of boycott and others part of Israeli retribution, people created systems of their own to deliver milk, service cars and get the sick and injured to medical help. Particularly striking was one change that reached deep into the fabric of Palestinian life: as more and more children were left behind by jail-going parents, Mubarak told my class, "Every woman became every child's mother." In that brief period when nonviolent energy was at work, the Palestinians found themselves doing much more than rebelling against an external authority; they were reinventing themselves as a civil society. To do this, interestingly enough, they were reawakening the timeless principle of the extended family that had indigenous roots in their society. Even in this flawed, provisionally non-violent struggle, then, loving community was created as a by-product. And yet it was not just a by-product. It was — and always is — a direct result of choosing nonviolence. In chapter two we saw the psychological health that comes to the individual who makes that choice. Now we are beginning to see the social health brought into the group at large.

Why, then, are nonviolent campaigns usually protests and disruptions? If they contain the seeds of creative order, why this popular perception of nonviolence as a kind of revolution, and why do nonviolent activists from George Fox to the Berrigan brothers go about breaking laws and generally disrupting apple carts? We will see that it is not just because protests and disruptions are the only expression of nonviolence people tend to recognize. It is because nonviolent actors are the ones who are clinging to order in societies where some kinds of disorder have been taken for granted — like the British monopoly on Indian salt and cotton or the segregation of buses in Montgomery. As Archbishop Romero said in a homily before his assassination in El Salvador on March 27, 1980:

> I don't want to be an opposition, as was said of me this week.
> I want to be simply an affirmation. When one says yes to
> one's own conviction, one is not confronting. . . . Naturally,
> some others don't think the same way and thus confrontation
> arises.

Apple carts that are going blindly over a cliff must sometimes be upset by people trying to save their occupants.

The Spiritually Poorest

So "the children of the stones" (as the intifada youth are often, and somewhat unfairly, called) hit on something very relevant to our own dilemmas. We traced the connection step by step from drug abuse to crime itself, and finally to a lack of purpose in the industrial culture we are surrounded with, each step getting closer to the cause of our problems. At the same time an answering path was revealed from *restorative* programs that can heal the alienation between the assaultive person and society, to *preventive* programs that largely focus on communities, to — What shall we call it? — the overriding *creative* program of restoring the value system whose deformation has led us into a world of so much crime, among other symptoms of disorder.

Mother Teresa shed some light on this goal in an observation I referred to earlier:

> You in the West have the spiritually poorest of the poor. . . .
> I find it easy to give a plate of rice to a hungry person, to

furnish a bed to a person who has no bed, but to console or remove the bitterness, anger, and loneliness that comes from being spiritually deprived, that takes a long time.

Overcoming spiritual deprivation is deeply personal work on one level, but on another it's building loving community with others — eventually, all others. The purpose of our life in the third Christian millennium is partly personal, and partly to take apart the entire social order wherever it has come to rely on violence and reground it in the other, the opposite kind of power.

Daunting. But we don't have to start absolutely from scratch. Along with all the other trouble he caused, Gandhi devised a social program with just this daring. And it nearly worked.

6 The Sweet Sound of Order

To reclaim our colonized political spaces, we
must reclaim our colonized cultural spaces.
— David Korten

One day in 1940 a young Indian importuned Gandhi, "What will it really take to get the British off our backs?" Gandhi replied brightly, "Phenomenal progress in spinning."

I like to imagine that this was one of those revolutionaries who didn't believe Gandhi was really serious about nonviolence. They thought — they wanted to think — that he was just biding his time, waiting for the moment to launch the real revolution. But nonviolence *was* the real revolution. Really, though, we are tempted to ask, with spinning wheels? Yes, with spinning wheels and everything they stood for. At the time Gandhiji made this rejoinder he had almost fifty years of experience behind him, and was no longer interested in sounding clever. We can take it that he meant just what he said. Why did he endow the humble spinning wheel with such power?

Nonviolence has two faces, that of cooperating with good and that of non-cooperating with evil. These two faces, or call them two edges to the sword of Satyagraha, have been expressed throughout history as what Gandhi would call *Constructive Programme*, where you create things, and make corrections in your own community, and what I like to call *obstructive program*, where you dig in your heels and refuse to go along with others' attempts to weaken or exploit you. When to do which is largely a matter of timing, yet most people who think about nonviolence at all are like that young man who importuned Gandhi in 1940 — they think only about the obstructive side. None other than Kenneth Boulding once quipped that nonviolence was good for offense but not for defense, which, humor aside, turns out to be wrong, as we will see in the next chapter. This blinkered perception, shared by activists, some scholars and lay observers alike, has done a great deal to hinder the development of peace and nonviolence. For ironically, it is the constructive edge that far outweighs in its importance the confrontational-obstructive one we're becoming relatively familiar with.

Once I met a French baron and his wife while I was working at an archeological site on the Greek island of Delos. M. and Mme. Evrard-Garbé invited my wife and me to their Paris apartment for dinner, which of course we readily accepted. Mme. was a superb cook, and the conversation was going splendidly when my friend M. le Baron casually remarked, "Oh, I completely believe in racial inequality." My wife blanched, knowing I was likely to make a scene. Normally I would have, but several things held me in check this time. The conversation was in French, for one, and that slowed down my repartee; then, too, I was in his home, eating his wife's gracious cooking, and most importantly perhaps, I had a year or so of meditation under my belt at that time. I held my tongue. Some moments later, as the conversation changed course, my host said, "You know, nothing in the world matters but love (*charité*)." I quietly said to him, "Do you think the races are unequally endowed with the capacity to love?" He was stunned.

I probably did more to reduce the racist burden of the world that evening than I had in a lifetime of activism. And yet, I wasn't an iota less angry —*tant s'en faut!* Unbeknownst to me, my anger was seeking a more constructive outlet, making me more alert to what my host was saying rather than less, even though I held it back not out of any conviction, really, but simply because circumstances so dictated. This was for me an

important personal experience of the efficacy of anger transformed —
and what I was later to understand as Constructive Programme.

As we'll see, the seed of Constructive Programme was planted at the
very beginning of Gandhi's public life, about a year after the shock of
Pietermaritzburg had worn off, or rather had sunk in. By the 'twenties,
shortly after he arrives back in India, that seed has grown into "Constructive Programme," a roster of eighteen projects designed to rebuild
India from the ground up. Not only has it become more elaborate and
comprehensive along the way, it is steadily moving to center stage in
Gandhi's thinking. By 1940 it is his main hope. He is fully committed to
the belief that while nonviolence had an impressive power to protest and
disrupt, its real power was to create and reconstruct. The tail of protesting wrongs would never wag the dog of building a society — this is what
he wanted his young interlocutor of 1940, and so many others, to understand.

Today, wherever you look for successful examples of social change,
it seems, it's the groups or individuals taking concrete, positive steps like
the reconstructive projects we looked at last chapter that are making the
biggest difference. Maybe it's as simple as the Environmental Defense
Fund's "Safe Harbor" program that rewards private landowners who protect endangered species, instead of punishing them when they do not.
Introduced in three states, it has "worked" beautifully; Safe Harbor Texas
alone has over a million acres under protection. Or the Educational Fund
to End Handgun Violence, which started a project called "Hands Without Guns" whose purpose is to show kids a world of fun and opportunity outside a world of fear and violence. The positive message struck a
resounding chord. In a Boston neighborhood, for one, teens organized a
gun buy-back and made a peace sculpture from the collected weapons.

One of the most successful environmental programs worldwide is
Dr. Karl-Henrik Robèrt's "Natural Step." Dr. Robèrt is an M.D. from
Sweden who became immensely concerned with environmental degrada-

tion and set out to bring many others into that circle of concern. He had, fortunately, patience to match his passion. What's unique about Natural Step is not so much its superb scientific homework and scientific credentials as its approach.

> First we educate business leaders, politicians and scientists in The Four System Conditions [four things that have to be observed for the earth to be a sustainable life-support system] and then we ask them for advice. Instead of telling them what to do, we say, "How could this be applied in your world?" This sparks creativity and recruits enthusiasm into the process instead of defense mechanisms.
>
> Any expert in her field . . . is much more clever than you or I. If you give her the overall principles, therefore, and then ask for advice, she finds much smarter solutions than Greenpeace or I or anybody else can. And we are very much in need of practical, creative solutions.

In the early days, before Natural Step had national organizations across the globe, Robèrt would go to corporations and ask to speak to their boards about the diminishing funnel of resources they were running into. Typically, they would dismiss him with a "Don't call us, we'll call you"; but in a week or so they *would* call him. The secret is that if you assume people are rational, it helps to awaken their rationality. It "forces reason to be free." This sometimes works even in cases on the high end of the escalation curve, when the intensity of negative passions seems to have stifled reason.

Long before Gandhi threw that cold water on his impatient questioner of 1940, twenty years earlier, when he launched full-scale Satyagraha against British rule in India, he did so with the daring promise of "Swaraj (freedom) in one year." It was daring, but not foolhardy. He promised freedom in one year *if* he got complete cooperation in Con-

structive Programme and spinning. Nothing changed his opinion between 1921 and the early 'forties. If anything he was more certain than
ever that nonviolence was the only way to go and that the true meaning of
nonviolence was not in the grand, dramatic confrontations like the
Dharasana raid but the slow, steady humming of the spinning wheel.

In fact, to appreciate fully how fundamental constructive work was
to his concept of nonviolent change we have to go back to the very beginning, to 1894, when he had wrapped up the law case he had been hired to
help with in South Africa and could now turn his attention to the "evil"
that had been in his face almost from the day that he arrived in May of
1893 — apartheid. For right here where it all began he made sure that,
alongside the community's direct struggle with the government, "the question of internal improvement was also taken up." These were to prove
portentous, and understated, words. In course of time, "also" would become "mainly"; the emphasis would steadily shift to constructive work
undertaken in the community itself, whether it be the Indian community
in South Africa or the disenfranchised Indians in their own country, even
though the drama that fascinated the world would always be the outright
clashes with British will and power. He meant it when he said his real
politics was constructive work. It was so simple that almost no one got it.

A nonviolent actor will naturally be a little nervous about putting
the blame for any wrong exclusively on others. When you are the weaker
party and are, in fact, being exploited, it's all the more important to remember that you, too, must have weaknesses that got you into the situation. No weakness, no exploitation. Though he had no illusions about
the ruthlessness and bias of Europeans, Gandhiji would nonetheless tell
his fellow Indians — in *Hind Swaraj,* one of the most fiery tracts he ever
wrote — that India was not taken with the sword and could not be held
by the sword. "We brought the English, and we keep them. . . . Our
adoption of their civilization makes their presence in India at all possible."

Whatever we may feel about the fairness or morality of the emphasis on correcting our own weaknesses, it is a powerful way to resist exploitation. Gandhi came to feel it was the best way. Like most popular movements, Satyagraha originated as a reaction to an outsider's offense; that was Gandhi's first reaction as it is anyone's. But where most movements stay fixed on "getting them off our back" he instinctively felt that this was only half the story — and maybe only the shadow half. The really powerful approach was, "Let's get up off our own backs." Two things give the approach power, as we've seen: the shift from "them" to "us" (and think how much more accessible we are than they, after all) and the parallel shift from an *obstructive* to a *constructive* mode of operations. Is it not obvious that, other things being equal, it is far better to build than destroy?

From Constructive Programme to a Constructive Program

How can we apply that insight today and in the West, facing the enormous changes we need to bring about? Here and there, many people like Dr. Robèrt are already hard at work at parts of this vast project, rebuilding neighborhoods, rescuing young people from gangs, doing nonviolence workshops in prisons, saving whales. What's missing, it seems to me is that all this has yet to gel. The whole that would make much more beautiful sense of all these parts is not yet very clear. One afternoon, a student of mine asked a well-known peace scholar who had given us a beautiful talk,

> As an activist, I find it frustrating that we're trying to stop a war here, stop genocide there, stop the arms race all over, and the minute we prevent one thing, there are three more. What we're not stopping is what's causing all these things. And I'm wondering if you have any sense of what that is.

She didn't. But I think we're beginning to. What causes "all these things" is called violence, and something called nonviolence is the antidote and something called constructive program would be the most effective shape for nonviolence, especially in between, and leading up to, climactic struggles like the Civil Rights Movement. It seems to me that two things need to happen that are not quite in place: we need to have a real grasp of the nonviolent principle, which will give us an articulate understanding of how to apply it (no inanities, Gandhi would say); and we need some overall design — some coherent, but all-embracing picture — in which we could feel that we're all working together even if we're not working on the same project. Not just a whale here or a prison group there, a beat-up nose cone here and a hugged redwood there, but a total nonviolent guided evolution.

The design of the Indian Constructive Programme offers us a model. For the program did have an overall design, which was extremely simple and could be visualized in a single, oft-repeated image: Constructive Programme was a "solar system," Gandhi would often say, and the *charkha* (the spinning wheel) was the "sun."

Since Gandhiji had a chance, as King did not, to develop his ideas on a mighty scale, we have in him the opportunity to see reform in action on that scale — to see, for example, the interesting relationship between charkha, the flagship project, the campaign to wrest back from British control India's once-proud textile crafts by cottage industry, and Constructive Programme *in toto.* The great advantage to this configuration was its harmonic coherence; if the whole, wide-ranging program was bewildering, you could understand it in the spinning wheel — so that, for example, he could say "phenomenal progress in spinning" and you would understand that it stood for the whole thing. It was not a pinch of salt here and a boycotted liquor shop there; it was the whole call to truth that those and other activities represented.

Watch your eyes; we're going to look first at the sun.

Epiphany at Ahmedabad

In the broad, comprehensive spectrum of those eighteen projects, charkha (Hindi for "wheel" and shorthand for the home spinning campaign) was the sun 'round which the rest revolved for many reasons. One has to remember that from ancient times India had been a "forest civilization" whose culture lay not in the great cities like Takshishela, Pataliputra or Kashi (modern Benares), but in villages, hundreds of thousands of them, in which people lived close to nature and to one another. The economic signature of these villages was self-sufficiency. Most village industries were carried out by families who had been organized for centuries into a system of interdependent castes. The exchange of goods and services, rather than money, was the main currency of this interdependence. Among many such industries, spinners and weavers were a part of "village economy" that reached far beyond its villages. Indian cloth was the pride of Asia. Clearly, the absence of central organization does not mean the absence of any organization, whatever the European rulers would later think. Cottage industry was the hub — the network of many hubs — of a vigorous trade throughout the subcontinent and beyond. Some fragment of that trade is being revived when you see a Kanjiveram silk sari ranking as high fashion at a San Francisco gallery opening or a Washington ball. And along with this economic self-sufficiency went a whole cultural system: religious institutions, education, and most of the governance and law and order that were based in and around the village and in the hands of people who knew each other.

Then, in the course of the nineteenth century, city-based industrial mills started pulling to themselves the many threads of this economy. In almost no time (if you take an Indian perspective) industrial cities like Ahmedabad, and the British monopoly on textile-making, idled millions of productive villagers, driving them off the margins of the social system. (Another, portentous aspect of the abuse was that most of these textile tradesmen were Muslims.) In 1928 Gandhiji visited those mills in Ahmedabad (the capital of his home state), and had an experience one might be tempted to call a vision: as he stood on the mill floor, looking at the clanking machinery, he wept. For where you and I would just see machines — noisy and unpleasant, perhaps, but just machines — he saw the structural violence and the greed that put them there: the city-dweller exploiting the simple villager, the impersonal corporatization replacing what had been a wide network of close relationships, the craze for profit overwhelming the dignity of work. Legends relate that once the Compassionate Buddha and his disciples were gazing at a particularly beautiful scene, and while they were admiring the snow-clad mountains and the clear river, he saw a river of sorrow — the flowing tears of suffering humanity — and mountains white not with snow but with the bones of the departed. Buddha's answer was to set in motion the Wheel of the Law; Gandhiji's was to turn the spinning-wheel of freedom — freedom from greed, centralization and structural violence.

The charkha showed that we can return to the kind of life humanity lived before the craze of the machine took over. Not only cloth was involved, but an ideology — not too different from what India had known centuries before — in which the rich would voluntarily "live simply, so that others may simply live," and the socioeconomic system would be one of human scale. Again, the fact that the system was decentralized did not mean that its components were isolated. As in the past, the spinner in his or her village was joined with the farmers who provided the cotton with those who manufactured, who sold, and finally who wore the *khadi* (homespun cotton). Even more than the intifada, charkha was rebuilding the infrastructure of a free India with her own, sustainable way of life.

From the 'twenties onwards Gandhi urged everyone, rich or poor, to spend a half hour a day spinning, if not carding, weaving or otherwise making cloth from India's own cotton, tirelessly explaining that the point was to make cloth for those who could hardly afford to cover their nakedness, to give back meaningful work to millions who had been idled by a system of subtle but ruthless exploitation, and in so doing to bring that system to an end. Many Indians, especially westernized city-dwellers, did not *like* wearing khadi, or *khaddar*. It's plain, it's rough, and definitely not chic. This kind of argument hurt Gandhi to the quick:

> We must be prepared to be satisfied with such cloth as India can produce, even as we are thankfully content with such children as God gives us. I have not known a mother throwing away her baby even though it appears ugly to the outsider.
> . . . Khaddar is the concrete and central fact of Swadeshi.

Swadeshi, briefly defined, is globalization in reverse. It means self-reliance and local action, growing outward from that position of strength to wide interdependency and global concern. Swadeshi embodied is homespun, as Gandhi says.

Charkha was exactly right in so many ways that it's easy to lose sight of the most important. "Food, clothing and shelter are basic necessities of civilized life," said one of Gandhi's granddaughters recently. "Most of us, at some time in our lives, have rolled out a *chapati* (flat, Indian bread). Similarly, every Indian should at some time in his life, feel and touch the charkha, for that is the *praan* or soul in all of us. We need cloth next to food." In Gandhian economics, there is a qualitative difference between the basic needs of food, clothing and shelter, and anything less essential. Everyone has a right to those three basic needs; if they are not met — for everyone — a society has failed.

Now recall Gandhi's other really great campaign. It's about salt — again, absolutely basic in a tropical country like India. With these two campaigns, the "obstructive" bid to get salt back from the government, and the constructive effort to make cloth at the village level, he sought to repossess two of the most basic life-sustaining elements of any economy, food and clothing. This makes Nehru's famous saying, that khadi was "the livery of our freedom," almost an understatement: in the fight for cloth and salt, India was fighting for control over the necessities of life itself.

Nothing could be more real, then, than a spinning wheel. Of course — thinking now of the real versus symbolic issue we dealt with in chapter three — the wheel is *also* a symbol. In India it's an ancient symbol of the world-process, the wheel of existence, of life and death (*samsara*); or as in Buddhism, the "wheel of the law." But what brought that ancient symbol back to political life? Not a slogan that you hung on the back of your bullock cart: "You're Following a Wheel-turner." It was people spinning real cotton for people who really needed it. From that concrete reality came many other gains: an income for idled, often starving people; hundreds of local networks getting raw material to spinners and their products to its market; providing and repairing the capital equipment of *takli*s (spindles), wheels, carding bows; an ethos of simplicity; a deep sense of solidarity with the poorest; and last but not least, political freedom once the British grip was nonviolently neutralized. A picture of a spinning wheel on a billboard or the nation's flag (where it resides today) could have done none of these things.

In addition to these major qualifications for charkha's "solar" status, namely that it was concrete, constructive and non-confrontational, we can more briefly cite a few of its other advantages:

(1) Everybody could participate. Working together creates a sense of shared destiny and unity, as almost nothing else does. We've already mentioned the now-classic experiment carried out at a children's camp where working together on common projects reunited rival groups of youngsters more effectively than seeing movies, eating together or any other common activity. Potentially everyone was united by khadi because everyone could spin — man, woman or child, rich or poor. No one was too humble or weak or proud or powerful to put their hand to *this* wheel.

In the grand days of charkha, even Congress VIPs came home and spun their half-hour every day — in fact, especially the VIPs. But khaddar was not only something you spun; it was something you wore, and this forged another kind of solidarity, since the rich could dress just like the poor, in simple, dignified homespun. Wearing their beliefs on their bodies, many well-off Indians found out first hand that brotherhood is more satisfying than status.

(2) You could do it every day. You did not have to wait for the right time, weather or circumstance, or depend on a big turnout on some special occasion; the ancient rhythm of the spinning wheel was tied only to the rhythm of day and night itself. It must have reminded and symbolized to the volunteers that they were in it for the long, long haul — the "relentless persistence" that makes the real difference in nonviolence, or almost anything worthwhile. It's interesting in this connection that Gandhi even claimed that daily spinning was a kind of spiritual discipline, because no Indian believed that spiritual results happen in fits and starts. You can make them happen only by sustained application over a long period.

(3) Charkha was *proactive*. You needed clothes, you made them. This is the heart of constructive program. Truth takes the lead, and events follow. Being proactive gives one a great strategic advantage, as any general knows. But it also involves the deepest principle of Satyagraha: truth is not a reflection or an absence of something else; it *is*.

(4) Finally — coming back now to the impatient volunteer's question to Gandhi in 1940 — spinning was unquestionably an act of truth which confronted the lie of colonialism at the deepest level, and therefore constituted the most effective resistance. The whole colonial system rested on a lie — the "big lie" of dependency, which tries to make one group of human beings think it has to beg its bread from another. That is not the way God stocked the Earth, but the mystique of superiority is compelling, even to those on the receiving end. India had come to believe

the implicit message, "You are dependent on us — you need us to give you salt and cloth (not to mention, administer justice, defend you from outsiders and keep order)."This is what Gandhi called that most "sinful" and unnatural connection between exploiter and exploited, and to it the charkha hummed back, "Thank you, we can clothe and feed ourselves — as we did for five thousand years before you came." In fact, if we listen closely, the wheel is saying no one needs anyone else's manufactured goods to stay alive. People need very few factory-made goods at all. Revolutionary enough?

In a world of falsehood, truth is inherently confrontational. A truly constructive program in such a world is like a swimmer against the current — he or she will bang into obstructions, even without seeking them. The Raj began as a trading company; it ended when their unwilling partners decided they would no longer go along with that kind of "trade." The British may have taught in their schools and speechified in their Parliament about "the flag" and "destiny," but as soon as the Raj became unprofitable it lost its grip, especially since Gandhi offered the double-sided resistance which Toynbee defined so well. "He made it impossible for us to go on ruling India, but at the same time he made it possible for us to abdicate without rancour and without dishonour."

So charkha only *appeared* non-confrontational; it was really going for the colonial jugular. A woman in her cottage, a youngster on the veran-dah, sometimes a whole village gathered in a festive moment on the *maidan* ("meadow") — the air humming with charkhas, they sat slowly, steadily undermining the whole economic system of the Raj, and the government scarcely knew what was happening. Or how to stop it if they did. Con-structive Programme provokes confrontation simply by what it is — or rather, what the rest of the world is. One hopes that Gandhi's impatient questioner grasped that.

At the same time, there was a noncooperative dimension to charkha which complemented the purely constructive one of spinning. One who clings to truth never clings to just one mode of operation. Khadi-clad Indians burned their British trousers with as much gusto as they had turned the wheel to make their own. The boycott of foreign cloth was so successful that nearly three million Lancashire millworkers found themselves out of work, and that at a time of worldwide depression when economic tempers were already frayed. Gandhi, in England for the Round Table Conference, made a special trip north to explain his movement directly to the Lancashire workers on September 22, 1931 that has become one of the high points of nonviolent history. "I am pained by the unemployment here. But here is no starvation or semi-starvation. In India we have both. If you went to the villages, you would find . . . living corpses." He did not mince words with them. "Do not think of prospering on the tombs of the poor millions of India. . . . Cherish no hope of reviving the old Lancashire trade" that charkha was rendering superfluous. "Don't attribute your misery to India. Think of the world forces that are powerfully working against you."

It was another miracle of Satyagraha: "May I say or need I say," one man wrote, "that I as a Lancashire cotton working man, who is to some extent suffering through the action of the Indian Congress leaders, have a profound admiration for Mr. Gandhi and a great many of my fellow workers share that spirit?" Said another, after Gandhi's stern words, "We understand each other now." Through soul-force we can divide opponents from their agendas while reuniting them with ourselves.

Heart Unity: Diversity Without Division

Constructive Programme was a comprehensive agenda of some eighteen projects that dealt with virtually every aspect of the injured country's condition, but throughout them ran an underlying thread, and that was to heal the "brokenness" of Indian society. The first plank on the platform was, accordingly, Communal Unity. Removal of Untouchability was the second — in other words, to restore harmony between Muslim and Hindu and eliminate caste arrogance within the Hindu fold. No less than six others aimed at "weaving back into the community" various groups who had been marginalized either by Indian tradition itself or the disruptive influence of foreign rule. Clearly, Constructive Programme as a whole was designed to build loving community; heart unity lay behind its every project.

Let's pause for a moment over this deceptively simple phrase. Heart unity means that I want you to be happy, notwithstanding our differences. In fact, to feel heart unity with others is to *enjoy* differences — what a flat, boring world it would be without them. And those differences can even include, for example, differences of wealth. Inequalities of wealth are an increasingly obscene feature of the global economy. The world's four richest men hold onto more wealth than about a third of the world's least developed *countries*. What else can one call this but obscene? Now, absent a concept of heart unity, the only solution that suggests itself is to wrest wealth away from the richest people by whatever means necessary and then spread it around until everyone on the planet has about the same amount. Wealthy people tend not to like this solution, and the result is bitter and unequal violence. With a heart unity framework, the approach is very different. You do not begrudge the comparative happiness of the rich (as Gandhi explained to the Lancashire workers), but you seek to awaken them to the shallowness of material wealth and the sorrow of extracting it from others who need. So you have to change the *minds* of the rich. This, of course, is not that easy; but it's actually easier than dispossessing them of their money. For one thing, you can demonstrate your own lack of concern for excess material wealth, even if you have access to it. This will work; in a culture that is not overly materialistic (which admittedly we don't have at the moment) it will even visibly "work."

Nor do you have to go on until you've made the whole world a level playing field. All you have to do is get the most destitute people enough to live on and to nourish the hope that they'll be able to grow and express themselves like human beings. You don't stop until you've achieved that, but on the other hand you can live with "rich" and "poor" as long as the poor have enough to get going on, *including respect.* You can't have rich and destitute, as we do, but you don't need to have everyone at the same economic level, only the same human level. There has to be empathy, which is the means and end of all heart unity techniques.

If people of different races have reached a state of heart unity towards one another, what possible difference can it make that they have differences of physiognomy? Or diet? Or taste in music? Or religion? Heart unity is key.

Other projects in the Constructive Programme addressed health, substance abuse, poverty and cultural deterioration. Taken together — and they were meant to be taken together — they were to make India a viable, whole society embracing its diversity. Charkha was no exception since, as you may recall everyone, big-shot or peasant, was supposed to be doing the "bread labour" of this basic work together — and wearing the results.

One thing is clear: if we would benefit from Gandhi we have to take him whole, not just try to imitate the iconic moments of high drama that punctuate his career. His trust for the future lay mostly in steady, constructive work — steady rather than occasional, work rather than protest; self-uplift rather than the obstruction of others; practical and concrete rather than symbolic. No one could fight with more determination when it was needed; but no one was as willing to get back to constructive work the minute it wasn't.

What can we learn from Constructive Programme? Not the individual programs, at least not without understanding and modifying them. We don't have 700,000 villages, so "village uplift" won't make sense in our world (although people doing community building in their neighborhoods are doing a version of village uplift). Our material resources are on a different order of magnitude from what theirs were then, so khadi itself won't be directly applicable. Not the structure of command, since we don't have a single leader of Gandhi's stature (and do have an individualism that balks at giving anyone the "dictatorial powers" the Indian masses gladly gave Gandhi).

The impressive thing about Constructive Programme, the thing we can still use, was its vision and articulateness — the way it addressed every hurting problem with one inspired energy. We can take the energy, and the organizational model. The energy is nonviolence; the model is a broad range of programs with a "solar" project holding them together and bringing them into range of a single vision, a project that everyone can take part in.

Perhaps its obvious what I think that project should be.

Sine Qua Non

There is a Canadian magazine called *Adbusters* dedicated to exposing and often satirizing commercialism. One of their first issues came out with an extremely clever cover.

You see a flotilla of small boats carrying men in colonial dress made up as Native Americans making for some old-fashioned three-masters sitting at anchor. Some of the "Indians" have already boarded the ships and are happily throwing boxes of cargo overboard. Sound familiar? But as you look closely you begin to register a few anachronisms: the little boats are actually rubber zodiacs, and the cargo that the "Indians" are ditching in the harbor is television sets. The caption is, of course, *The Boston TV Party*.

There is a very serious point to this irreverent pun. In a sense, we have been "colonized" by people who don't have our interests at heart — any more than the officials of the Raj cared for India's well-being. Our colonial masters do not come from another country; they move among us with the same skin colors and speak the same language we do; and yet they systematically victimize us, the "viewing audience," by making us buy things we don't want, goading us to run after a happiness that material goods cannot provide, while covering up the unity and purpose that could make us happy. Unlike India's colonial oppressors, who came from a different civilization, speaking a strange language and touting an upstart religion (which they hardly followed themselves), our oppressors walk the streets with us and follow exactly the same religion that most of us do — materialism. Commercial television has so altered the minds of young people that teachers are hard pressed, those who still try, to convey anything to them that doesn't follow the materialist-competitive paradigm. As I put it last chapter, the mass media are practicing education without a license. It is time to rebel.

Let me give just one example of what David Korten, in our epigraph, means by the colonization of our political space and our colonized cultural space. Millions of Americans watched the Clinton-Bush television debate on October 19, 1992, myself among them. When it was over, a network official came forward and announced, "We'll have the results of this debate for you in just a moment." The results? He meant, of course, who had "won." Since I virtually never see commercial television, this was quite a shock. I thought the point of a public debate was to help us make up our *own* minds, not to be told by some arbitrary "authority" what we had just seen. I thought political debate was to air issues, not to identify winners. Many commentators before me have pointed out that the media, particularly television, have changed politics as we knew it, changed it from being at least partly a decision-making process to a popularity contest — a fight. They have reduced democracy to a power struggle. It is from the beachhead established by materialism and competitiveness that they have moved this far into our political space.

It is an irony, but it's true, that after fighting so many wars to defend

our way of life from foreign aggressors we have given up our most meaningful freedom — freedom of thought — without a struggle. We will
certainly not get it back without a struggle. But the method of that struggle
and the manner of it must be different in kind from the forces that got us
into this morass. We must put at the very center of this struggle a key
project that begins in personal choice — to break the hold of the mass
media over our values and culture. Where the Mahatma's rallying cry was
"Boycott foreign cloth," I propose "Boycott foreign *thoughts*." Where he
put the wheel of the charkha in motion, I say we should spin the dial of
the mass media — to "off."

Thoughts of hostility, revenge, competition, materialism and greed
can truly be called "foreign" to our essential nature — such, at least, is
my confirmed belief. It is in this sense that my late friend Willis Harman
used to use the term "pseudo-values" for making money and "getting
ahead" at the expense of having deep relationships, a vibrant family. The
former are goals that those who have gotten a taste of service and compassion and loving community no longer take seriously. This world of
turmoil and darkness that we have devoted our ingenuity to creating is
not the essential expression of our nature. Despite their long evolutionary pedigree, greed, lust and anger are foreign to us in the very real sense
that they impede us from realizing our most profound aspirations.

Children are not born prejudiced, for example. They "have to be
carefully taught," as the old song says, and they can be untaught remarkably easily, as we shall see. We can become so conditioned that it becomes
second nature to respond to a different skin color or accent or belief
system with fear and hostility; but it never becomes our first nature. The
opening verse of the central text of Buddhism, the Dhammapada, reads,
in Eknath Easwaran's translation, "All that we are is the result of what we
have thought." If our thoughts have been put into us by out-of-scale,
impersonal interests . . .

Getting Real

The reclamation of our cultural space is an everyday, everybody activity — just like charkha. And while it begins, unlike charkha, with a "no," it's open to all of us to "spin" some time each day — the very time we save by not watching television or going to a gory movie — on constructive alternatives. Within the "no" there are constructive, network-building aspects: writing letters, spreading knowledge, maybe organizing a media boycott in our kids' school, or church, or just among friends.

Media cleanup can be as rewarding as spiking trash alongside the freeway or draining a toxic swamp, and though it starts in personal choice it can give rise to a network, a campaign — a movement. One day a few years ago I received a call from the Santa Rosa, California school board asking for some help. A well known director was making a horror film in which teenagers are terrorized, complete with realistic, gory violence, and he had the brilliant idea of making it right in picturesque Santa Rosa High School. Why not let the young people participate in their own degradation? Would I come to a public meeting as an expert witness? Coincidentally, a former student of mine who now works with the Media Violence Project had just sent me some of the latest studies on screen violence and horror movies in particular, so I told the concerned parents and school board members I'd be happy to speak, little realizing that by the time I got there the meeting would be front-page news. I arrived at the high school early to find the auditorium already thronged with an intense, buzzing crowd. Film making, I had forgotten, is one of California's largest industries. The director, who shall remain nameless, had threatened to blackball our community, perhaps even our state, and the then Governor — always concerned with our (fiscal) welfare — had backed him with threatening noises of his own. But these powerful men had reckoned without their host. Over eight hundred people soon filled the seats and both aisles were filled with prospective speakers waiting their turn at the mike (including "spies" from the studio — attractive young women trying to sweet-talk some of us men out of our resistance). It was a disciplined, intense, high-level meeting, one of the best I've ever seen and perhaps the closest to an old-fashioned town meeting I'll ever find outside New Hampshire. The issue was crystal clear: accept $30,000 in cash from the director or protect the minds and hearts of your children.

Speaker after speaker came forward and delivered good arguments, with almost no ranting, almost all of them against the filming. One man concluded his defiance of the film company and the Governor by going up to the stage and plunking down thirty dollars from his pocket to compensate the school's financial sacrifice. (I pointed out that a certain infamous betrayal in our civilization had been bought for thirty shekels of silver, and while I wasn't sure how much a shekel would go for in today's dollars the choice we were facing looked uncannily similar.) A woman who spoke made it onto the next day's front page. The director had sent a message that, "In twenty-five years of film making I have never encountered such resistance." To which she replied, "It's about time!"

Those parents made their point, and the filming was turned down. I had never felt so good about "the American system" even when the film ended up being made in an old house in the country, across the road from where I live!

Satyagraha is always a form of education. The more we can get people to focus on what the issue really is, as in this case money versus the well-being of our children, the sooner and the less abrasively we can solve it. The networks — thinking of television again — are in the business for ratings; they have no ideological attachment to vulgarity and violence as such. Even one letter that politely explains, "I have stopped watching your program because of its gratuitous violence," with a "cc" to the advertisers who support that program, makes a difference. More make a bigger one. A movement based on truth may not catch on as quickly as some, but it doesn't go away as easily either.

Boycotting television and most other media is, it is true, less than inspiring as a *constructive* undertaking: what does it build? Or what are we "putting *in* business" with this kind of boycott? Actually, quite a bit. Families that have stopped watching television have started rediscovering each other. Over and over they have found that it's far more satisfying to interact with someone, even if it's someone you have a problem with, than to stare at pictures of someone who isn't there. "The children spent a great deal more time doing creative things," writes officer Brawley, a New York City policeman who turned off the tube for two weeks as part of an experiment; and he goes on:

> I could begin to see where the children spent more time
> doing things which would be of importance to them in their
> school work in the future. . . . For the first time since I had
> been in school, I was completely caught up with all the
> reading for my courses. . . . We began to visit different
> families who, during the winter months, we lost contact
> with. The children seemed to fight among themselves more
> often. . . . At the same time the children became closer to us
> as we participated in doing things together.

"The family, I feel, is pulling together tighter as a result of No TV," wrote one participant in a school's experiment in Denver. Watching television can be an isolating experience — which is to say a pre-violent experience even before we get to the horrendous content. Conversely, whenever and to the degree that people or families or friends have abstained from watching television, they have found relationships flooding back in, whether it's playing games with the kids or talking about family decisions, or just talking. Five minutes of in-depth conversation is more fulfilling than five hours of vicarious absorption in images of someone else's life. People and families have just about universally reported a sense

of relief, of discovery, a sense that they were better off and more "func-
tional" when they deep-sixed their set.

They have scientific support. In an interesting study reported by
Israeli sociologist Urie Bronfenbrenner, children who grew up in new,
postwar housing developments in West Germany where they were given
wide yard-space to play in were found, surprisingly, to have done less well
developmentally than comparable kids in more cramped quarters in older
German cities. The reason, the researchers concluded, was precisely that
space — it allowed the children to run away from each other whenever
they couldn't get along, instead of working out their difficulties and becoming more intimate in the process, as Officer Brawley discovered. We
need human space to grow up in, not physical space.

My grandchildren have grown up in a world where gas-station at-
tendants sit in glassed-in cubicles and the cashier at the movie talks to
you through a speaker tube. This is a form of dehumanization, and by
virtue of that fact, an indirect cause of violence — other forms of which,
ironically, it's trying to prevent. Here we go again, making the problem a
little worse in the long run by isolating ourselves from one another at the
heart unity level, in the name of preventing (or rather, thwarting) a certain manifestation of violence in the short term.

Since I'm digressing a little, let me make the most of it. Being a
classroom teacher in this era has had its shocks, and most of them are due
to the appearance of a generation who not only grew up on television but
whose parents had grown up on television, and so they knew nothing
else. Among the downsides you hear about — that freshmen don't know
anything (that is, anything of permanent, cultural value) and they have a
terribly short attention span (so they can't *learn* anything of permanent,
cultural value) — there is one you may not have realized. I remember the
first time when I was talking away about something and a fellow in the
second row just got up and walked out. It still goes on — and so does my
sense of shock. My students don't lack respect for me or interest in what

I'm saying. It took me a while to realize what the problem is. *They don't quite realize I'm real.* They walk out to get a snack when the tube is on, and they're not totally aware of the difference when they're listening to a real live person.

Remember my observation in chapter three, that when the military uses video games to train combat soldiers it's primarily training them not to shoot straight, but to shoot without remorse, to kill without awareness that what they're shooting at is alive. It is also true that those who kill within our own society, in our streets and workplaces and homes, often testify that they did not see their victims as real human beings, but like moving dolls, or images — "virtual" people, just targets. Just as nurse Black overcame violence by seeing the person behind the would-be killer, reversing that process, those who would kill or injure fail to see the person for the label, or something even more dehumanizing. Susan Atkins of the Manson cult literally said that her victims "didn't even look like people. . . . I didn't relate to Sharon Tate as being anything but a store mannequin." No, I'm not personally afraid of violence happening in my classroom; but I'm quite afraid that our culture has, by making us progressively less real to each other, planted the seeds of violence in students before they get there.

The constructive alternative: if Gandhi could bring back the charkha we can dust off "charades" — or some cool modern equivalent. We can wait for films that don't find it entertaining to grind the human image into dust. In the early years at our meditation community we saw every Ian Carmichael comedy available; we saw *Casablanca* almost as often as *Gandhi*. If we all support a film like *Groundhog Day* or *Mr. Holland's Opus* it will help convey to producers that not everybody likes dialogue dripping with cynicism or thinks that people betray each other and use a gun to solve problems as a matter of course. When producers or newspaper editors say, "But this is what the public wants," they overlook the simple fact that they trained us to want that. Their supply cultivated our demand. Their progressive breakdown of standards created our insensitivity and taste for the dark side on which they now feed. Who can break the cycle? Both parties. We, by abstaining from the violent and explicit entertainment we've gotten used to; they by risking some short-term profits at the box office until the public's sensitivity returns.

If someone were to ask me, "What is it *really* going to take to get violence off our back?" I would answer without hesitation, "Phenomenal progress in culture."

Loving Community as Planetary System

Constructive Programme was, as the name implies, constructive rather than obstructive. It was proventive rather than after-the-fact; and those characteristics gave it a strong bent toward healing. The projects sought to weave back into the community the economically depressed, marginalized or rejected, using the simple but potent concept of heart unity that informed all of Constructive Programme, as it did all Satyagraha. The healing energy worked on all those who now had a self-transcending purpose to live for in the great struggle. It worked between individuals, like the newly khadi-wearing rich and the traditionally khadi-wearing poor, the first by choice, the second by necessity, and in the much tougher cases of intercommunal bitterness. In the end it even worked some of its magic between the rulers and ruled.

The coherence of the solar system model would give us a way to follow our individual passions (save whales, perch in redwood trees, educate around the death penalty) without feeling we are off doing our own thing in isolation; the healing energy of nonviolence will unite us.

Television is said to be a form of communication, but the communication is pretty one-way. In fact, television-watching as we know it does nothing but isolate us. Each in his or her techno-cocoon, we commune with the unreal. By form and content it is, at least as we use it now, the very technology of alienation. Even the fact that forty million Americans watch the same news at the same time has an isolating effect, for this is a good example not of *unity* but *uniformity* — a paradox we'll be revisiting in chapter nine. The thrust of our constructive program, like its great predecessor, has to be overcoming that isolation, getting back together.

In 1936 a delegation of African-Americans headed by Dr. Howard Thurman, made a pilgrimage to Gandhi in India. The Harlem Renaissance, that great cultural revival, was in full swing in those days, and we can imagine the hope with which African-Americans had been following the rise of the great Indian leader. Bear in mind that Martin Luther King, Jr. was seven years old back home in Atlanta when this conversation took place.

> Mrs. Thurman: We want you to come to America. . . . We
> need you badly.
> MKG: How I wish I could, but I would have nothing to give
> you unless I had given an ocular demonstration here of all
> that I have been saying. I must make good the message here,
> before I bring it to you.

Gandhi had long ago learned the lesson of swadeshi, which meant not only the use of native rather than foreign goods, especially khadi, but the profound principle of operating within your own circle of influence. It was for this reason he had had to renounce work among the Zulus in South Africa and get back to his own country. By working in your own sphere of influence you create a resonance in widening circles; but if you overextend yourself, if you try to do everything too soon, you lose power here *and* there.

And in that very connection, Gandhi added a prophetic remark. "Well . . . it may be through the Negroes that the unadulterated message of nonviolence is delivered to the world."

Twenty some years later, Rosa Parks refused to yield her seat to a white man on a Montgomery bus, setting off a chain of events that punctured the legitimacy of institutional racism in the United States.

We know now, thanks mainly to Sudarshan Kapur, that that "ocular demonstration" of India shaking off her colonial shackles through nonviolence came to the United States as a force embodied in quite a few flesh-and-blood satyagrahis who came to the South to advise and support the movement of the 'fifties and 'sixties. We also know that for both countries the lofty movement that collected around these great leaders is unfinished business. We teach it in schools, but we don't carry it forward in our lives. Of late, we've actually been losing, not gaining, ground to prejudice.

I had been in denial about this for some time when I gave a talk at Berkeley in the 1970s to a group of alumni who wanted to hear about my nonviolence course. I spoke enthusiastically, as I recall, about what you can do with this great force and how much it had done for us in the Civil Rights struggle. But this was Berkeley. One of those alums had been in the thick of that movement. She came up after the talk and tried to say something about how could it be — how could we possibly be going back to race-hatred after all they had suffered and achieved? She tried, but she could hardly speak through her tears. That broke the spell for me and I had to admit — first of all to myself — that even though the conscience of the nation had been roused by purely nonviolent principles for that brief, shining era, we were actually now going back into the stupidest and most destructive hatreds.

I needed an explanation. And after reflecting over what she'd said for some weeks, it did come: Martin Luther King, Jr. delegitimated racism, but he did not delegitimate *violence*. He wanted to, but he never had the chance. Before he could get that far, someone killed him. Violence stayed in the warp and woof of our culture, and along with it the energy of hate that it bears, and so racism, a form of hate and violence, was bound to return. You cannot expect steam not to leak out through the most convenient crack in the boiler: you have to seal all the cracks — or get sensible and turn down the heat.

What The Weissers Did

It is not possible — at least it doesn't seem possible right now — to reignite the Civil Rights Movement, nor would Martin Luther King, Jr. necessarily want us to. I am quite sure he *would* want us to continue his legacy in the form of constructive action. In fact, that was the direction he himself was taking before reaction cut him off. And it would not have to start, necessarily, as a great movement. Think now about one of the most gripping news stories of 1992, the healing conversion of a Grand Dragon of the Ku Klux Klan, Larry Trapp, by a Jewish couple, Michael and Julie Weisser.

Michael Weisser is the cantor of the South Street Temple in Lincoln, Nebraska and a prominent supporter of democratic issues. In 1992 he and his wife started getting a series of threatening phone calls and hate mail. The police warned him that a prominent local Klansman, Larry Trapp, was behind most of those calls, and though they put a tap on Trapp's phone they could not quite prove he was the one harassing them. So Weisser was not able to do much to protect himself — by the usual methods. One day Trapp was yelling at him over the phone and he decided, with his wife's support, that he had to resolve this for himself. "I was real quiet and calm," cantor Weisser recollects. "I knew he had a hard time getting around [Trapp, who has since passed on, was in a wheelchair] and offered him a ride to the grocery store. . . . He just got completely quiet, and all the anger went out of his voice, and he said, 'I've got that taken care of, but thanks for asking.'"

The Weissers had much more in mind, however, than just stopping the harassment. They wanted, if possible, to relieve the hate that this man was suffering, who (they later found out) had been disabled for life by a beating he received from a group of blacks. They now took the initiative, and called *him*. Not long after they went to his apartment for a friendly visit, taking a dinner they had made. When he opened the door of his apartment to meet the Weissers, Trapp pulled two rings off his fingers and handed them over to his still slightly apprehensive guests. They were Nazi rings. He was symbolically, and actually, renouncing the Klan forever.

Larry Trapp, by his own admission, had been one of the most hard-case white supremacists in the country, a man who "wanted to build up the state of Nebraska into a state as hateful as North Carolina and Florida." Perhaps it is for that very reason that his conversion, compared to some of the other card-carrying supremacists who have made the break, was so complete. "I denounce everything they stand for," he said of his former Klan associates,

> *But it's not the people in the organizations that I hate.* . . . If I were to say I hate all Klansmen because they're Klansmen . . . I would still be a racist.

This shows a sophisticated grasp of true, redemptive nonviolence — of heart unity. I would submit that this story takes us to the heart of loving community. The Weissers' brilliantly successful act is a model of how to apply courage and compassion to the curse of racism, which has responded to virtually nothing else.

At the same time, you cannot disestablish racism — or any division — by waiting until a spiritually ready hater who is beginning to look for a way out meets a particularly courageous and nonviolence-aware couple like the Weissers. We need not just more individuals like them, but programs such that, if there were enough of them, they would make emergency cures like the Weissers' unnecessary. That means we are talking about young people and education.

Elias Jabbour is an Israeli Arab and a Christian. He has lived in Israel his whole life and has yet to see the peace process work. One day, in 1987, he decided to stop waiting for peace to come from policymakers and started to ask himself what he could do himself. His scheme was simple: turn his home into an "oasis of peace" (like the famous school of that name, Neve Shalom/Wahat Sala'am). The children spend their days "in a colorful, warm, nurturing environment where it doesn't occur to them to treat one another differently based on race or religion" — until, that is, they go on to public school, and are once again segregated. Those who have the privilege of working with young people get to see how easily the conditioned responses of prejudice can sometimes be peeled away. In Los Angeles, when members of the Fourth Reich Skinheads were brought together with a group of blacks and Jews their own age, once again they quickly came to accept their new friends, leaving the "Reich" and "Skinheads" stuff in the dust.

Jan Øberg, head of the conflict mitigation team of Sweden's Transnational Foundation for Peace and Future Research, recently returned from the foundation's thirtieth mission to former Yugoslavia, where he conducted a series of "reconciliation seminars" in Eastern Slavonia with 120 Croat and Serb gymnasium students from Vukovar, Osijek and Vinkovci. For most of them it was the first time they met "the other side," even though many of them lived in the same town. Various techniques such as fish bowl, role play, group discussions and brainstorming were used. The students got to know each other and exchanged views, made friends and sang songs. They cried about the hurt and pain they had experienced during the war, but were careful not to say things like "you did this to us," just to give vent to their grief. They allowed themselves to brainstorm fascinating ideas and visions about a peaceful Croatia, Eastern Slavonia and Vukovar. And here is the payoff: Øberg found that, "It took Croat and Serb students less than an hour to find out that they have a lot in common, in contrast to what they have been told by their government, the media and, often, their parents since 1991."

Less than an hour. How many people or groups are willing to give that hour for the young people of the world, to heal the wounds that come from and perpetuate war?

There are not many, so far; but I would like to show how much good they're doing — and how to build on it.

Coffee Epiphany: Toward a Thermodynamic Model of Community

This question of renewing a culture can sometimes be understood best by comparison with a familiar model, the second law of thermodynamics. This law states that a physical system spontaneously goes to a state of higher entropy over time, meaning that it seeks a kind of equilibrium where everything is mixed up uniformly; its order, or from another viewpoint its "information," decreases, eventually to zero. Things degrade. "Isolated systems move spontaneously toward maximum entropy." The most dramatic example is the living organism, which without exception degrades irreversibly to the state of death. The universe itself, it is thought, is eventually approaching a state of "heat death" to become an undifferentiated cosmic soup of mass-energy. Any smaller system, however (and most of them are!), can reverse that entropic drift by receiving energy from outside itself. One important example is our planet. To quote the *Encyclopaedia Britannica*:

> The state of nonequilibrium of the Earth irradiated by the much hotter Sun provides an environment in which the cells of plants and animals may build order — i.e., lower their local entropy at the expense of their environment.

This is how we stay alive, even though "there is no evidence pointing to any ability on the part of living matter to run counter to the principle of increasing (overall) disorder as formulated in the second law of thermodynamics." A biological community is not dissimilar. Inbreeding can cause a dangerous loss of diversity, meaning a loss of its resilience and vitality, unless new genetic information comes into the gene pool from another source.

Imagine now a society as a "black box," or isolated system. In such a closed system, be it a test tube or a galaxy, energy inevitably runs down over the course of time; disorder increases and meaningful information is steadily lost. Similarly, do not cultures lose their vitality over time, their focus blur, their priorities start to drift as people lose their sense of what it is they're supposed to do in life? One obvious sign of this declining vitality — one we're only too familiar with — is that decision-makers keep coming up with the same unworkable solutions to problems that go on increasing. Is alienation eroding our security? Let's put more people in jail. Is there a rogue state in the international system? Hit them with more sanctions — and if they don't fall in line, more bombs. On one level violence, as we've seen before, is a serious lack of imagination.

One of the most studied decision-making processes in modern governmental history is that by which a series of American presidents, particularly President Johnson, kept on deluding themselves that they were about to win the war in Vietnam. Psychologists invented a new concept, "crisis decision making," to explain this cramping of the imagination (not to mention, of compassion). One way that worked was as drastic as it was simple: President Johnson surrounded himself with a small clique of men, a black box within a black box, who would scornfully dismiss any but the "more war" mentality. Anyone who came up with another idea was out; and so we were doomed to stay the course — until we sank.

It was extreme, but President Johnson's war cabinet was also symptomatic of the way our thinking about violence in general is cramped by narrow, self-defeating notions. We need new ideas and fresh energy to break out of the closed circle of discourse surrounding violence, as living things on earth need energy from beyond our planet, from the sun, to organize themselves biologically and overcome entropy. The prevailing culture is "running down" towards thermodynamic death for want of a new energy that can vitalize new patterns of order that can help us respond to the crisis and opportunity facing us.

Nonviolence is that new kind of energy. It is not really new, of course, any more than sunlight is new, but we have so turned our back on this dimension of life that we find ourselves trying, absurdly, to solve problem after violent problem as though that energy did not exist. One way of looking at Constructive Programme (and Gandhi certainly saw it this way) was as an attempt to introduce nonviolence-energy into the social order on a grand scale. Through Constructive Programme, for example, Gandhi and his close disciple, Vinoba Bhave, birthed institutions of every description — hospitals, schools, rural institutes, spinning centers — no less than 1,200 of which are still going strong in India today. The innate power of nonviolence is so impressive, as this institution-building hints, that you might think of Constructive Programme as the Van Allen belt, filtering the immense power of nonviolence and stepping it down to useable amounts and wavelengths so it could enter society with minimum disruption and maximum ordering potential, the way the Great God, Shiva, absorbed the immense power of the Ganges onto his divine head so he could meter it out to bring life and purification to the Gangetic plain.

Where our thermodynamic analogy breaks down, however, is that in our case the "outside" of the social system is really an "inside." Nonviolence is first and foremost a kind of energy that resides within an individual human being. We do not need different individuals in power, so much as we need a different kind of power in individuals. Some of the key campaigns of the Civil Rights Movement — the Montgomery bus strike and the Greensboro, North Carolina lunch counter sit-ins — were not sparked by Martin Luther King, Jr. or Bayard Rustin or by "outsiders" coming from up North. They were initiated, respectively by a black seamstress named Rosa Parks, and by four local college students who took it in their heads to take the actions that would eventually culminate in a higher level of social order.

We tend to know more about how the leaders went through the profound inner changes that allowed them access to new faith and courage, simply because of their public exposure. We know that Martin Luther King, Jr., for example, was at first unprepared for the level of hatred that rose like an angry sea that threatened to take, and eventually would take, his life. He passed through a profound crisis, his Pietermaritzburg if you will, that almost broke him. It came to a head on Friday night, January 27, 1955, the day after his first jail experience, when a series of obscene and hateful phone calls shook his confidence. At midnight that night, after a particularly ugly and threatening call that left him unable to get back to sleep, his anxiety mounted.

> And I got to the point that I couldn't take it any longer. I was weak. Something said to me, you can't call on Daddy now, he's up in Atlanta a hundred and seventy-five miles away. You can't even call on Mama now. You've got to call on that something in that person that your Daddy used to tell you about, that power that can make a way out of no way. . . .
>
> And I bowed down over that cup of coffee. I never will forget it. . . . And it seemed at that moment that I could hear an inner voice saying to me, 'Martin Luther, stand up for righteousness. Stand up for justice. Stand up for truth. And lo, I will be with you, even until the end of the world.'

Whatever we believe this inner voice was, however we explain it, it had the immediate effect of lifting King to a higher level of functioning. "Almost at once my fears began to go, my uncertainty disappeared." Three days later it allowed him to accept calmly the news that his house, with wife and children inside, had just been bombed. "My religious experience a few nights before had given me the strength to face it." In fact that experience came back to him repeatedly over the months and years of struggle. It was his enduring strength.

We could not find a better example of what I was calling a different energy coming into "the system," in this case American society, through the deep experience of an individual. We should not be surprised that King was looking much more towards constructive work when death overtook him.

What, though, does this mean for the rest of us? These rare experiences do happen to people — to a rare leader in a crisis, to a group kneeling on the Birmingham sidewalk, to a nation roused by a Gandhi, but we can't count on them. We can't plan them; but maybe we can institutionalize them. That is, maybe we can make institutional and cultural changes that will encourage such experiences and make longer-lasting use of their effects. There is at least some indirect evidence that this must be possible.

According to an important anthropological theory of violence, human groups have a kind of mob instinct which has been carried along the course of social evolution and has been observed very clearly, for example, among primates. Because of this instinct (or whatever name we should use for such a pre-rational behavior) certain kinds of tension within a community can precipitate a destructive frenzy that often, indeed typically, expends itself on available victims who may have little to do with the original problem. Such a response has been inscribed, as it were, in the cultural code of many societies, expressing itself in varied institutions that would fit the term "scapegoating." The Holocaust was a huge example — note that the word "holocaust" itself is drawn from the context of ritual sacrifice, which was a major form of victimization in archaic cultures.

Without going further into this fascinating theory, which explains so well how violent impulse becomes violent institution, we can use it the way we have used other aspects of violence in this book — we can stand it on its head. If destructive energy can be encoded and institutionalized, surely so can creative energy. This is what Gandhi's ashrams were supposed to do. "The Ashram holds that . . . society can be built up on the foundations of ahimsa," he explained, and it "conducts experiments with this end in view." This is what I had in mind when I pointed out how Joan Black, when she was confronted with a deranged individual in her emergency room, responded with behavior that was curiously like the pattern laid down by ancient rhetoricians for that kind of emotional work.

Apparently the ancients, with their relatively slow pace of life and stable institutions, observed how some talented individuals here and there had calmed down someone in a dangerous fury, or bucked up somebody mired in a depression, and they literally wrote the script for anyone who needs to do this. And this is what Gandhi, King and others lived for: so that no matter how much they had to suffer to show the power of nonviolence in their flesh and their lives, we could come along and understand what was involved and learn how to make it work more systematically, eventually to make it not some odd exception or unexplainable fluke, but the way conflict is resolved and life is lived. All science works by serendipity; so does the evolution of culture. So should we.

For this reason we have, in the above discussions, peered into the abyss of crime and the abyss of racism to see how nonviolence can send a ray of light even into those areas of profound darkness. In a moment, we will do the same with war. We have already seen moments of great illumination happening in sudden emergencies, at the climaxes of movements, and most importantly in the defining moments of certain individuals. And we already know that, if we don't want to go on lurching from one emergency to the next, we have to let ourselves down the chain of causality, from spectacular late interventions like the Weisser's to earlier and less hair-raising ones like Elias Jabbour's, or numerous projects like those mounted by the Search for Common Ground and many like it. The one thing needed for such moments and such projects to thrive is cultural support — which is why substituting better media and programming takes pride of place as the sun around which other healing projects of our constructive program should revolve.

Early intervention, and especially earliest intervention at the foundations of culture itself, are what constructive programs are about. I have little doubt, as I've mentioned, that had King lived, he too would have moved from protest marches and sit-ins toward "cooperating with good," once he got past the necessary first step of "non-cooperating with evil." The instinct was already there, even in the first campaign, which was designed not to put the Montgomery bus company out of business, but to put justice *in* business, "to achieve justice for ourselves as well as for the white man." The arc from integrating buses to securing voting rights to building economic opportunity was bending toward an American Constructive Program; how do we complete the circle?

I have stressed two modalities, privileging the first: personal engagement. As King said, "Nonviolence in the truest sense is not a strategy that one uses simply because it is expedient at the moment; nonviolence is ultimately a way of life that men [and women] live by because of the sheer morality of its claim" — or, as I've been putting it, because of the quality of its energy. The other mode is institutional change, starting with the "institution" of our basic values and how we shape and communicate them. Why are we never told in school that the human being has an innate need for integration with others, and "as far as in him or her lies," with all life? Why are we never told that no one can live fully without realizing that his or her life has an overriding purpose? Are we to turn our back on our deepest needs simply because advertisers have no way to exploit them?

In these last two chapters we have been exploring how nonviolence — in "the truest sense" as King puts it, a nonviolence universal in scope and deeply founded in individual commitment — could be systematically applied to two huge social problems, crime and racism. We explored, or at least began to explore, how the nonviolent moment can be regarded as a kind of epiphany, a sudden appearance of some underlying reality that can be better understood and systematically instituted to give us a much saner future than the one we now face. Our theme was loving community; our preferred mode of action was constructive. And so they will remain, as we move on to grapple with "the scourge of war."

7   A Clear Picture of Peace

If passive resistance could conquer racial
hatred . . . Gandhi and Negroes like King
would have shown the world how to conquer
war itself.
— W.E.B. DuBois

Some six weeks after the bombing of Hiroshima and Nagasaki a group of distinguished nuclear scientists met in Chicago. It was here that Fermi had carried out the first nuclear chain reaction; now the bomb had shown its awful power and humanity had to face the question of how to live with it. The scientists were acutely aware that history had opened a window of rare possibility for them. On the one hand, the world was shocked and sickened by the horrors of the war, and on the other, they who had created the weapon that ended it were held in an almost priestly authority. No one else had quite the prestige they enjoyed to chart a course for humanity that would lead toward peace. "Yet," Glenn Seaborg sadly recalls,

> No clear picture emerged of how we could achieve the objective nearly all of us had in mind — a world without nuclear weapons. It was as though the seeds of a nuclear arms race were embedded in human nature and political institutions.

The seeds of a nuclear arms race are indeed embedded in human nature and political institutions, and so are the seeds of stable peace. Human choices, individual and collective, nourish the soil that determines which of those seeds will flourish and predominate. As we have seen often, there is absolutely nothing in human nature, as far as human nature is known to scientists or sages, that predetermines which of these outcomes civilization will eventually reach. If by "nature" we mean the deepest aspirations discoverable in the human psyche and the evolutionary mechanisms designed to implement those aspirations, then the cards are, in fact, fairly obviously stacked toward peace. If we are heading right now in the other direction, that is not nature calling, but a kind of perverse conditioning that is diverting us from the course of our rightful destiny.

This was the picture the scientists did not see — understandably, because while they were brilliant men in their field, their expertise, no matter what the public might think, was more or less irrelevant. As Kenneth Boulding pointed out, the field of integrative power has been left fallow. No one — that is, no category of "experts" we currently recognize — makes it their special study to learn and teach how to fertilize the field of peace and reap its rich harvest. Scientists and well-meaning people that they were, the Chicago group were nonetheless caught in the same constricted vision as the rest of us; like us, they tended to see the world and its potential from within the shadow side — the sad, media-constricted image of what is possible.

I have a reason for stressing this point. For a while, I was part of a remarkable series of meetings with nuclear weapons scientists, theologians and professors convened by the Bishop of Oakland, California, when the American Catholic Bishops' pastoral of 1983 had expressed grave concern about the morality of the nuclear arms race. Our discussions in the privileged atmosphere of a Catholic retreat house in the hills above the Central Valley were remarkably frank, and searching. It was one of the best opportunities I had ever had to present nonviolence to an influential audience. I noticed, however, that a physical science colleague from Stanford laid claim to — and was granted — special authority because he was "the guy who knew how to restart the Stanford Linear Accelerator." I was impressed, like everyone else; I can barely restart my computer when it crashes. But what, exactly, does that have to do with the nature of violence, or the psychology of deterrence? Have we become so obsessed with machines and technology that we've forgotten that the most important things in life are neither?

I believe it was George Bernard Shaw who said that there are some subjects about which almost anyone could enlighten you more than the experts. Peace is one of them. In the search for peace, "experts," like the solemn "news" reports of the media or the pronouncements of the elite that makes our foreign policies, often do little more than obscure the common-sense intuition that, after all, can light up the path.

The Nobel Prize for Peace in 1979 went to Mother Teresa of Calcutta. The world's reaction, basically a paean of joy, was one of those sparks of intuition. "Now the mother of Bengal is the mother of the entire world," said an ecstatic Bengali on the streets of Calcutta. Mother Teresa had been honored by Pope Paul eight years earlier with the first Pope John XXIII Peace Prize, and now she was awarded the Nobel, though she had never played a role in a negotiation, signed a treaty, or used her influence to prevent a large-scale conflict. Yet world opinion rapturously approved the award, unconsciously sharing in the logic it implied, that he or she who lifts the human image out of the gutter, as Mother Teresa had so literally done in the streets of Calcutta, does more for peace than haggling statesmen or threatening armies.

And in fact, Mother Teresa demonstrated her peacemaking power dramatically in 1982 when, upon hearing that an orphanage for disabled children in Beirut had been abandoned to its fate during intense fighting, she announced her intention to enter the city and rescue the children.

And so she did. For ten days the mere presence of the diminutive nun who owned virtually nothing and had access to no state authority brought the spasm of raging conflict which no UN-brokered force, no Syrian presence, no Israeli armies had been able to control, to a strange peace.

So the Nobel award, and the world's approval, were one golden thread of bright intuition in a fabric of confusion surrounding peace and war. In the Beirut rescue drama there resided, however, one of the wilder ironies of modern times. Mother Teresa's antagonist in this struggle, the man who ordered the rain of bombs and rockets on South Lebanon, was the Prime Minister of Israel, Menachem Begin — who had been awarded a Nobel Peace Prize the year before! This award was not given in cynicism. Prime Minister Begin and Egypt's Anwar al-Sadat had jointly signed an agreement which put a temporary slowdown on hostilities between Israel and Egypt. (The award had been given to Le Duc Tho and Henry Kissinger for a similar achievement in 1973.) This is what is called "negative peace," arguably better than positive war, and in this sense the award to Begin and Sadat was not made in cynicism. But it was certainly done in confusion, the confusion between the two definitions of peace that are now, as Emerson said, "reigning in the minds of many persons" — the confusion between "negative peace" (à la Begin) and "positive peace" (à la Mother Teresa), between a standoff characterized by the absence of physical war and an island of loving community nourished by the presence of spontaneous mutual concern.

Incidentally, the attack Prime Minister Begin had launched on Lebanon in 1981 was code-named "Peace for Galilee." *That* was cynical.

None other than Robert McNamara said, "Mother Teresa deserves Nobel's Peace Prize because she promotes peace in the most fundamental manner, by her confirmation of . . . human dignity." But in her own acceptance speech at Oslo, speaking in what she calls "her own special brand of English," Mother Teresa defined even more simply the contrast between her kind of peace and that promoted by presidents and prime ministers: "I am called to help the individual." Violence is always against the individual; the human individual is always the source, and individuality the ultimate beneficiary, of nonviolence.

This makes all the more arresting the idea that nonviolence can be used in war, which is the largest-scale form of violence, in which the actors are large groups or states.

Can nonviolence be used to defend a whole state — can it lead to a replacement of the war system? Even in the largely unworked field of peace itself some scholars will declare that nonviolence is not relevant to the solution of international conflict; it just can't reach that far: "Nonviolent action has never been and will never be a replacement for warfare." But that glittering thread of intuition we picked up in Calcutta and traced through Beirut and Oslo seems to be leading to a "yes." As W. E. B. DuBois said, it indicates that those who cultivate the "arts of love" like King and Gandhi and Mother Teresa are the ones who bring peace to the world, not those who hold others at bay in an uneasy equilibrium of naked power. DuBois was speaking incredulously, even sarcastically; but I will be confirming it in all seriousness. To Gandhi, it was very clear: *only* nonviolence can replace warfare. "I can say with confidence that if the world is to have peace, non-violence is the means to that end, and [there is] no other."

I. I. Rabi, who received the Nobel prize for physics in 1944, later said ruefully of the nuclear arms race. "It gets worse and worse. I don't know why we failed. It's a mystery. It's the great mystery of the postwar period. . . . Anything that reduces nuclear weapons, I'm for."

But isn't it intuitive that we cannot get to peace through the designs of war? The reason the way to peace is such a mystery is that most of us cannot get from the intuition that we share with Mother Teresa to a coherent idea how we ourselves, who don't have her vocation, can nonetheless follow her lead. Politicians give lip-service to her kind of contribution, but who tries to move that acknowledgment from the lips to somewhere near the heart? I suggest that the way to see the "clear picture" sought by the nuclear scientists, so far in vain, is to step out of the shadows. That is, not to be always thinking how to stop war so much as how to start nonviolence.

Body, Mind and Spirit I: Thinking Peace

When, in 1961, Joan Baez led the first group of protesters into Sproul Hall on the Berkeley campus, launching what is now known as the Free Speech Movement, she stopped at the head of the long, wide stairway for a moment, turned and said with her famous smile to the huge crowd of students who were all but intoxicated by the historic significance of their entry into the forbidden building, "Remember, we're not going in here angry; we're going with love in our hearts. We're going to be nonviolent in thought, word and deed." She was echoing what Martin Luther King, Jr. before her and many nonviolent activists before and after her have said. Real nonviolence comes from the whole person, from within her or him. We have to do something about our thoughts, our speech *and* our outer behavior to have a nonviolent effect on the world.

The trouble is, or was, that in 1964 even those who were inclined to agree with Ms. Baez didn't have the faintest idea how to be nonviolent in thought. To get any sort of systematic handle on your thoughts was never discussed in education; indeed it was scarcely dreamed of, anywhere. Meditation was still an empty or a badly misunderstood word outside of the rarest circles. How quickly that all changed. By the time the Free Speech Movement was over, in little less than a year, alongside the political style that went back to centuries of student rebellion, now filtered through what we took to be Marxism (none of us ever *read* Marx and Lenin, to my knowledge) was the "new age" consciousness that was to create yet another subculture. Where we had sat discussing Camus and Fanon over a cup of coffee some of us now talked excitedly about Vivekananda and Buddhism over lattes.

Time will have to sort out what is real in this new way of thinking and what is romantic wish-fulfillment. It is still difficult to talk about — even think about — the mind in this still very material age. In the 'seventies, there was a *Reader's Digest* series on health, called "I am Joe's foot" or "heart" or some other organ. As Sri Easwaran began to collect enthusiastic meditators around him on the Berkeley campus in that era, one of his oft-expressed desires, not entirely tongue-in-cheek, was to write an article called, "I am Joe's mind." He even had his opening sentence: "Joe thinks he's me." It would have made the *Reader's Digest* a journal for all time.

Peacemaking is nothing more nor less than the application of soul-force to human violence at its greatest scale. Therefore it must begin, somehow, with deep changes that take place within the person — where the soul is. It doesn't stop there, to be sure. The fact is, it's nearly impossible to keep soul-force from having effects on the world, eventually quite visible ones on the material aspect of the world. To begin to show how soul-force, somehow resident in or reachable through the human mind, could become a peace system in the world, I am going to envision three steps, or projects, which, in the spirit of Joan Baez's rallying cry, illustrate three stages of the great change that has to happen — three threads to weave into an eventual fabric of peace: thought, word and deed.

Whatever else the "new age" paradigm may have accomplished, or failed to, it has made it easier to talk about the baffling problem of large conflicts by making it somewhat more natural to bear in mind their connection with consciousness. Consciousness is within, but not limited to, the individual. However vast, however complex and "out there" the war system may finally play itself out, it is crucial to remember that "wars begin in the minds of men." Emerson had long ago foreshadowed this truism of the UNESCO Charter in his musing about the Concord armory that I've often quoted. "It is really a thought that built this portentous war establishment, and a thought shall also melt it away." The nonviolence which can overcome war must also begin in the minds of men and women. Any and all of us. During the Cold War that followed hard upon that resounding, but ignored, first clause of the UNESCO Charter, British historian E. P. Thompson was dismayed by the dangerous fixation on nuclear weapons — prophetically, because this trivialization of war was to reach a climax in the Gulf conflict some years later. He remarked then, rather chillingly, "The deformed human mind is the ultimate doomsday weapon." Where Emerson had said that "timber, brick, lime and stone have flown into convenient shape, obedient to the master idea reigning in the minds of many persons," Thompson was only re-reminding us that now steel, silicon, glass and radioactive isotopes have obediently flown into shapes far more destructive. Our thinking has not improved, and so the "improvements" in our technology take us backwards into grave danger.

I would, however, propose a more compassionate, and in the end a more practical, revision of Thompson's grim observation: the *undisciplined* human mind is the ultimate doomsday weapon. Minds become deformed by lack of discipline, and formed by discipline. As the Buddha said, "More than those who hate you, more than all your enemies, an undisciplined mind does greater harm. More than your mother, more than your father, more than all your family, a well-disciplined mind does greater good." An undisciplined mind is the most dangerous kind of loose cannon. Whoever owns such a mind will feel insecure no matter what situation you put him or her in, will spread insecurity to all those around, which in course of time can become the mass insecurity known as war.

The most powerful, direct and immediate way to discipline the mind is the method I extolled in chapter three: meditation. Meditation — again, as I understand it — is "choosing responsiveness over violence" over and over again, systematically and doggedly putting the mind back in a positive channel (in my case the inspirational passage) every time it starts wandering, as it will, to hell and gone. The relevance for nonviolence of such a struggle is that distractions are not as random as we think. Scratch any thought that's trying to distract you from your chosen train, and you'll find that even the most innocent-seeming, the most pious train of associations is leading you into an ambush only two or three associations off the trail.

"Ah, that's a great verse."

"Wonder why more people don't realize that."

"I'm so profound!"

"Why on earth doesn't Genevieve appreciate me. Like the other day when . . ."

And off you go. When our thoughts are slow and positive (and slow and positive tend to come together, just as fast and negative do), it is relatively easy to keep them off that most boring of subjects — ourself. The mind quickly regains its native responsiveness, i.e. to the needs of others. The fact is, when we speak of an uncontrolled mind we are being a bit inaccurate. A mind over which our better judgment does not preside is not really uncontrolled, it is controlled by forces we would not approve of. Meditation is thus an ever-deepening tug-of-war between our better judgment and forces like anger, fear and greed, which are in turn driven by the ultimate, chaotic principle within us; call it the ego or something more colorful, it is the "doomsday machine" in our own consciousness. We definitely dismantle that machine when our better judgment gains spontaneous, unbroken control over the thoughts, images and feelings produced, now more slowly and less seemingly randomly, in the factory of the mind.

In the centuries after Jesus' passing, tens of thousands of men and women took to the deserts of Egypt or the hills of Syria to practice what they called the "secret regimen." Later they would call it "the prayer of quiet" and practice it in monastic enclaves all across Europe, or at enclaved moments during otherwise normal lives. Today, relearning from the East what we have forgotten from our own traditions, we call it meditation — the name matters little. Millions of our fellow human beings have recognized that the mind as we know it is a problem that has to be solved for our own fulfillment and the world's peace.

Mass media have, seemingly by their very nature, obscured this recognition. D. W. Griffith, one of the pioneers of film, made some innovations in the early days of the silent movie that illustrate this all too well. He drastically accelerated scene-changes in the typical one-reeler of the day from about a dozen separate shots to as many as sixty-eight. This is the same man who, you may remember, produced one of the most pro-violent films of all time, the notorious *Birth of a Nation* (1915), a film that glorified the Ku Klux Klan and, as the title implies, what Griffith saw as the nation-building significance for the United States of vigilante racism. To watch MTV today is to see the mind being made jerky and uncoordinated and — once you understand the connection — prone to violence.

In meditation you are dealing directly with that mysterious connection between speed, fragmentation and violence. Key to the practice of meditation is not only the positive content of the passage you're meditating on, but your efforts at slowing down the rate at which you're going through it. I sometimes feel that you are like a cowpoke, grabbing the mind by the horns and wrestling it down, causing it to go through the passage as slowly as you can, until the blessed day when compulsive thinking does actually stop.

And along with it all its violence. This is the ultimate in making — and experiencing — peace. Then we will know for ourselves why Emperor Ashoka declared that there is nothing like meditation for making progress in the law of life.

Body, Mind and Spirit II: Talking Our Walk

To the extent that we can make peace rule our thoughts, to that extent our speech and actions will be pure peace. When Gandhi said, "I have not the shadow of a doubt that any man or woman can achieve what I have achieved," he was not talking about founding spinning centers or leading salt marches. The perfecting of this long, long process, however, is a long way off (judging by myself), and people are causing each other death and suffering all over the world even as we speak. What can we do now, while trying to work these deep changes on the mind, to lay the secure foundations of peace from below?

There is — and we are leading up to it — a form of direct action ordinary people can take part in which, in my opinion, will help to roll back the monstrous momentum of the war system more effectively than urging our representatives to sign treaties or withhold some monies here or there from the military budget. But there is also an important middle ground between thought and action.

What causes, or allows, a human being to do inhuman actions? Here are the statements of two such people who found themselves swept up in World War II. Former Japanese soldier Shiro Azuma participated in the massacre of civilians in Nanking. Sixty one years later, stricken with remorse, he explained quite simply, "We were able to kill them because we despised them."

Respect is indeed a powerful antidote to violence. Once after I had given a talk in Pasadena for the American Friends Service Committee, a man came up and told me that he and his wife had grown up in a small suburb of Berlin, where her father was the Rabbi and was much respected in the whole community. As persecution intensified in the late 'thirties, orders would come from Berlin to inflict greater and greater indignities on the Jews. But in this community people found themselves unable to carry out those orders, at least when it came to his father-in-law. They were not particularly opposed to the Nazis, he told me, and certainly not openly trying to resist the government; they simply could not overcome their innate respect for someone. A respect which nonviolence itself had roused, it occurred to me, in the case of the Birmingham marchers.

But it is the testimony of the second witness that I want to focus on: Adolph Eichmann, who was hunted down and brought to Israel to stand trial for his war crimes. Eichmann reportedly said that it hadn't been hard for them to send tens of thousands of people to their death, thanks to their language. Hannah Arendt explains that all the Gestapo leaders were ordered to communicate in a bizarre code of euphemisms. No one spoke of killing, but of "final solution," "evacuation," "special treatment."

> The net effect of this language system was not to keep these people ignorant of what they were doing, but to prevent them from equating it with their old, 'normal' knowledge of murder and lies. . . . Eichmann's great susceptibility to catch words and stock phrases, combined with his incapacity for ordinary speech, made him, of course, an ideal subject for [these] 'language rules.'

We may be getting somewhere. If we look back on the Cold War era, it can give us a weird feeling of disorientation to see ordinary people like you and me blithely contemplating the extermination of the planet, and how we thought and spoke about it. It was not a time of democracy, but one in which a small elite had a handle on our way of thinking, which they seemed bent on cranking in the direction of more and more anxiety and war. A number of us scholars who were looking for a way out of this freakish condition hit on the idea of studying the language of the Cold War discourse going on among these "experts." Perhaps we could understand something of how we had gotten into that crazy way of looking at things and help them, the "defense intellectuals," understand it too.

The approach had attractive features. We know how maddeningly difficult it can be to get someone who's opposed to us to change their thinking. A nonviolent moment can turn that trick; but we know how rare that is. So it occurred to us that you could look at the imagery, metaphors, nuances and suggestions in which people speak and write and, by putting that aspect of their language under scrutiny of reason, help to show them — and the general public — how they were deceiving themselves. Wording began to look like the place to stir up the dovecote (or should we say hawk-cote). It was anyway more constructive than simply despising those who went in for endless discussions of megatonnages and throw-weights or trying to talk to them about the morality of the arms race, which would evoke nothing but a cold shoulder, which we perhaps deserved. To shock a person into feeling bad about what they're doing rarely works. Usually it just guarantees that she or he will stop listening, to protect their smarting conscience.

When the Peace and Conflict Studies program was just underway at Berkeley I used to invite a captain from the Army ROTC (now called Military Science at Berkeley) to talk to the introductory course. He usually stood up to my students' impatient criticism very well; but on one occasion he casually mentioned, as people do, that of course "there have been wars as far back as recorded history." Fresh from reading Marija Gimbutas, I piped up, "Do you realize that isn't actually true? First of all there's the whole 'Old European' civilization, then there are scores of societies, for example a broad swath of Native American cultures, who did not. . . ." It was too late. He had changed the subject already. Wherever people are faced with the fact that their behavior doesn't accord with what they say, "The theory of cognitive dissonance suggests that [they] change their beliefs to be consistent with their behavior," not the other way around.

Thus we felt the need to explore the world of language and metaphor, where we could hope to engage the defense community in constructive dialogue — and I now want to add, we can all do some constructive work today. People are not going to take charge of their thinking process in great numbers any time soon, for this involves the hardest disciplines in the world and the farthest removed from the mainstream culture's field of vision; but language is the key to thoughts, and language can be worked on independently. Whether or not we are systematically trying to control the *process* of our thinking, i.e. through meditation, we can pay some careful attention to its *content*. So what did that content look like in the Cold War era?

In an influential article called, "Sex and Death in the Rational World of Defense Intellectuals," psychologist Carol Cohn led the way. Spending two weeks in a seminar with Cold War civilian "defense intellectuals" ("a feminist spy in the house of death," she fancied herself), Cohn shed some rather frightening light on the way this elite community was shaping the most fateful decisions of our time — indeed, if they had their way, perhaps of time itself. These men (and an occasional woman) thought of their mission as formulating "'rational' systems for dealing with . . . nuclear weapons." But what Cohn picked up, listening in as a woman and a political outsider, was an odd language shot through with interlocking metaphors of eroticism and violence. Weapons "marry up;" some are called "slick-ems;" they try to achieve "deep penetration." One's stereotype of these men had it that they were, if anything, *too* rational, with their cold calculations of "megadeaths" and innumerable chilling euphemisms like "surgically clean strikes" and "countervalue attacks;" but in an important way they were far from rational. With the lives of every one of us in the balance, there they were psyching themselves up on the sex-and-violence appeal of Armageddon!

Cohn's important study focused on the key issue of gender and the rather bruising concept of maleness that's served up in our modern culture, but her work has even broader implications. Language — all levels of language from the individual word to the complex argument — is a powerful handle on the mind. Within the interstices of our own language we can often encode — and thus in a sense conceal — arguments we do not want to spell out. Modern language is so pervaded by aggression now that we no longer notice we're using the language of conflict, even when we're doing peace:

> UNESCO distributes rucksacks to institutions which are
> part of its Network of some 4600 associated schools in 147
> countries. Teachers and educators can add material *targeting*
> the specific needs of the region or community. . . .

Oh dear, "targeting" peace materials at schools! But we all do this — when we say, "This project is *targeted at* inner city youth," instead of designed for them, or we say we are going to "impact" something instead of have an effect on it (making a verb out of a noun, to boot), or when we say something is "competitive" when we mean it's good. Noticed or not, these locutions — and the implications behind them — register in our consciousness. If they did not, there would be no such thing as poetry. Or advertising.

You might think with some justice that the words and imagery we're discussing here are too subtle to be called violent. But the effects of such speech are not so subtle. Some time in the 'seventies, I recall, an Irish revolutionary was taken into custody in this country and the British wanted to get their hands on him. Should we extradite? The life or death outcome of this question, at least as far as the press was concerned, hinged on whether this person was a "freedom fighter" or a "terrorist." These are extremely polarizing words. In reality, of course, he was neither. In reality he was a person, one who had used violence to get what he wanted. We could certainly have talked about what to do with such a person — but the possibility for such discussion disappeared behind a debate over which stereotype defined him. This is dehumanization.

It is when we go from labels like these to the imagery and metaphors in ordinary language, however, that we really see the power of words to construct and at the same time conceal. Consider this remarkable passage from an interview with General Oscar Humberto Mejía, the military dictator (or was he chief of state?) of Guatemala who describes here his campaign against the nation's guerilla army in the 1980s.

> It's a curious thing, but sometimes the population supports the guerilla more than they support their own army. I don't know why. We were just doing our duty. We didn't *start* the war. But the population was the water and the guerillas were the fish. We realized that to kill the fish we had to drain out

the water. We had to pull the indigenous population over to one side, and this is why we created the civil patrol system."

The guerillas were the fish. That's a long way down the food chain from being human!

But the indigenous people fare even worse in this conceptual fantasy; they are water, i.e., not even animals. They are inert and passive (like the army, which "had to" expel them), hardly relevant except as a hindrance to killing the fish. And so one of the cruelest campaigns of the cruel twentieth century, in which an entire people was reduced to living in terror, became easy, just as it became easy for Adolf Eichmann to mastermind the slaughter of tens of thousands of human beings. It became easy when the perpetrators imagined they were not killing and destroying, they were just "pulling the indigenous population to one side." I can almost hear the words of Mike McCullough, research director for the National Institute for Health Care Research: "Imagery is a major vehicle for increasing anger."

It's enough to make one stop using images or metaphors altogether — except that we would soon find ourselves unable to speak, or even think very much. Language is entirely based on metaphor; even the word "metaphor" is a metaphor, being a Greek expression meaning "carry across" (i.e. from one frame of reference, one meaning, to another). Rather, what I'm exposing here tells us to be careful how we metaphorize and create images for people. Just as we have sensitized ourselves to the need to watch our traditional language around issues of race, gender, etc., we can sensitize ourselves to the power of language to disguise and promote violence.

Carolyn Merchant showed in her eye-opening book, *The Death of Nature,* that the guiding myth of our culture profoundly determines how we see everything around us. By changing the traditional underlying image of the earth as Mother to that of an inert thing, a process Merchant correctly calls "desacralization," our immediate ancestors destroyed a safe-guard against the despoiling of their own environment, paving the way to the near-destruction of the planet that is now facing us. I said "by chang-ing," but who actually carried out that change? In the case of a huge cultural shift like this, a shift that goes on under the surface of our aware-ness, it is hard to identify who changes the surrounding language that makes such a shift possible. Do we all do it together? Do we follow cer-tain leaders, who may themselves be scarcely conscious what they are doing? The images just seem to shift by themselves — but of course this is impossible. Rather, the elusiveness of this controlling process should make us aware of the potential importance of each speaker, of you and me.

Relearning to talk — this is about as much fun as relearning to walk or eat. That is why James O'Connor opened the Cuss Control Academy in Chicago and wrote *Cuss Control: The Complete Book on How to Curb Your Cursing;* because if people can learn to communicate better, he rightly says, they will also learn to cope more easily with life's inconveniences, thus leading straight to less violence. The rise of cursing is keyed to the decline of idealism and compassion; but it's only part of the story. We have to painstakingly revisit old habits and make ourselves conscious of many things that were automatic. Are we using euphemisms as an anaes-thetic? Are we indulging in the "techno-trivialization" that now takes the place of our thinking about war? Have we succumbed to the "pseudospeciation" that turns the people in your own country first into guerillas and then to fish — drops people out of sight by reducing them to labels and finally to objects?

Cultivating right speech is annoying, vexatious, socially awkward — and definitely worth it. There is a famous verse in the Bhagavad Gita describing the highest kind of happiness, which applies here. "What is poison at first but turns to nectar at the end" (18. 37). Well, "nectar" may be a bit of an exaggeration; but if my own experience is in any way typical, we do enjoy a sense of realness, of solidity, when we begin to drop misleading euphemisms, evasive technicalities and dehumanizing stereotypes — a sense of relief.

Euphemisms in particular repay close attention. They can be as dangerous as stereotypes. Scrupulously calling things what they are is a form of Satyagraha — clinging to truth. Underneath all its conditioning, the human mind still inherently rejects violence. We have seen evidence for this in the etymology of the word "violence" itself, in behavioral science and in numerous historical examples. There is enough innate rejection of violence inside a person that Satyagraha can often work just by making the violence in a situation unmistakably visible.

Euphemism has another side, which became all too manifest in the horrors of the Cold-War rhetoric Carol Cohn analyzed. Remember that the all-important issue in violence is dehumanization, so graphically accomplished by the language of General Mejía. It is in this sense that "truth is the first victim in war"; the truth of the others' humanity is denied in all violence. In a way, this is understandable. You have to reduce people to "enemies," or even better to objects, before you can bring yourself to kill them. But during the Cold War, the sword violence wielded against truth in speech cut two ways. In this discourse the living were dehumanized (cities became "targets," disasters became "statistics") and nonliving objects were artificially invested with a life. Think of what it means to say a "rich harvest" of nuclear "kills" when we're talking about destroying enemy missiles; when missiles from the same side colliding with each other was called "fratricide." Think about the implication of "smart" bombs. This is the language of life — only what it's actually describing is certain death.

The choice between God and Mammon is, in a fundamental way, a choice between honoring life where it is, in living beings, or transferring that reverence to matter, where it does not belong. Materialism, in other words, is fundamentally linked to violence. In an age of materialism we slide all too easily into the mental violence of calling cities "targets" and then turning around and naming missiles as though they had personalities. (The two atomic bombs actually used in war were dubbed "Little Boy" and "Fat Man.") We have to worship *something*, as Dostoevsky reminded us — that is one of the redeeming features of the human being. But under the spell of violence we can end up putting that worship where it does not belong. In order to carry on war we have drawn a cloak of denial over the sanctity, or if you prefer, the supreme value of life, and then we find that some of us have turned around and vainly imagined life in inert machines — in the machines, in fact, of death. We denied life and worshiped death. Would the word blasphemy be too strong for this mistake?

One more example before we get from peace in thought and word to peace in deed.

Mr. Bill Kennedy is a financial guru (think about *that* metaphor for a minute!) who gives highly successful seminars for the rich on how to get very rich. Kennedy is a forthright sort of man. He likes to refer to his program with a rather unusual, attention-grabbing moniker, and here he explains why.

> I came to the decision that "war college" was an appropriate
> name. . . . What better metaphor than war for the battle of
> accomplishment every person must wage to survive . . .
> amidst the financial firefights that are sure to follow the
> inevitable crashes of the 1990s.

Social Darwinism can go no further. All life is a fight, in fact a war, a classic Malthuso-Hobbesian war of each against all. Human accomplishment, nay, survival, is making more money than other people. "Investing is not a win/win proposition," Mr. Kennedy blandly tells us, so do come to study with this "truly illustrious faculty . . . famous military leaders, acclaimed scientists, economists, journalists, historians and foreign dignitaries . . . Defense Department, and CIA." The paranoia of violence is here too, worthy of a Milosevic. (The crashes, which never happened, are "inevitable.") And by the way, only people with half a million in assets can apply to the Kennedy War College, so don't be too hasty to get out your uniform.

There is another element in this bizarre construction of the world that I can only touch on, not so much because of limited space but because of my personal inability to deal with it. As a teacher, I have found the dedication of education to money-making that is now the norm so personally painful that it's one of the few issues I don't trust myself to talk about. This use of the word "college" and "faculty" — this idea that education is to help individuals fight each other for money — this is grim news for the culture of human beings at the beginning of the third Christian millennium. Recently I was put on hold while waiting to talk to the produce clerk of a nearby food market which was, it happened, trolling for new employees. Naturally, I was not paying too much attention to the announcements, until I heard them say, "After all, working for us will give you more experience than any other educational institution." Any *other* educational institution? This is Safeway State? I can only say again that the unremarked shrinking of education to fiscal prowess that has overtaken our whole society over the last twenty or so years is profoundly relevant to the rise of violence, for if the purpose of education is to make money, what does that say about the purpose of life? This deserves a book in itself; but I can't be the one to write it. Not yet.

The main point this description of the Kennedy War College raises for our concern with nonviolence and speech could be put as a question: What do war, sexual aggression, business, sports, politics and criminal justice have in common? As activities, next to nothing; as expressions of the urge to compete, however, practically everything. They can all be reduced to forms of competition, all played out in a paradigm of scarcity and separateness, as zero-sum, win-lose propositions — if that is how you think about life. But why stop there? After you've done this to everything that can reasonably be construed as a fight, everything that has at least an element of give-and-take, go on to make *everything* a fight, even relationships between doctor and patient, student and teacher, and — of course — husband and wife. I remember a divorce being covered by the papers some years back in which the husband explained that he was fighting his ex for custody of the children because, "I have to get *something* out of this relationship."

This is why a certain amount of control over our speech can be effective. Because we nowadays tend to think of every sporting event, every business decision, every diplomatic exchange, and more and more personal relationships in terms of "winning," we have become incapable of seeing that they could be, instead, links in the net of loving community and peace. During the 1994 gubernatorial race in California, Congressman Tom Hayden was asked what he thought of his opponent, Kathleen Brown. He startled the journalist by saying, "She's not my opponent; she's my friend. We're running for Governor. It isn't a sport." A few more remarks like that and we could put an end to politics as we know it, and start returning to politics as it was meant to be — the decision-making process of a democracy, not the power struggle of the arena.

While most of us are not "defense intellectuals" or congresspersons, we all constantly participate in a speech-and-thought environment with its various subtexts of love and hate — over which we have a certain measure of control. It's a quiet but very real part of building a peace culture, open to everyone. Personally, I try never to say something is "competitive" when I mean that it's good, never "target" anyone when I mean I'm doing something for them, never say "impact" instead of have an effect on. I don't use euphemisms like "three strikes, you're out" when I'm talking about putting people in prison for the rest of their life, and for some reason I don't even say that a particular restaurant has pasta "to die for." When unsuspecting people say to me that "this will help the economy grow," I calmly reply, "You mean 'expand,' don't you? Only living things grow, right?" I make myself thoroughly obnoxious, but I do this because the thoughts and images and feelings that go on in my own mind create the very intimate environment that I live in, and they condition my contribution to the mental climate of the world around me. It's worth it. Even when I think, much less speak, I try to be as careful about dehumanizing and shoot-em-up images as I am about sexist bias.

Feminists have made good progress getting us to change language biased with regard to the issues that concern them. We should take that lead and go on, go deeper, to the issue that concerns every one of us as human beings. The other day I was in a big hardware store, standing behind a customer who apparently was looking for a certain kind of hinge. When the clerk behind the counter told him that they didn't have it in stock he said, in the casual violence of the day, "Oooh, I hate you!" I happened to be looking at the man behind the counter, and I saw him flinch. These things matter. In the long run, they matter much more than hinges. Whatever we are talking about, under the surface we are carrying on a constant dialogue with one another, about one another, about our relationships. When you say "I hate you" instead of "Rats," you are sending a damaging message when you could easily have sent a neutral, maybe even a healing one.

A friend of mine was told by the same store a few weeks later on the telephone that they had a certain item that she needed in stock. When she got there it turned out while they do stock the item, they didn't have it in stock that day. Up came the usual words in her mind, "Why on earth did you . . ." Never mind. She silently repeated her mantram and decided to smile, stay calm, and say something soothing. It probably helped that clerk a lot; it *definitely* helped my friend, who felt better about it for days after. Instead of spreading "road rage," "air rage," workplace rage, why not try to spread loving community? Then instead of war we might finally have peace.

The effect of each individual thought or word is very small, yes; but taken together, the effect of our thoughts and images is not at all small. When certain kinds of thought and image become a habit, they can become a worldview. What can we do about all this when it is so pervasive and so automatic? No matter how sweeping the changes that have to be made, or how remote the minds of an Eichmann or a General Mejía may be, we can begin with what appears to be the smallest and most remote point of leverage — you and me. This they can never take away from us. It matters what we say and in what terms we think. As far as the issue of violence/nonviolence goes, it matters crucially. Whether we refer to a city as a "target" or a bustling community of human beings matters as much as whether we call a thirty-year-old woman a "girl" or a black adult "boy." The only difference is, in the latter case we know whom we're hurting, and so we've tried to stop.

Yet if hurting somebody is bad, hurting everybody is surely worse. When the subtle violence of our speech "escapes the barrier of our teeth," as the poet Homer used to say, it hurts everybody at once on some level. And so, just as surely, the opposite is true: taking some care to use nonviolent, accurate words and imagery becomes second nature in course of time, and creates an incalculable influence toward peace. The habit of truth also is formed by small, repeated, doable efforts — only in this case they have to be *conscious* efforts over a long period of time, because the whole speech environment we live in is tilted the wrong way. I don't hesitate to call such humble efforts constructive program. They constitute, each of them, a truth act, available every moment, to everyone; they are non-confrontational, even unpolitical, if you will, and yet so powerful. To speak and eventually to think as though life were sacred and human relationships mattered — that would be so powerful. Because, after all, it is so true.

8   Fighting Fire with Water

> Perhaps the careful study of man's past will explain
> to me much that seems inexplicable in his discon-
> certing present. Perhaps the means of salvation are
> already there, implicit in history, unadvertised,
> carefully concealed by the war-mongers, only
> awaiting rediscovery to be acknowledged with
> enthusiasm by all thinking men and women.
> — Vera Brittain

By liberating our own minds from the culture of violence where that culture is being most actively promoted — in the mass media — and by consciously making our own thoughts and speech peaceworthy, we are preparing ourselves to act effectively for peace. It is now time to consider what that action might look like.

Body, Mind and Spirit III: Armies of Peace

I want to focus on a dramatic way that peace activists are confronting manifest, sometimes extreme violence, and I choose this way not only because of its high drama, but because while it's been done by a rather special set of people so far, there is room for everyone to take part and help them. Bear in mind that while the work done on our thoughts and speech could often be proventive, and is therefore indispensable, we will now be talking about much later-stage interventions; not so much about what to do before conflicts get out of hand as what we can still do when they have.

I met Ernesto Cardenal at Berkeley during the early 'eighties when he was Minister of Defense in the Sandinista government in Nicaragua — and by no means an advocate of nonviolence. I was eager to ask him whether the Witness for Peace groups in his country had helped to deter Contra attacks. These are the groups, you remember, in which volunteers like my friend Sue Severin stumbled upon the protective effect of an unarmed presence. At the same time I was a little apprehensive about asking him because I knew nonviolence was not his thing. I need not have been. "We need more of these groups and need them quickly," he told me with great feeling. "Wherever they have been there has been no violence!"

A little later, when he was speaking through a translator to the small group who had gathered to hear him at the faculty club, he repeated what he had just told me privately. Wherever these little groups of internationals went there were no attacks, no violence. At this point his translator unconsciously made a slight "correction." Evidently unable to quite believe what he was hearing, he said, "There has been *nearly* no violence." Cardenal caught that at once and slammed his fist on the table: "I said, *absolutely* no violence!" I beamed. Cardenal was not a believer in principled nonviolence. But he was man enough to believe what he saw, and not to "normalize" it away. This is all we need to see the antidote to war that is there, as intuition tells us, in nonviolence.

What Cardenal did not know — even I was not quite aware of it at the time — is that the idea of "armies of peace," volunteers trained in nonviolence instead of threat power who could intervene in large-scale conflict situations, was about fifty years old when my friend Sue Severin and others left their safe homes and careers in the U.S. to stand with villagers in the "low intensity" hell of Nicaragua. Gandhiji, who seems to have wrestled with every problem in the modern world, did address the question whether, and if so how, nonviolence could put an end to war. As soon as he began to see the power of the "new" method he was using in South Africa, he began to realize that it could be used not only in the social struggle of the disenfranchised Indians there, and any downtrodden groups like them, but against the "principalities and powers" that had led mankind into endless wars since the dawn of recorded history. Satyagraha was the opposite of war; it could be the cure for war. But how could a method, albeit highly successful, that was devised to resist injustice *within* a country be applied *between* them?

He must have sensed, probably from the earliest days when he realized that "passive resistance" was the wrong word for the Indians' struggle, that the seed they were planting in Africa would one day give rise to a plant strong enough to break its way through the centuries-old concrete of the war system, to bloom into a world order that was truly, not cynically, new. This conviction never wavered; even at the very end of his life, when the newly separated India and Pakistan went to war over Kashmir, he held out the claim that the Kashmiris, whose cause was just, could have protected themselves through nonviolence.

At the same time, Gandhi knew perfectly well that the nonviolent construction of peace lay, as he put it, "in the womb of the future." It would fall to others to see this particular promise of nonviolence through to fruition. His job was to rebuild India, midwife her out of the British grip and, by so doing, expose the illegitimacy and fragility of colonialism — enough work for a single lifetime, even by his Himalayan standards! There could be no doubt, however, that the "ocular demonstration" of Satyagraha's power being staged in India was meant for the whole world. He stressed repeatedly that what may appear to be India's problem — exploitation, greed, violence, race hatred — is the world's problem, and stressed even more explicitly that the technique used against communal strife in India, "though apparently conceived to apply to a corner of this world, is really intended to cover the whole world."

Similarly, once we understood the power of nonviolence, we would see that it applies, *mutatis mutandis*, to all forms of violence, not excluding the biggest. Nonviolence does not stop at national boundaries any more than the law of gravity does. On this point Gandhi was not inclined to mince words. "It is blasphemy to say that non-violence can only be practised by individuals and never by nations which are composed of individuals." In his own imagery for the South African struggle the words "army" and "soldier" occur frequently — even more often than "pilgrims."

By the year 1913, around the time he felt destiny was calling him home to confront the British Raj in its lair, he was talking openly about *Shanti Sena*s, "armies of peace," bands of trained volunteers whose nonviolent presence and nonviolent skills would make the police and national guard unnecessary. They would be locally based, thus ending the reliance on outside power. (A society that cannot manage its own disorder can never be free.) And even more important, they would be completely nonviolent, thus ending the age-old reliance on threat power that so entangles everyone:

> The Congress should be able to put forth a non-violent army of volunteers numbering not a few thousands but lakhs [tens of thousands] who would be equal to every occasion where the police and the military are required. . . . They would be constantly engaged in constructive activities that make riots impossible. . . . Such an army should be ready to cope with any emergency, and in order to still the frenzy of mobs should risk their lives in numbers sufficient for the purpose. . . . Surely a few hundred young men and women giving themselves deliberately to mob fury will be any day a cheaper and braver method of dealing with such madness than the display and use of the police and the military.

Gandhi is here talking about a nonviolent equivalent to the police, and the military used as police. It's only a short step to replacing the military where they are normally used, in war. In 1942, when India and the Raj were cowering before the prospect of a Japanese invasion, he took that step. While the British rattled their sabers and many Indians themselves rushed to enlist, he startled everyone by proposing that India could defend herself with nonviolent armies of peace. It seems that the army Britain had brought into existence in India was not only not capable of protecting the country (the cardinal justification for holding India at that time), but was attracting a Japanese attack. Ironically, in view of popular concepts of strength, while Churchill was trying to prepare Roosevelt for a British collapse, Gandhi was "preparing his unarmed countrymen to resist to the last man rather than submit, if the Japanese landed on Indian soil."

He was never given a chance to put this bold vision to the test. The British put him in prison, conveniently, for most of the war years, and even most of his own Congress Party members found they were not ready to follow him that far. Historically, wars always thin the ranks of pacifists. When danger stares one in the face, it is difficult to keep faith with an untested future.

One man, however, had already taken Gandhiji at his word. By far the most dramatic Shanti Sena the world has ever seen was organized in what was then the North-West Frontier Province by the Mahatma's close disciple Khan Abdul Ghaffar Khan; and the Khan did this not among gentle Hindus but among the notoriously warlike Pathans. These are the same people who, along with other Afghans, would stand up to the overwhelmingly superior military force of the Soviet Union half a century later — and then, tragically, tear themselves to pieces in armed factions. But that was later, when they went back to more traditional methods of fighting. Our story concerns those days, under Khan's inspiring leadership, when nearly 100,000 Pathan fighters — all devout Muslims —

vowed to resist the British without weapons in their hands or violence in their hearts, and kept that vow under unbelievable provocation, adding immeasurably to the unstoppable drive toward freedom.

Abdul Ghaffar Khan first heard Gandhi as a young man at the All-India Congress party meeting at Calcutta in December of 1928. He had heard *of* Gandhi, of course, and must have been intrigued that the Mahatma was doing in grand style what he had been doing for his own people through village uplift, education, empowerment of the women and a steady weaning away from violence; but he had not come to Calcutta to hear Gandhi. At that time the honeymoon between Muslims and Hindus that warmed the first part of the decade was largely history. There was not much love lost between the two communities as a whole, and Khan had come to Calcutta only to attend a meeting of the Muslim League.

It was, however, an unruly and distasteful meeting of the League that year; in fact it soon broke up when one irate delegate pulled out a knife. So, more or less at a loss what to do with himself so far from home, Khan dropped around to the Congress pavilion. There, as it happens, Gandhiji was speaking to the accompaniment of a relentless heckler. Strangely, rather than being rattled, Gandhi seemed to get no end of amusement from his unruly "friend," and went right on speaking through his chuckles. Khan was deeply impressed. A leader himself, and gifted with an eye for the outwardly small things that reveal nonviolent power, he at once understood what he was seeing in the Mahatma's good-natured, unflappable control of the situation. He went back to one of the Muslim leaders and suggested, rather naively, that they might get further with a little of that forbearance themselves. "So," the irate leader cut him off, "the wild Pathans have come to teach us about tolerance!" This is exactly what the Khan would do.

We must tarry here a second because Badshah Khan's story explodes no less than *four serious myths about nonviolence,* and the Muslim leader's curt rebuff illustrates one of them — namely, that *nonviolence is only for gentlefolk.* Gandhiji would explain that you had to be capable of violence before you could renounce it. It was precisely the Pathans, whose frontier-style traditions of revenge and violence went back uncounted centuries, who would most readily follow their Badshah, their leader, when he created a new kind of army without weapons. These were the famous Khudai Khidmatgars, or "Servants of God." Years later, when Khan himself was at a loss to explain how his Pathans were still nonviolent when most of the Hindus had bolted, Gandhiji explained to him, "Nonviolence is not for cowards. It is for the brave, the courageous. And the Pathans are more courageous than the Hindus. That is why the Pathans were able to remain nonviolent."

A second widely-accepted myth, as we've encountered often, is that *since nonviolence is weak it can only work against weak opposition.* It only worked in India, we are repeatedly told, because the British are so fair-minded; (get ready) "It would never have worked against the Nazis." The British, however, were not so fair-minded with the Servants of God. They dubbed them "Red Shirts," and used their control of the press at home to play on age-old fears of communism and invoke the mystique of the Great Game Britain had played out for over a century against Russian influence in the Hindu Kush — quite an irony, considering that it would later be the Pathans who would thwart Soviet power in Afghanistan and thus be instrumental in bringing down the Soviet regime. When the Red Shirts refused to knuckle under to ordinary methods, the British sealed off the North-West Frontier Province and set to work humbling the proud Pathans in the way of imperialism everywhere, as though they had not heard that they themselves were supposed to be a civilized people. Homes and crops were razed, people beaten, stripped and dragged through cesspools — civilians were bombed from the air for the first time in human history (ten years before Fascist planes bombed Guernica, which is usually cited as the breakthrough in this form of barbarism). They regarded the Pathans as "leopards," and treated them accordingly.

The following is an eyewitness description of the attack on a crowd of nonviolent demonstrators protesting Khan's arrest at the Kissa Khani Bazaar in Peshawar on April 23, 1930. It does not give the impression of a people whose fair-mindedness made them a pushover for nonviolence.

> All of a sudden two or three armored cars came at great speed from behind without giving warning of their approach and drove into the crowd. Several people were run over, of whom some were injured and a few killed on the spot. The people . . . behaved with great restraint, collecting the wounded and dead.

Despite this, the Congress Inquiry Committee report notes that,

> The troops were ordered to fire. Several people were killed and wounded and the crowd was pushed back some distance. At about half past eleven, endeavors were made by one or two outsiders to persuade the crowd to disperse and the authorities to remove the troops and the armored cars. The crowd was willing to disperse if they were allowed to remove the dead and the injured and if the armored cars were removed. The authorities, on the other hand, expressed their determination not to remove the armored cars and the troops. The result was that the people did not disperse and were prepared to lay down their lives. The second firing then began and, off and on, lasted for more than three hours. . . .

Gene Sharp continues:

> When those in front fell down wounded by the shots, those behind came forward with their breasts bared and exposed themselves to the fire, so much so that some people got as

many as 21 bullet wounds in their bodies, and all the people stood their ground without getting into a panic. A young Sikh boy came and stood in front of a soldier and asked him to fire at him, which the soldier unhesitatingly did, killing him. . . . This state of things continued from 11 till 5 o'clock in the evening.

Enough said. The fierce repression gained the imperial power, in the end, a pyrrhic victory. The Khudai Khidmatgars' leader was jailed over and over again, and his organization was disbanded and passed from the scene. The Raj that did all this soon followed. The Khudai Khidmatgars had played a signal role in the liberation struggle, and their efforts worked where they may have seemed not to "work," showing again that nonviolence can prevail, in its own way, against cruel and determined opposition.

Myth number three: *Nonviolence is OK for Hindus and Buddhists; it is not for Muslims* (or, some have tried to tell me, for Jews). Whatever may be our stereotypes of "Islamic terrorists," the *Jihad*, and so forth, the religion of the Prophet was not based on violence. No religion is. Like all other major world religions, Islam has a core devotion to positive, inward peace however unevenly this commitment has been carried out in practice. Of course the Prophet and his followers fought for their place in history. Of course many Muslims today believe, as many Christians and Jews believe, that they must fight their way to peace through the sword. But those who pray, "In the name of God, all mercy, all compassion," cannot believe that their Prophet was primarily a bringer of the sword, their Prophet who said "those who commit violence, — God has given them respite only until the day their eyes become glazed." There is another important *hadith*, or traditional saying, to the effect that the Prophet one day told his followers, "Help your brother, whether he is an aggressor or a victim of aggression." When one of them asked him, "How are we supposed to help the aggressor?" he replied, "By doing your best to stop him from aggression." The religion of the Prophet, in other words, entails not just a sentiment but a sophisticated comprehension of nonviolence.

And Badshah Khan was quite aware of this.

> There is nothing surprising in a Muslim or a Pathan like me subscribing to the creed of nonviolence. It is not a new creed. It was followed fourteen hundred years ago by the Prophet all the time he was in Mecca. . . . But we had so far forgotten it that when Gandhiji placed it before us, we thought he was sponsoring a novel creed.

Myth number four, which is the "blasphemy" that we're primarily concerned with here: *Nonviolence can't be used in, or instead of, war.* At its height, during the repression of 1930, the Khudai Khidmatgars numbered more than eighty thousand. They were trained, drilled, uniformed and organized. They were committed to their leader and followed his orders even when they did not understand him — even unto death, as they demonstrated at the Kissa Khani bazaar. That is, they were an army in every sense of the word, except that they were not armed with the physical instruments of death but rather, as far as they understood it, with the inner powers of life. The Servants showed that just as people can be trained and organized and steeled for war, they can be trained and organized and steeled for peace.

A Vision is Born

When the British invited Gandhi to the Round Table Conference in 1931, they also invited his subversive ideas on peace. During his visit to Romain Rolland in Switzerland on his way home, Gandhi had a chance to air those ideas when a sceptic questioned the applicability of nonviolence to national defense.

By enacting a Thermopylæ in Switzerland, you would have
presented a living wall of men and women and children,
inviting invaders to walk over your corpses. You may say that
such a thing is beyond human experience and endurance. I
say that it is not so. It was quite possible. Last year in
Gujarat, women stood *lathi* charges unflinchingly, and in
Peshawar, thousands stood hails of bullets without resorting
to violence. . . . The army would be brutal enough to walk
over them, you might say. I would then say . . . an army that
dares to pass over the corpses of innocent men and women
would not be able to repeat that experiment.

In our time, we have seen so many "killing fields" that the Mahatma's
faith may seem naive. In reality, though, those massacres are not the kind
of suffering he is talking about. He is talking not about people herded
unwillingly to their death, but people going out willingly, when all else
fails, to meet their death. This is not passivity, but endurance, the capacity of suffering voluntarily borne to awaken conscience. There is some
evidence that he was not so naive, after all. In Rwanda, a tribal militia
bent on genocide herded children out of their school and ordered them
to separate themselves into Hutus and Tutsis. The children knew what it
meant. They refused. The soldiers yelled at them, but the children were
undaunted. The soldiers gave up and went away. Amid all that slaughter,
when the value of life had all but disappeared, the mere willingness of
some school children to suffer for justice made a blood-crazed band of
soldiers "not able to repeat the experiment"; in fact, not even carry it out.

Some ten years after the Thermopylae speech, back home in an India panicked by the prospect of a Japanese invasion, Gandhiji would elaborate how this strange, new kind of defense would work. One of his talks
is worth quoting at some length, because it shows that he not only had
perdurable faith in the possibility of nonviolent defense, but had worked
out its main principles in some detail.

Japan is knocking at our gates. What are we to do in a non-violent way? If we were a free country, things could be done non-violently to prevent the Japanese from entering the country. As it is, non-violent resistance could commence the moment the Japanese effect a landing. Thus, non-violent resisters would refuse them any help, even water. For it is no part of their duty to help anyone to steal their country. But if a Japanese had missed his way and was dying of thirst and sought help as a human being, a non-violent resister, who may not regard anyone as his enemy, would give water to the thirsty one. Suppose the Japanese compel resisters to give them water, the resisters must die in the act of resistance. It is conceivable that they will exterminate all resisters. The underlying belief in such non-violent resistance is that the aggressor will in time be mentally and even physically tired of killing non-violent resisters. He will begin to search what this new (for him) force is which refuses co-operation without seeking to hurt, and will probably desist from further slaughter. But the resisters may find that the Japanese are utterly heartless and that they do not care how many they kill. The non-violent resisters will have won the day, inasmuch as they will have preferred extermination to submission.

Bear in mind that we're talking about the most difficult possible situation, way up on the high end of the escalation curve, when all dice are loaded against you. This is outright invasion by a determined enemy with overwhelming military force, in other words, conflict at the most advanced stage and the biggest scale. If we look closely at Gandhi's plan for such an extremity, however, we see nothing that is not familiar from the principles of classic nonviolence. It may call for qualitatively greater sacrifice because the conflict is so far advanced, but the dynamics are the same: the consciousness-raising impact of the "new" force, the way non-violent resisters mobilize that force by refusing to identify the humanity of the individual aggressor with his intention (the sin is not the sinner), and finally the dramatic declaration that success is primarily spiritual and long-term rather than visible and immediate. These are all familiar land-marks of nonviolence, and each of these principles has been known to work. That much is history. So is, as he pointed out in the Thermopylae speech ten years earlier, the possibility of self-sacrificing courage on a big scale. The only thing different is the boldness of imagination, Gandhi's signature, the audacity to make such a scheme public in all seriousness, as though every one of us were capable of so much more than we realize. And who knows. . . .

"If we were a free country, things could be done non-violently to prevent the Japanese from entering." This again is a very important point. If the Government had not tied their hands, the Indians could have be-gun nonviolent preparations much earlier. If they had, Gandhiji claims, they may well have put their bodies on the line to prevent the invaders from entering the country in the first place. Would that have "worked?" Absent those preparations, would the kind of defense he outlines above have actually thwarted a Japanese occupation? Unfortunately, we will never know. It's always easy to say, "Nonviolence wouldn't have worked," if you don't give it a chance.

Gandhi's way was to extrapolate from the known successes of non-violence to the biggest cases where it had not yet been tried. Nothing said to him that armies of ordinary citizens steeled for nonviolent resistance would not work, and even "work." He called for organized nonviolence when fighting broke out over Kashmir right after Independence, as I've said. He called a major meeting on the Shanti Sena for the beginning of February, 1948. Only death called off that meeting, for the assassin's bullets struck his chest the evening before he was to leave for it.

The dream of nonviolent substitutes for war, however, did not die on the path to the prayer meeting at Birla House on January 30, 1948.

A Vision Lives: Civilian-Based Defense

While the Mahatma was making his great plans, other people began to notice how spontaneous, unarmed crowds, here and there, were getting in and plugging up the war machine — something that had probably been going on, all unnoticed, forever. Excited peace activists have recently been documenting them:

- Fighting broke out in Algeria in 1962 between the regular army in exile and rebel forces in control of the country. There were over a hundred deaths, whereupon workers, women, seniors and children got in between the two groups and stopped them, leading to an agreement.
- Philippine citizens, with the full blessing of Cardinal Jaime Sin, protected heavily outnumbered troops of General Fidel Ramos from government forces still loyal to dictator Marcos. Peace observers were not blind to the irony that you had unarmed civilians protecting a segment of the armed forces rather than the other way around. "Both [General Enrile] and Ramos no doubt . . . realized that they and the rebel forces were being protected far more by unarmed supporters than they could be by the equivalent number of armed supporters."
- In 1968 in Beijing, when the "cultural revolution" raged, two Maoist student groups, each claiming to have the "right line," opened fire on each other from different corners of the University. About 50,000 people moved peacefully and spontaneously into the University; they got between the two groups and shouted slogans like, "Use your sense: nonviolence." One group stopped firing at once; the other went on, wounding over 700 people, but laid down their weapons the following day — "unable to repeat the experiment."
- The Tienanmen Square demonstrations ended in slaughter, but the

debacle "should not make us forget that, at least twice, the military command to retake Tienanmen Square could not be carried out because thousands of Beijing citizens had placed themselves between the army and the students." My own campus was witness to a mini-version of this when members of a small group called Berkeley Students for Peace positioned themselves between Callahan Hall, then home of the ROTC, and a large group of angry protesters descending on the place with rocks and bricks. Crisis averted.
As we've seen, thousands of unarmed citizens stopped bloody confrontation between coup and government forces in Moscow in 1991.

All these cases were civil uprisings in the sense that they involved rival factions of the same country and the third parties were the citizenry of that same country. But we have already looked at a case that was much tougher, and more like a war: the Prague Spring resistance to the Soviet invasion of 1968-69. I mentioned at the time that the eight-month success of this resistance was gained even though no leaders could advise the people how to proceed with their chosen strategy, if they even knew what to call it.

What we call it today is Civilian-Based Defense (CBD). We know of cases involving external invasion, as in "Prague Spring and internal takeovers, like the miserably failed Kapp Putch in Weimar Germany in 1920, when Wolfgang Kapp's attempt to unseat the fledgling Weimar Republic was aborted by workers' strikes. Ideally, "classic" CBD could be said to operate on three principles:

(1) The resisters do not physically prevent invading troops from entering their territory, which is often a costly symbolic barrier. They are more concerned with the integrity of their institutions.

(2) Everyone participates in the resistance — men, women and children. This is not merely a matter of numbers, of course, and goes beyond

the solidarity function we touched on when we were considering charkha. It has to do with taking responsibility for one's own defense, rather than delegating it to an elite. In military defense you cannot avoid creating an elite, and that has all kinds of unpleasant repercussions for the preservation of democracy.

(3) Ideally (again), the resisters are scrupulously careful not to reject their opponents as people, while firmly non-cooperating with them as invaders. When your intended victims stop relating to you as "Sergeant so-and-so" — not to mention as "pig" or "fascist" — but as a potential comrade, a person, that tends to remind you that under all the trappings that is, after all, what you *are* — human like them.

Prague Spring undoubtedly owed something to the fact that the Czechs had a long history of honoring nonviolence. In the fifteenth century, for example, Peter Celcický published *The Net of Faith*, arguing that Jesus meant it: Christians should not swear oaths, they should definitely not be trying to live by the sword. This was the beginning of the Czech Brethren, who would maintain a nonviolent witness for decades. Celcický's classic would go on to influence Tolstoy, so the influence of the Brethren did not die with them, in Czechoslovakia or the world. Whatever the reason, the Czech people were able to respond to their dire situation with an element of humor as well as courage — a superb mix for nonviolence.

There are times on this planet of ours, however, when the people, trained or untrained, cannot save themselves from spiraling violence. The conflict may be so unequal that all resistance is crushed before it begins — think of some of the regimes of Central and South America, or Burma, or Cambodia. Merely to make your presence known sometimes in such regimes is to be "disappeared" by shadowy paramilitaries, accountable to none; or — as in Kosovo for one long decade — by heavily armed Serbian police put there by Belgrade to make life impossible for the Albanian majority. There are times when conflict reaches such a pitch of madness that even if there is no clear victim and victimizer mutual slaughter erupts before anyone can, or will, intervene: Somalia, Rwanda, Croatia. Sometimes the chaos is so extreme there are not even "sides" properly speaking, as in Madrid during the Spanish Civil War, or more recently the Balkans. It is here that we need a somewhat different mechanism than CBD, and to create it contemporary visionaries have carried the Mahatma's scheme a step further.

What if there were a network, they have dared to imagine, of "rapid response teams," which instead of belonging to the government of one nation or another were composed of international volunteers, and instead of being military were recruited and trained to carry out nonviolent intervention. They would be courageous, these volunteers, peace-oriented, knowledgeable about the region they were going to and about nonviolence — possibly they would somehow have developed a knack for it. The raw material is not lacking. People, mostly but not only young people, are volunteering as we speak to go to dangerous places and try to interpose peace. If they were better trained, better supported, acknowledged, funded, could they not, when the "international community" is paralyzed between passivity and brutality, supply that "third way" by going and standing in the way of war?

It's easy to imagine that they'd simply be crushed, swept aside; but as we've so often seen in this conflict business, it is easy to imagine many things that are not true. The women at the Rosenstraße prison were not swept aside — they saved their men. Karen Ridd was not swept aside — she went in facing handcuffs and a blindfold and came out alive and well with her friend Marcella. In the three cases we've just mentioned, in the Philippines, Beijing and Moscow, the people who stood between hostile armies or between a hostile army and its intended victims were not swept aside, and this is only a fraction of the cases on record.

Building on the salutary shock of their voluntary presence, these groups would do a variety of things, depending on the situation on the ground. They would curb rumors (as Shanti Sena members often did in India), offer themselves as intermediaries between the hostile factions,

stand in solidarity with the threatened, aid and comfort the injured, and
— in the worst case — interpose themselves in the line of fire, making
their bodies speak where no one will listen to anything else.

Maybe they would be killed, in the worst case, and then maybe another group would come, the way wave after wave came on at Dharasana.
The way, we hear, when the Shah's soldiers killed a Mullah who had
stood up to address a crowd, another Mullah stepped forward to replace
him, and then another, until one soldier couldn't stand it anymore and
turned his rifle on his own commander — and then on himself. Maybe.
And if so, then the world would have seen that there is something other
than conquering others that's worth dying for. Martyr means "witness."
In the worst case, they would have borne witness to the world that there
is another kind of power, there is another meaning and definition of
human relationships. And in course of time and suffering the shooters
would strangely find that they could not repeat their experiment.

But that is the worst case, and even it is far better than the appar-
ently bottomless pit the world is enduring right now — in Kosovo, East
Timor and Aceh, the Molukus, Tibet, the Sudan, Colombia, Algeria, ·
Afghanistan, Ethiopia/Eritrea, Rwanda, Israel/Palestine, Armenia, Iraq.
As Hans Scholl, the young leader of the White Rose conspiracy, said
before his execution, "Better an end in terror than a terror without end."

You have to start small. Absent a Gandhi to inspire and organize
such a worldwide "army," a number of international groups (about twenty,
as I write this) have taken on specific, doable small-scale peacemaking
tasks that can become the "points of light" in this brand new picture.
One kind of work that can be done by very small groups indeed is to
accompany human rights workers and others whose lives are in danger. It
has been remarkably effective. When they were faced with the systematic
assassination of their leadership in 1985, a daring human rights organization in Guatemala, Grupo de Apoyo Mutuo (GAM), asked members
of Peace Brigades International to accompany them. When team members moved into the apartments and offices of remaining directorate mem-

bers, Liam Mahoney writes, the assassinations stopped. This had the effect of opening up space for political dialogue in Guatemala. PBI members think they played a key role in moving Guatemala from armed chaos into a peace process, and so do I. This activity is what brought Karen Ridd to Guatemala, as we've seen; it's called protective accompaniment, and it is here, one on one, that we can often best understand the dynamic of nonviolent rehumanization. Karen was, if you will, a peace team of one when she voluntarily interposed herself between the Guatemalan soldiers and her *campañera*, Marcella Rodriguez. The power of her interposition was not physical, of course, but psychological. As Patty Motchnick, the PBI volunteer who had the honor of accompanying Rigoberta Menchú and her associates through five harrowing days of death threats testifies:

> The actual physical protection I offered her was absurd, and
> to myself in that moment, laughable. I was absolutely
> vulnerable, and so were they.

But they all survived. And made a mark for peace. Military force works by amplifying the weak physical power of the individual, and loses the spiritual power. Unarmed accompaniment renounces the negligible physical power and somehow gains spiritual influence that is not only protective but peacemaking. Large or small scale, the principle on which this works is the same, and it's been well expressed by another of these groups, Quaker Peace and Service (QPS):

> While demonstrating a willingness to see the humanity of
> everyone in the conflict [in Sri Lanka], QPS could also help
> to break down misconceptions the various groups had of
> their alleged "enemies." This aspect of the work was funda-
> mental to QPS's belief in the power of reconciliation.

Incidentally, when PBI began that fateful accompaniment of the otherwise-doomed women of GAM, the PBI "team" was one person, Alain Richard, who had to leave the country just then to renew his visa.

The dream now is that third parties can do this on a larger scale. At the Hague Peace Conference in the summer of 1999, two North American peace activists, Mel Duncan and David Hartsough, discovered that they had been working full-time on this vision of a standing nonviolent army for peace without knowing about each other for several years. At the time of this writing, the idea of something called "Nonviolent Peace Force" has grown to a worldwide tide of enthusiasm. Nobel prizewinners, the UN Millennium Forum, organization-savvy business people, an occasional head of state and hundreds of volunteers have signed on as the overworked visionaries, with their modest organizational experience, scramble to make it all happen.

This has created three levels of opportunity for anyone who sees the power of this vision and wants to put a hand to an oar and help to pull us there. (1) Support any organization involved in third-party nonviolent intervention or Peace Brigades International with time, money or both (details at the back of this book). (2) Support a volunteer financially, logistically or emotionally — peace team work requires as much or more courage, training and support from the home front as war work. (3) And if you're over twenty-five and think you have a taste for it, go ahead and sign up for a dangerous, thankless mission that will probably be the most rewarding experience of your life.

It may not be out of place to reiterate how nonviolent intervention works, and often "works." The first requirement of war is polarization; our then Secretary of State John Foster Dulles defined the mental framework of the Cold War perfectly when he declared that it was "immoral" to be neutral. A third party suddenly stands outside that framework; he or she dissolves that simple polarization by embodying the longing for peace that is above all labels and hatreds. A French peace team coordinator put it this way (my translation):

Even as a foreigner from far away, each of us can act so as to
bring to bear a little of our own humanity and solidarity.
Even if the volunteers do not interpose themselves between
the belligerents, their action contributes to . . . rein in the
logic of war and the hate in people's hearts. Inasmuch as it
does that, it is nonviolent action.

A Vision at Work

The worst had happened. The Contra soldier was leading away a
Nicaraguan villager at gunpoint, his thumbs wired behind his back, when
suddenly an American journalist ran up, camera clicking, and shouted,
"International incident!" That villager lived. A group of plainclothes
policemen in Sri Lanka, waving their clubs, bore down on women protesters, when a foreigner stepped in front of them and raised his camera.
The police lowered their clubs and went away. A group of angry Israeli
Defense Force soldiers was threatening a small band of Palestinians in
Hebron; but between them stood a Christian Peacemaker Team (CPT)
of three people, one of whom, Marge Argelyan from Chicago, stepped in
front of a soldier and told him, "Every time you point your rifle I'm
going to point my camera." "After a while," she reports, "the soldier's
grip would loosen and the fury would dissipate."

The above incidents are a mere sample of what happens to come
across my desk every day in the form of newsletters or e-mail. As Gandhi
gave voice to the "dumb millions" of colonized India, international volunteers are giving visibility to those who suffer in darkness. They are
giving eyes to a world that did not know, or perhaps very much care
about, their suffering.

Of course, there is another kind of example, too. In one particularly
telling exchange, also in Hebron, CPT-member Cliff Kindy was roughed
up by a very angry settler while trying to protect a Palestinian being
beaten by soldiers. "I don't think we've ever met. What is your name?" he

asked the settler, holding his hand out. "My name is Hate and I hate you!" the settler said, and pushed Cliff off the sidewalk. The CPT team has been in Hebron for a relatively long time and the salutary shock value of their third-party witness has worn thin with these ideologically blinded settlers. Yet even in this case (and it's a relatively infrequent type, except in Hebron) the mirror did some good. It forced the settler to confront, or at least name, his own evil. No one can do that indefinitely without eventually rendering oneself, as Gandhiji says, unable to repeat that experiment. However enraged, however blinded, the nonviolent mirror will always awaken dormant responsiveness to some degree. You can't count on such a person to snap out of it then and there, necessarily, as "Mr. Hate's" example shows. The committed nonviolent actor is willing to take that chance. She or he is willing to wait for the inevitable good her or his witness evoked.

As any school yard monitor can tell you, stopping fights must have been a part of life since before history was recorded. Nonviolent intervention, *sans* the name, must have helped keep societies from destroying themselves with their own violence long before we became human — the evidence of de Waal and others makes this conclusion inescapable. The Buddha is said to have prevented a war between rival kingdoms by his presence, and in the Chou dynasty, four centuries before Christ, the philosopher Mo Tsu made it his habit to travel to distant kingdoms whenever war threatened to break out between them, putting his philosophy of "universal love and mutual benefit" to the test. So there is nothing new about individuals and groups trying to stop wars by getting between the conflicting parties. (One of the small peace-movement groups that arose during the antinuclear days called itself the "Mo Tsu Project.") What is new today is the conscious attempt to do it systematically, on a global scale. The goal here is not to stop this war or that war, but eventually to stop war itself — by providing a nonviolent alternative to the whole system.

More Non-Bang for the Buck

As you start to think about nonviolent intervention, its vast innate advantages over known, conventional methods really start to shine. For what are those conventional methods? They are two: fight or flee, threaten or ignore. Don't be fooled by the debate between sanctions and bombs, as so many were in the case of Iraq; from the nonviolence point of view it is a "choice" between threat power and threat power. The sanctions imposed on Iraq have killed more than 1.2 million human beings, the majority of them children, the majority of these not even born when their president made his fatal move. It is not a humane alternative. As Gandhi said, "I care little whether you shoot a man or starve him to death by inches." In a way, shooting is better: it makes more noise.

The alternative, not getting involved, may keep our hands clean, but it has dire consequences on the human level, even for ourselves. As Bishop Tutu said in connection with Bosnia, "Our own humanity is affected very deeply" when we ignore such suffering.

> You can't watch people behaving in a debased and dehuman-
> ized way and not, in fact, be affected. If we don't recognize
> that we have a common humanity, we are all going to be
> losers. . . . We are affected very profoundly, even when we
> don't at the time note that this is actually happening to us.

What's actually happening to us is, we are living a lie. When we ignore the suffering of others, the message is, "Tough, but we're not you." This is simply not true; every teacher of wisdom we possess in human culture has stressed the precise opposite, that we are all co-involved in each other's happiness. Gandhi classified passivity (and cowardice) in such cases as a form of violence.

To be torn between doing nothing and dropping bombs is, again, to face a "choice" between violence and violence. In terms of the real forces that move human destiny, this is no choice at all.

Armed peacekeeping, again from this nonviolent point of view, is only an apparent exception that proves the rule, even if we mean the work of the "blue helmets" — United Nations peacekeeping, as mandated by Section VII of the UN Charter. (A young friend I worked with, a Kosovar Albanian, was tortured in a Serb prison *after*, and no doubt partially as revenge for, the "liberation" of Kosovo by NATO bombing. Thus I may be forgiven a trace of bitterness about this kind of operation.) While motivated by the best possible impulses, UN peacekeeping is nonetheless, when looked at from the point of view of nonviolence, a badly mixed bag. It tries to reach positive ends with hurtful means — to make peace with weapons. Having weapons and not using them (UN contingents are generally supposed to return fire only when attacked) is the violent person's idea of nonviolence. Real nonviolence, remember, is not abjuring the instruments of threat power, but wholeheartedly using the wiles of integration; not pulling punches but extending a hand.

There may be a place for armed peacekeeping in certain cases, but because its means and ends are so fundamentally at odds we can never expect it to be more than a marginal solution. It is because of this inherent contradiction, certainly not because of any lack of courage or will in the men and states involved, that the history of UN peacekeeping shows a few modestly successful operations but nothing like enough peace power to meet the demand for interventions which suddenly increased in the flare-ups of ethnic conflict after the Cold War. The record boasts a few modestly successful operations, like the Cyprus Resettlement Project, but when UN peacekeeping was leaned on as the way to move forward with peace as a whole, projects began to meet with ignominious collapse.

A friend of mine was in Somalia, trying to maintain a badly-needed orphanage during the chaos of that region's competing warlords. (One morning, symbolically, the UN compound was attacked by machine-gun fire, and Jim, who had been meditating, went out and shook his fist. "How the hell's a guy supposed to meditate with all this going on!") In those days, Jim reported, convoys of food guarded by UN contingents would head out towards the refugee camps, only to meet up with a ragged unit of fighters off in the desert. The bandits would fire a few shots in the air, and the UN escort would immediately surrender its weapons. The fighters — often seventeen-year-old boys — would jump into the trucks and giddily drive them off — weapons, food and all. The UN soldiers were plenty brave; they were well trained and had the latest equipment. Where did it go wrong? Where we usually go wrong in the modern world: in the big picture, the basic understanding of the dynamics of violence and its opposite, the awareness that opposites are opposite, weapons don't create peace. It's not that the blue helmets lacked courage; it is that, like Shakespeare's Edward, they could not be valiant where they were not honest. Peacekeeping with weapons is doomed to fail in the long run. It lacks the power that comes from matching right means with consistent ends. Another example:

> Khalil Atout of Pharmacists Without Borders was assessing medical needs of refugees at St. André School in Kigali, Rwanda, accompanied by a French photographer. Hutu militia surrounded the school and began shooting through the windows and walls, seriously wounding adults and children in the school, and also the photographer. Some were killed. UN observers were in vehicles outside the school, either unarmed or armed only with pistols, and were unable to help.

Who *could* have helped? A peace team, that was *heavily* armed with soul-force. They could have stood in front of the militia and taken the suffering on themselves. There's a good chance the militia could not have gone on with the experiment very long.

I have said that the volunteers who tried to be of some help in Bosnia in 1992 were hastily recruited and virtually without training. That doesn't mean they didn't have good instincts. A group of them managed to reach the outskirts of besieged Sarajevo in a few beat-up old buses. Before them lay "sniper's alley," to enter which was death for anyone the hidden Serb riflemen felt like shooting. The UN peace force for the region, UNPROFOR, offered them protection. They could put an armored vehicle or a tank before and after their column and guide them into town, they offered. After a brief consultation the volunteers politely declined. That kind of protection, they explained, would vitiate everything they were there for. And they went down to Sarajevo on their own. And no one shot at them. When ends and means meet, there is a special power.

When they do not, there are incessant contradictions, and that applies not only to the international arena but to violence closer to home.

Joe Loya is a writer who served time in Southern California for bank robbery. (Hopefully not all of us end up that way.) After his release, when two New York City policemen were charged with torturing a Haitian prisoner, Abner Louima, Loya was able to shed some light on this act of violence that shocked the city and the nation with its brutality. Don't pick on these two policemen as though they were solely to blame, Loya urged, or on New York in particular. It's the prison system itself that inexorably turns responsible, feeling people into cynical, even potentially sadistic tough guys. "I saw a lot of new corrections officers come into the prison, fresh-faced, young, eager and sometimes a bit idealistic," he writes. But in course of time "they all began to resemble us . . . using gutter-level profanity, swaggering like hoodlums and ironically . . . [they all] adopted our contemptuous attitude toward the 'good guys.'"

Alas, Loya observed, "It never worked the other way around. Inmates didn't begin to look like the fresh-faced boys who first came to law enforcement."

Loya was seeing the important principle that when a system is based on threat power, it cannot but reduce the human beings who move within its assumptions to creatures of threat power. Reading his comment, I was struck by the parallel to the perceptive observation of Dr. Aziz in E. M.

Forster's novel of the Raj, *A Passage to India.* "They have no chance here. . . . They come out intending to be gentlemen, and are told it will not do. I give any Englishman two years."

The prison system, the imperial system, and the war system — all are based on threat power. The answer is not to just get rid of those systems, much as we may like to, because to some degree the first and third at least serve necessary functions that no contemporary society can do entirely without, nor is likely to for some time to come. But as we know these systems today, they are pure conduits for threat power — they were set up at a time when that was the only kind of power generally understood. The answer is to reorganize these systems and let them act as channels for another kind of power. Nonviolent intervention in severe conflicts is the perfect example.

In *Gandhi's Peace Army: The Shanti Sena and Unarmed Peacekeeping,* one of the earliest books written about peace teams, Thomas Weber quotes from an Indian Shanti Sainik, or peace army volunteer, who served in Cyprus. "Whereas intimacy was a hindrance for a violent army, it was an essential for an effective nonviolent army." This is the exact converse of what Joe Loya and E. M. Forster observed. In a threat system, intimacy is a disaster. World War I almost came apart because one Christmas, "enemy" soldiers who had been pinned down in trenches within hailing distance of one another declared their own truce and milled around in no-man's-land, swapping stories and sharing photos of their loved ones back home. Panicky officers on both sides had to threaten the men with draconian punishments to restart the war. In other words, war engages the wrong energies and cannot but lead to the wrong results. To quote journalist Chris Hedges, who has seen more wars than he cares to think about, "The very employment of violence corrupts those who carry it out." When Lieutenant Max Plowman was court-martialed for resigning his commission in World War I, he explained to the judges that, "Disorder cannot breed order. Doing evil that good may come is apparent folly."

There are, it could be argued, two legitimate functions of the present war system: intervention, when that is necessitated by severe conflict, and defense. What we have seen now is that both can be addressed by peace teams. That would put us on an entirely different road, the road that leads eventually to stable, positive peace. "Nonviolent action implants, by anticipation within the very process of change itself, the values to which it will ultimately lead. Hence it does not sow peace by means of war. It does not attempt to build up by tearing down." Johan Galtung has actually defined nonviolence as "peacemaking by peaceful means. "

Because it treats people with concern and respect, never dehumanizing them, nonviolent peacemaking succeeds even when it "fails," while peacemaking-as-usual fails to bring us closer to a more peaceful world even when it "succeeds." Think of the old Roman paradox, "If you want peace, prepare for war." In the ever-spiraling dynamic of the Cold War, as in all arms races before or since, we experienced the folly of trying to live by such a paradox; yet what's a threatened country to do? Well, a population that would ready itself for the two-edged response of disobedience-cum-fraternization that Gandhi envisioned for India, and that Czech citizens partly carried out in Prague, offers no threat whatever to the safety of other societies. It would be able to prepare a defense without provoking an escalation. Nonviolence threatens no one except dictators, and then only if they understand what it can do.

In chapter two we talked about the testimony of Sue Severin who, with other volunteers from Witness for Peace, stumbled onto the power of protective accompaniment in 1982 — how she found the psychological reward of it "addictive." She was not alone. Randy Bond went to Hebron with a small band organized by Michigan Peace Teams and writes, you may remember, "We were a small group of ordinary people doing some rather extraordinary things in a hurting part of our world. We had to stretch ourselves and our capabilities to do these things; that's the only way we grow." The Vietnam War, by contrast, went on killing Americans long after the last helicopter evacuated our servicemen and women from Saigon. It killed by the anguishing psychological pressure of having to do horrible things to people for what seemed to many to be no good reason. A friend of mine came back unhurt in body from that conflict but for years went into cold sweats and panic every time he heard a helicopter. It took about a year after he'd learned to use a mantram to cure himself, and most were not that lucky. The posttraumatic stress has been so ubiquitous that it was once believed that the number of Vietnam veterans who committed suicide after getting "safely" home to the States was more than those killed in action over there.

Yet a marine who, by contrast, served in Somalia to do famine relief in 1992 told the press, "This was the most satisfying work I've ever done," echoing what nonviolent actors often say; for example Marge Argelyan whom we've just heard from in Hebron. "This experience had the most integrity of any work I've done." People are people; the kind of action you put them into very largely determines how they will develop.

Make Love *Replace* War: The Vision Goes Forward

The point of this discussion has not been that peace teams can end war. It has been that nonviolence can end war. We have now thought some about the three levels of change that have to happen — thought, speech and action — for the creative influence of soul-force to be applied by ordinary people toward the creation of a peace regime. For this is what we want: a robust system of conflict-absorption able to deal with war in such a creative way that it results in meaningful and lasting peace. Like all dynamics of major change, like the "catastrophe theory" that tries to account for how an argument becomes a war, or a bunch of water that's cooling down suddenly turns to ice, there would be a point at which a certain amount of peaceful change is enough to tilt the balance, and it would be possible to imagine the world free from war. No one knows exactly how much that amount is; but there is clearly what Gandhi called a "law of progression" such that successes build on earlier successes. Clearly the amount of energy needed to start the changes is very high when you begin the process; but later, when there is a discernible momentum, less can do more. All big changes are like that, and all real changes start out looking outlandish and at a certain point become the norm.

When I first had something to do with meditation courses at Berkeley, in 1970, one had to explain what meditation was from the ground up. Often there were raised eyebrows on the faces of parents. Now I have to specify what *kind* of meditation I'm talking about, such is the smorgasbord available in most progressive college towns of America or Europe. ("Passage meditation," we decided to call it.) Fairly often students tell me, "My parents got me into this — they've been meditating for years." Once it was a grandfather. The rhythm by which the world does finally phase from a war system to a regime of stable peace may be like that.

Peace teams play a special role in nourishing this vision, for several reasons. Peace teams, along with Civilian-Based Defense, are the kind of nonviolence that you could use to stop a war even after one has been launched. You can use them in extreme emergencies such as are endemic now in various parts of the globe, or slow-fuse emergencies like the "low intensity" conflicts that were waged throughout Central America, where protective accompaniment was born. You could use them in inner-city conflicts throughout the industrial world, which would be something more like the form in which Gandhiji first conceived of them. The most common objection to the idea of using nonviolence in war is that "it would never work in a tough case." But these are tough cases. Often, in terms of dehumanization, the very toughest. If we can show that nonviolence can work here, we will be on our way to understanding that it can work anywhere.

Imagine a well-trained peace team defusing a war where the standard methods had failed — say in a far-gone situation like those that seemed to appear out of nowhere in Bosnia, Somalia, Rwanda or Indonesia. The international volunteers would show, first of all, that the world does indeed care what happens to other human beings, even when there is no strategic concern like oil or other "practical" interest they have to protect. Further, the successful nonviolent intervention would begin to change the bottom line in global security, showing that nonviolence, not violence, is the ultimate sanction we can rely on for international peace and defense. That would shake the war system as it has not been shaken during all these turbulent centuries. And that was just the hope of over a thousand volunteers who flocked to the makeshift offices of Seeds of Peace and Balkan Peace Teams in Italy, Germany, Holland, the United States and elsewhere during the grim winter of 1991, when human beings forgot they were human beings in Bosnia.

They were not to meet with success that winter in Mostar, in Sarajevo, or in Tuzla — and I daresay that if they had, the world at large, given its priorities right now, would not have noticed. An "ocular demonstration" doesn't work if nobody's watching. This pretty clearly defines the two changes, in the movement and in the world, that we should work on to get peace teams off the drawing board and into the historic drama of leading us down the path of stable peace — stage a success and prepare people's minds to grasp it.

Remember: all the experiments so far have been carried on with a "chronic lack of resources . . . inadequate infrastructure, poor communications, and limited training opportunities," not to mention the near-total cold shoulder from the mass media and "little popular understanding of the dynamics and history of this manifestation of nonviolent action." Just imagine what could be done with adequate resources, a good infrastructure and communications, with public support, with active media. Imagine what the picture would be like if there were not a few thousand but "lakhs" of volunteers, well trained, decently supplied and appropriately recognized. We could make compassionate response teams a fixture.

Nonviolence of any kind requires special preparation; how much more when it's deployed in the crucible of an advanced conflict in a foreign country. The triumphs and tragedies of former Yugoslavia showed the peace team movement that before volunteers go into situations of intense conflict they need to have careful training.

They also need support. And this is where we come in. For every soldier in the trenches during the Great War there were hundreds, no thousands, of supporters back home: the ladies who knitted socks, the kids who collected scrap metal, the speech-makers, the decision makers and, at last, the taxpayers. Likewise, the institutionalization of peace will open up needs for supporters with many different talents. That support will be more moral and less financial (far less financial); and it will also need something that a conventional war does not: it will need what's called "interpretation." The world at large does not understand how non-violence works. Even a dramatic "win" by a nonviolent peace team would likely be ignored or so mishandled by the press that it would not have its educational effect. We have seen so many examples of this, not only in individual cases (Joan Black), but others on a handsome scale (the intifada, Kosovo), that we can't afford to hope that even a well-carried-off peace-making operation using the kind of power appropriate to peace would make its mark. The logic of war may be deeply flawed, but it's dreadfully familiar, and paralyzingly simple. It follows directly from what we like to think we know about human nature: that people respond only to force. This is not the case with the logic of peace. Good writers, speakers, artists, every kind of culture-maker and communicator, academics and laypeople who talk to their neighbors — all have a highly creative job cut out for them in explaining peace teams, and peace itself. The stories have to be told, just as we tell the stories of wars *ad infinitum, ad nauseam* today, and their meaning has to be spelled out.

Even protective accompaniment, the smallest, one-on-one kind of intervention, has already had wide repercussions, as we saw with the creation of "political space" in places like Guatemala, where it turned a process of pure terror into one of grudging dialog. A Haiti team of only sixty-four people mounted by a PBI coalition defied the deadly FRAPH militia for six months, saving countless lives. At one scary moment in Guatemala, as we saw, the PBI presence was a team of one. Nonviolence can be done, if you have to, without large numbers. The thing is, it cannot be understood and institutionalized without large numbers.

The famed ethologist Konrad Lorenz — not a wild-eyed idealist but a distinguished scientist — decided after extensive scientific investigation that war is not programmed by nature. "Modern war has become an institution, and . . . being an institution, can be abolished." What we are saying here is the converse, and the missing practical component of Lorenz's discovery: *peace can be institutionalized.* When it is, then people will be willing to send war on its well-deserved way to the cabinet of bad memories.

Looking Ahead

Everything we know about paradigm shifts — for that is what we're talking about — tells us that this kind of enormous change is tricky, but possible. It tells us that as far as timing goes, and the exact pathways that will be taken, we are in the realm of the unpredictable. We do not know, and may never know with much certainty, the rules for the dynamics of a shift of paradigms. How does it start, what constitutes the mysterious breaking point where the new becomes the norm, how can it be guided and facilitated? What can be said with certainty about this particular shift is, it will need more conscious direction than many shifts that have taken place in times past. This is because the interlocking global situation we now face is so complex, and the speed with which the conversion to truth has to occur is now so great. There won't be much left for humanity to rescue if we wait for this process to happen by itself.

To understand the needed change we should think about a slightly different kind of shift than the ones on which Thomas Kuhn based his *Structure of Scientific Revolutions,* the book that made "paradigm shift" a household phrase. We should think about the incredible shift of consciousness awakened by the suffering of the first Christian adherents, followed by the hard work of the Fathers of the Church (and the Mothers) who crafted a universe of thought that put the sanctity of the individual and the One God at its center. That great shift, too, came from a deep groundswell of belief and needed a lot of careful thought to explain how the new system worked. Absent divine intervention, we have to work on this huge job in many ways.

So it is helpful to remember the two big things that make such an enormous change possible. The first is that peace is the deepest drive of our being. Underneath all our conditioning, "There is no human heart that does not crave for joy and peace." Appearances can be very dark. Right now they are very dark, indeed; but they still are only that, appearances.

> Think of men who are bent on war. What they want is to win, that is to say, their battles are but bridges to glory and peace. The whole point of victory is to bring opponents to their knees — this done, peace ensues. Peace, then, is the purpose of waging war. . . . Notice that there can be life without pain, but no pain without some kind of life. In the same way, there can be peace without any kind of war, but no war that does not suppose some kind of peace.

Even those who wage wars do so to reach some kind of peace within the limits of their understanding, as Augustine says, and these are limits which we can always push back by culture and education. "Peace is the quest, nay the hunger of every soul." Through conditioning, people can come to think that threat force and destruction are unavoidable; but nonviolent logic rises to show up this superstition, and we quicken. Yes, it is a huge task to eliminate war; but it's the task we've all been called to, and we will not rest until it's done.

The second encouraging truth is that, while many things have been tried in our sporadic approaches to this great task, one has not. Soul-force has never been systematically put to work to create the conditions and institutions of sustained peace. So, as Norman Cousins used to say, "No one knows enough to be a pessimist." Before the twentieth century we never had the tool to apply nonviolence to world peace systematically — or did not know we had it. Gandhiji lived and died to show us that we do. The women of Gujarat whom he mentions, the Pathans of the North-West Frontier — many groups and countless individuals have lived and died to show us the utility of this force. This is the time to learn their lesson. Let me restate what I think their work and suffering has to teach us: *the task is not so much to stop war as to start nonviolence.*

The Chicago scientists had no way of knowing it, but the clear picture they sought when they met that day in 1946 was already beginning to emerge.

9 Toward a Metaphysics of Compassion

It is plain that the law against the slaughtering of
animals is founded rather on vain superstition and
womanish pity than on sound reason.
— Spinoza

Compassion is the radicalism of this age.
— His Holiness the Dalai Lama

Before I took to meditation, the two things that
kept me in touch with reality were poetry and
nature. There wasn't much nature in Brooklyn,
to be sure, but my family would spend summers high in the Adirondacks,
and the resinous smell of their deep pine woods on a hot summer afternoon has never quite left me, even when I hike the aseptic eucalyptus
glades of California. As for the poetry, I grew up in a warm household
that was television-free until just before I went to college, and that left me
relatively able to preserve my sensitivity to the nuances of language —
and the human comedy in general. For the first part of my academic
career I spent many fruitful years studying the earliest and greatest poet
in western civilization, Homer, whose epics, the *Iliad* and the *Odyssey*, were
to a large degree constitutive of the value system most of us grew up in.
There were many things that held my ear to his music, one of them being
his profound understanding of war, and what Wilfred Owen called "the
pity of war," and what that kind of violence does to women and to the
family, and what kind of society you have if the only kind of peace you

know is an uneasy respite in the shambles of intermittent conflict. One line of Homer in particular keeps coming to my mind to this day. It is spoken by the god Apollo in the final book of the *Iliad*, Book 24, or as scholars say, Omega, line 54:

κωφην γαρ δη γαιαν αεικιζει μενεαινων.
For look, he is outraging the mute earth in his fury.

"He" is Achilles, the semidivine hero who represents war incarnate; and the offense he's committing is grave indeed. He's dragging the dead body of his enemy Hector round the camp at the back of his chariot. This haunting hexameter concludes Apollo's speech to the assembly of the Olympian gods whom he is persuading to intervene and stop the desecration. In life Hector was a warrior who in the course of defending Troy, his homeland, slew Achilles's companion; but in death, the Greeks believed, he no longer belongs to his city *or* to Achilles, who slew him in turn. He belongs to the earth. Hector is no longer the individual person he was when alive; his human accounts are settled. Now he belongs to the cycle of nature itself. Achilles can take Hector's life — that is the warrior code — but not his *psyche*, his soul. What Achilles is trying to do now by refusing to relinquish Hector's body to the earth goes beyond that code. It is an outrage — in other words, violence. (The same word in early Greek, *hybris*, means both.)

Just prior to verse fifty-four Apollo has made a point about violence that is as sophisticated as this line is poignant. "For Achilles himself cannot but lose by doing this." By desecrating the body of his fallen enemy and thus violating the prevailing war code, he will destroy the very value system on which he himself depends for the meaning of his own life and honor. Again, the innate contradictions of violence. Violence begets more violence, Apollo implies, and no one wins.

The "mute earth," however, is a striking image, one with as much resonance in the Vedic poetry of ancient India as in Homer's tradition (the two were distantly related), and it resonates to this day. The mute earth is Draupadi, whose humiliation at the court of the Kurus launches the gigantic Mahabharata war; it — she — is Sita ("furrow") abducted by the archdemon of the Ramayana epic; she is the Trojan women of Euripides' classic plays; she is whatever and whoever cannot make her voice heard in distress; she is the Victim. Achilles killed many men, and the warrior code absorbed that; what Achilles is killing now is pity. No culture can absorb that, and live.

Who will hear the cry of the earth? Apollo has been magically protecting Hector's body (and Achilles' reputation) from harm throughout the dragging. Now he persuades the gods to intervene, since nothing less than the whole value system, and by extension the world order, is at stake. Interestingly, there had been a plan to steal Hector's body, but the gods had not gone along with it. That would not work because what the system needs is the hero's change of heart. Although Homer doesn't explicitly talk about interior life as we do, he clearly tells us in the gods' unanimous rejection of the stealing idea that the change has to be inside Achilles; it has to come from his will.

Achilles' mother — Thetis, a goddess — appears to persuade him, with very maternal logic, to give Hector's body back to his family for proper treatment, but it's almost unnecessary; the hero is already persuaded. The great scene that follows, between Achilles and Hector's father Priam, when the old man steels his courage to kiss the "man-slaughtering" hand that took his son's life, is a gripping climax of hard-won reconciliation. With it, the poem is ready to wind down.

Poetry is powerful where it speaks to all of us. We are all a little like Achilles. On our own scale, we too become blind to pity — and like him we can all open our eyes again. In the absence of Homer's genius and tradition, perhaps the following thoughts and images can help:

> Earlier this month, [May, 1998] several members of the Iraq
> Sanctions Challenge stood at the bedside of Mustafa, one of

at least a dozen dying children in a crowded, wretched ward
of the main hospital in Basra, Iraq's southern port city. His
mother, tall, thin and quite beautiful, sat cross legged on the
mattress beside him, waving away flies, as the doctor explained to us that the child, hospitalized for the past twenty
days, now suffered from dehydration, diarrhea, acute renal
failure and extensive brain atrophy. Lacking equipment and
medicine to diagnose and treat Mustafa, the doctors could
only stand by, helpless and frustrated, while the child's
condition worsened over three weeks time. If Mustafa
survives, he will be severely crippled. Ima Nouri, his mother,
is 35 years old. Her serious eyes, large and luminous, followed us as we paused before each bedside. She seemed
surprised when we asked her to tell us a little about herself.
We learned that she lives in a rural area north of Basra and
has two children at home whom she misses very much. We
asked the doctor to tell her that we are so very sorry, that we
want to tell people in the U.S. her story, that we will try hard
to end the sanctions. She smiled slowly, nodded. Then we
mentioned that people in the United States were celebrating
Mother's Day on this day and asked if she had a message for
mothers in our country. Ima suddenly became animated.
"Yes," she said, "I have two messages. First, tell them, from
Iraqi women, that these are our children and we love them so
much." Stroking Mustafa's face, she continued, "Ask them to
please try to help us protect them and take care of them.
And, for American women, — I want them to feel what I am
feeling."

If we only could. The appeal made me think of Saint Francis in the
valley of La Verna, when, as one tradition has it, he asked Jesus to give
him the uncompromising love He had felt for all that lives, and for the

stigmata He had borne in his very flesh because of that love. The word compassion means literally "suffering with." Of course it hurts. But isn't it better to suffer with others, and grow to that extent, than to close our hearts against them and inwardly die?

In Hebrew, the word for compassion is *rachamim*. It is the plural of *rachem*, "womb." To have compassion is to be towards someone, in a little way — or not so little — what every mother is to her own child.

Let me try now to put this eternal issue in a historical context. The painting that you see on the following page was done by Joseph Wright of Derby in 1768, sixty-four years after Sir Isaac Newton taught that matter was built up of "solid, massy, hard, impenetrable, moveable Particles," established by God to be forever inviolable; in other words near the beginning of modern materialism and its decisive break with millennia-old traditions of an organic human relationship with the living earth.

The adult facing us is a traveling science lecturer, a circuit rider of the new religion of scientism, if you will, demonstrating a vacuum pump to the rapt onlookers. He is pumping the air out of a glass cage and to make that fact visible there is a bird inside the cage. By watching the bird gasp for breath, in other words, you could see that there's no more air in the cage and be impressed with what technology can do. But what other impression are we to receive? The real dramatic interest in the painting, what takes and holds our eyes, is the children. For them, this is not about the wonders of science. In their innocence, they do not follow the explanation of the pump and the air; they just think a man is killing a little bird.

The real story of the painting is in the contrast between the glazed lecturer holding the audience spellbound, a kind of high priest of technology, and the distress of the children — and the fact that they are just children and the adults ignore them. When we hurt nature, it is not that we lack warnings. Not everyone loses their sensitivity all at once. The real tragedy is to ignore those who are still aware of what we're doing — the way, in an early book of the *Iliad*, Hector and his wife, Andromache,

An Experiment on a Bird in the Air Pump, by Joseph Wright. (National Gallery, London).

laughed at their little son Astyanax when he was frightened by his father's war-helmet. Shortly after that laugh, after the epic as we know it closes, Hector dies in that helmet, and shortly after that, the Greeks throw Astyanax from the city walls so he can't grow up and avenge his father. Who is to be laughed at? Who's vision was more realistic?

Flaubert, who saw "An Experiment on a Bird in the Air Pump" in 1856, noted in his journal, *"Petite fille qui pleure. Charmant de naiveté et de profondeur."* That is, "A little girl crying. Charming in its naiveté and profundity." It is the naiveté (if you want to call a child's unmediated awareness of life naive) that is the profundity.

Today we stand at the other end of the arc which began when Wright painted his enthusiast demonstrating the vacuum pump, and the power of man over nature. Science and technology have risen to heights even his eighteenth-century audience could hardly have imagined, and we now stand, or we should, aghast at the results. What we have done to the environment, and to the fabric of human life within it, could not have been imagined in 1768. Spinoza notwithstanding, we must take "womanish" pity — along with our sound reasoning. We can no longer afford to set aside the simple, unmediated responses of the children.

Who even understands children today? The other day I went to my granddaughter's ballet recital — a form of art that has brought joy to millions of young people since the seventeenth century. But in the twenty-first, I was appalled by the choices of the well-meaning directors, for none of the pieces bore resemblance to anything a child could relate to or enjoy. As the parents applauded wildly a particularly sexy number, the phrase we often use, "children without a childhood," came sadly to mind. The plight of children today makes Dickens' London seem like a paradise. In the decade 1985-1995 two million children died in wars, and nearly half a million fought in them. Somewhere between four and five million were forced into refugee camps around the world, twelve million left homeless, and some 200 million were engaged in child labor. In the U.S., six million children under age six, that's one out of four American children from that age group, live below the poverty line. Juvenile crime increased fifty percent in the five years from 1989 to 1994 (though at the moment it's participating in the downturn of violent crime). Los Angeles Superior Court Justice Charles W. McCoy, Jr. noted that "When a juvenile is tried in court, more than half the time no parent even shows up." And economic sanctions imposed by the UN have killed a million children in Iraq.

By the time we see Achilles dragging Hector's body behind his chariot — the way American soldiers dragged the body of a Viet Cong soldier behind their tank in an infamous photograph; the way three KKK members dragged a black youth to death in 1998 — the hero had lost all sense of compassion in the madness of battle. He lost what the Greeks called *eleos* and *aidôs*, pity and respect, and became more like a lion than a man, capable of eating his enemies like a savage beast; but by the time his mother comes to him with the gods' message he has already come back to his senses. If we tend to think of Homer as war poetry, it may be surprising to encounter such a change of heart — such a recovery of heart — serving as the climax of an epic that furnished war ideologies to two millennia of Western cultures, but it is not unrealistic. We've seen several such recoveries in the preceding pages. There is nothing unrealistic about the tension between compassion and savagery in the same person, because that is the condition in which we find ourselves.

Science and Compassion

The Nazi occupation of Denmark was an uneasy business. The Danish underground was well organized, bold and effective, with a galling habit of executing collaborators. One thing the Danes did not like at all was the Nazi plan for their Jewish population. That plan loomed to its climax one fall day in 1943 when Berlin gave the order to take the Danish Jews to Theresienstadt and other concentration camps. Their time had come — or so it seemed. What the Germans did not know was that someone had tipped off the underground. During the night 7,200 people, virtually the entire Jewish-Danish population, was smuggled out under the noses of the waiting transports to make for safety in neutral Sweden. The motley flotilla, made up of fishing vessels and everything that would float, pitched and tossed in the rough sea, but made Sweden with its huddled, seasick cargo by morning. Then, just when everyone thought they were finally safe, word came that the king of Sweden was afraid to give them asylum — frightened of the Nazi presence. Perhaps he feared it would even jeopardize Sweden's neutrality.

As it happened, though, a famous Danish physicist was hiding out in Uppsala. When he heard about the dilemma he calmly sent word to the king that if the refugees were not taken in he would turn himself over to the Nazis with them. The famous physicist was none other than Niels

Bohr, and the king immediately relented and accepted the refugees. Bohr will form a heroic thread through later stages of this narrative.

One could argue that the king was moved more by political expediency than a true change of heart in response to Bohr's Satyagraha — for that is what it was, consciously or not — but I think the Scandinavian royalty had better blood in their veins than that, and they were perfectly capable of courage and compassion. There is a story, perhaps apocryphal, that in Denmark the Nazi authorities had once sent an order that the Danish flag be joined by the Swastika. The king said that if the Swastika flew over his palace a Danish soldier would climb up and pull it down. He will be shot, replied the Nazis. I will be that soldier, the king calmly replied, ending that scheme.

But we need not probe King Gustav's heart to search for courage and compassion in this story. We need look no further than the person whose tip-off cheated the Germans of their next victims. It was their own naval attache, Georg Duckwitz.

Dumb Earth or Deaf Humanity?

Homer told his story in a language that came embedded with ideas much older than himself. One of these, which comes to the surface in Omega 54, is the conception of Earth as a living, sentient being, a goddess. Fitting, that when he wanted to image our crying need for compassion he depicted a warrior outraging the "dumb" earth, himself oblivious to the pain that only the gods could hear. It makes me think of the stunning line I once heard, either a Russian proverb or a line of poetry: "Every bullet finds its target in a mother's heart."

Seeing connections like this is the basis of nonviolent consciousness. Recently one of my students offered, as we were groping for a definition of nonviolence, "If you're damaging anything you're damaging the big picture." For example, the earth; it should be so much easier to see this today, when enormously destructive bombs and rockets, not to mention chemicals and toxic organisms are our weapons, and how prescient Homer appears when you remember that he sensed this when his warriors were fighting one-on-one with swords and spears. His was the poet's deep vision that sees that violence is violence, "damaging the whole picture," even if only the gods were aware of it. He was indeed prescient, but at the same time he had an advantage over us thanks to the myth he implicitly believed in — and sometimes I wish we still could — that Earth was alive.

The Greeks also had myths that told how Agamemnon had to sacrifice his own daughter so he could get to Troy. How much it helped them respond to the connection, I don't know, but in the generic language of myth the message was unmistakable, that war-fighting, which has been the traditional preserve of males, and the family, traditionally woman's preserve, are in eternal opposition. One has to destroy the other, because underneath the complexities they are based on fundamentally different values: destruction and preservation, triumphalism and nurturance. But in our age, when mothers appear in the news in their combat uniforms, leaving their children in America so they can go and bomb other mothers' children in Iraq, what will awaken us?

One reason I chose the story of Niels Bohr is that I sense some intriguing connection between his kind of science and his kind of courage. Bohr was the genius behind the "Copenhagen Interpretation" of quantum theory, the interpretation that even Einstein could not accept, namely that those shocking data really are telling us that the "solid, massy, hard" particles established by Newton's God are actually an unimaginably strange, shimmering "foam" of interconnected forces. Between the universe of the "new physics" and the universe of the timeless mystics, with its deep sense of interconnectedness and privileging of consciousness over matter, there is a suggestive but little understood resemblance — just as Newton's world of separate, solid particles, "even so very hard, as never to wear or break in pieces" seems in hindsight a somehow inevitable parallel to the world of violence against nature and living beings that we are now struggling to escape. For one thing, the world of material mechanics, which is still the "master idea" reigning in most of our minds, is a world of scarcity — because matter is finite, because it has a limited capacity to fulfil beings like us whose consciousness is not. So our present fascination with matter spawns violence by telling us that we are separate, that I can hurt you without hurting myself, and that there isn't enough for both of us, so I may have to.

Ironically, science itself has now left Newton's deterministic world far behind. The "new" physics that came from the astounding breakthroughs of Einstein, Planck, Heisenberg and Bohr, and which is almost a hundred years old, supports none of the views of nature or creatures that would make violence logical. In it "things" are not matter at all, but energy. Ultimately they are, or at least they fundamentally involve, consciousness. Nothing, not to mention no one, is separate from "us" but is co-involved with our being, however that being is to be understood. Nothing occurs as random isolated events but in a mysteriously connected entirety.

I wish that we were closer to understanding how this metaphysics of interconnection, which ties back so unexpectedly to the earliest myths of our culture, is to be lined up with the ethic of interconnection behind all nonviolence and ecology. We cannot follow that intuition with our rational minds as yet — but it is there, brooking no denial. Bohr, the scientist, cannot be separated from Bohr, the human being, who, in the name of his Jewish mother, because of whom he had had to go into hiding in Uppsala, refused to be safe while his people were in danger, but stepped out of the shadows to die, if necessary, to protect them.

Here is perhaps a trace of that connection. In the summer of 1938, just before his flight to Sweden, the "grandfather of quantum theory" addressed an international gathering of physicists in Copenhagen. Bohr was best known to the general public, remember, for his famous theory of complementarity, that there is a built-in limit to human understanding of the outside world, so that to describe anything "out there" completely we always need at least two mutually exclusive models, like particle and wave. The photon, or the electron, or any quantum entity, which means ultimately anything, is neither a particle nor a wave; it is something that will appear as either depending on how we observe it. On the occasion of this distinguished international gathering he applied his famous idea to things a bit bigger than the electron.

> We may truly say that different human cultures are complementary to each other. Indeed, each such culture represents a harmonious balance of traditional conventions by means of which latent possibilities of human life can unfold themselves in a way which reveals to us new aspects of its unlimited richness and variety.

At this shocking suggestion, Richard Rhodes laconically points out, "The German delegation walked out." As well they might. They were, after all, Nazis first, and scientists afterward. This was not just "Jewish physics" they were listening to, but a worldview utterly inimical to Nazi values, a challenge to their whole monoculture of superiority. That human differences are part of a natural scheme to be cherished, that every race and community and even every individual has his or her role in the scheme of things and that we need one another if any of us is to be fulfilled as a whole family — all this is gall and wormwood to fascists.

From Paradox To Paradigm

Nazism represents the logic of violence carried to its ultimate and unsubtle conclusion. We can see in it, then, several things that come along with the decision to use brute force to get what you want. The first of these — and probably the first thing to consider about any worldview — is its image of the human being. Hitler was kind of blunt about this. It's said that he once explained to an American journalist, "You know, every man has his price — and you'd be surprised how low that price is." Violence is keyed to the lowest image of the human being. Nonviolence is keyed to the most exalted. This is one of the reasons violence drives us apart, while nonviolence appeals directly to the mysterious unity among all of us, which is the hidden glory in each of us. It is one of the reasons that a nonviolent attitude leads to works that confer a sense of meaning while a life of violence confers at best fleeting and shallow satisfactions. From today's Germany, where many youth have taken a lead in putting the Nazi legacy behind us, I recently received a handsome brochure blazoned with "Nonviolence" along one side and "Self-image" across the bottom. Intuitively right connection.

Bohr's disruptive words were ahead of his time and we are still barely catching up to them. He saw that at the heart of the fascist worldview was a concept of order utterly contrary to what we know to be true of biological life. Every biologist knows that the essence of life is diversity; but they held that life was an extreme hierarchy. Only one race, one regime was legitimate, clean or whatever, while everyone and everything else was beneath, or wrong, destined only to be assimilated or subordinated to the One Right Way. The most direct antidote to fascism on this level, then, to a worldview we might call "disunity through uniformity," was the very different idea Hegel had called "unity in diversity." Unity in diversity is really a way to acknowledge the unique value of each life, through grasping its connection with all of life. Note Bohr's expression, "latent possibilities of human life can unfold themselves." This is exactly the definition of nonviolence which a young fellow-Northman, Johan Galtung, would propose some years later, "the fulfillment of the individual," while violence is any "avoidable compromise of human needs" which inhibits that fulfillment. In this spirit the Dalai Lama, speaking from the margins of the UN-NGO Human Rights Convention in 1993, said, "If we are prevented from using our creative potential, we are deprived of one of the basic characteristics of a human being." And he added, "It is very often the most gifted, dedicated and creative members of our society who become victims of human rights abuses. Thus the political, social, cultural and economic developments of a society are obstructed by the violations of human rights."

We are trying to get a sense here of the connection between a force and a concept; between compassion and the vision that all life is precious in its diversity and its unity. Otherwise put, I am trying to trace out the legitimate extension of biodiversity, which we understand relatively well, to cultural and individual diversity which we do not. I am trying to do this because unity in diversity goes hand-in-hand with nonviolence. Unity in diversity is, if you will, the theology of compassion.

The human family is growing on past six billion individuals. That does not matter. From the standpoint of unity in diversity each of them is still invaluable. That foundational insight is growing dimmer instead of brighter at this time. The euthanasia movement, the reinstatement of the death penalty, the countenancing of grotesque human rights violations, even the letting slip of the family and the support systems that nurture a child — these are all ways we are compromising that principle because we see no other choice but to keep on using violence to control violence. But for Gandhi, as for every nonviolence advocate from all time, it has been axiomatic that life is sacred, i.e. invaluable, that while the sum total of all life is in a way more precious than that of a given individual, in a way it is not. Infinity = infinity.

In totalitarian logic, "One death is a tragedy, a million deaths is a statistic," or, "If you've seen one redwood tree, you've seen them all." In nonviolent logic, it doesn't work that way. Rather, "Each is good, and taken all together very good, for 'Our Lord made all things very good.'"

So to the nonviolent, one death is a tragedy and a million deaths is a million tragedies, even though our imaginations may not be able to grasp that enormity. That's what the sanctity of life means.

Now, for Gandhi, as a traditional Hindu, there was a solid metaphysical basis for this, and he liked to quote a traditional wisdom proverb which articulates it: *Yatha pinde, tatha brahmande.* "As with the fragment, so with the whole." This is not the way we generally view things; but why should we think that when we're walking around in our normal buy-and-sell consciousness we're seeing things as they really are? Quantum physicists, mystics, the world's faith traditions with their awkward belief in the sanctity of the individual — and a lurking suspicion in all of us in our more reflective moments — keep returning to this vision again and again. This vision prompted George Orwell, for example, to muse, as he watched the movements of a young Hindu over whose hanging he was about to preside, "One life less; one world less." This is what drives good citizens to the picket lines when the state decides it has the right to snuff out a life, what makes them say the death penalty is "the supreme moral issue of our time," as a recent mailer from *Death Penalty Focus* said, because life is so precious that we dare not snuff it out under any circumstances, however impractical that may appear. The challenge instead is precisely the reverse: to make that very treasure, the supreme value of each life, the basis of our practicality.

To do this, we turn to the positive corollary of the injunction against killing, namely that in this microcosm that is each one of us are the seeds of the whole world order. We know the drop is in the ocean, but it's a mysterious truth that the ocean also is in the drop. This is why the Talmud, and the Koran, say in nearly identical language, that "Whoever saves a single life, saves the whole world." In a very real sense, he or she does. It only took one individual, waking up and slowly unbending his back, to break up the colonial system and evaporate the myth that "it is natural for the weaker to lie down before the stronger." Physically, a ridiculously small fraction of our DNA is brought into play to manifest our bodies while the rest lies latent and unused. Analogously, in the depths of our consciousness, there is enough "information" in each of us to regenerate a world.

Nonviolence states, negatively, that life is sacred. Each life, regardless how humble it may seem to us, is too precious to be destroyed. And it states, positively, that the resources for creating a world-order we want are born every minute, though they become fully realized only once in many centuries.

Every spring I show my class a stirring film about the Civil Rights Movement that features a snatch of a sermon by Martin Luther King, Jr. delivered in Montgomery. I can hear these words (and the audience chiming in) as I type them:

> And we're not wrong in what we're doing. (No!)
> If we're wrong, the Supreme Court is wrong. (Uh huh!)
> If we're wrong, the Constitution of the United States is wrong. (Yeah!)
> If we're wrong, God Almighty is wrong. . .

I feel, in a small way, that we've just been paraphrasing him. If nonviolence is wrong, then unity in diversity is wrong; then the sanctity of life is wrong, then the basis of civilization is wrong. If we give up on the sanctity of life, which we are doing right now, step by step — for the convenience of assisted suicides, for the convenience of abortions, for the convenient delusion that executing "criminals" makes the rest of society safe — we are giving up on the principle of our civilization.

Of course, the idea of unity in diversity seems a bit paradoxical. "The more clearly one studies the character of individual human souls," writes Rabbi Abraham Isaac Kook, "the more baffled one becomes over the great differences between personalities. . . . It is, however, precisely through their differentiations that they are all united toward one objective, to contribute toward the perfection of the world, each person according to his special talent." A certain amount of paradox is OK, no doubt, especially when a worldview is just being shaped, but in fact nonviolence gives us a simple way to resolve this paradox. The unity we're talking about is heart unity, it's a unity *beneath* the surface, while the diversity we're talking about is *on* the surface — a diversity of outward characteristics. Gandhiji never wanted Muslims to give up their religion or Brahmins to stop teaching or performing rituals and take up washing dishes to make their living. He wanted everyone to stop feeling superior, or inferior, or indifferent to each other — in other words, stop feeling alienated. Brahmins would stay Brahmins, Christians would become good Christians, but all in a context of identifying with one another's welfare.

Heart unity, the empathetic desire for the welfare of others, can also be called rejoicing in diversity. Our unity comes from our underlying consciousness, which has no divisions. I am in touch with that unity when I want you to be fulfilled, in the way you can be fulfilled — not necessarily the way I'd be fulfilled. That we can and should both be fulfilled is a cardinal principle of faith in the world of Satyagraha; that we have different ways of getting there is equally cardinal. So you really can't have one without the other; unity of aspiration is as important as diversity of attributes, of individuality. And this is not unduly paradoxical because unity is the signature, the fulfillment of our inner life, diversity the natural characteristic of our outer life. Now, Gandhi did want Hindus to wean their Muslim brethren from cow slaughter, by means of love; he wanted Brahmins to take some time off and do "bread labour," but voluntarily. Accepting everyone does not mean accepting everything. Similarly, as the world grows smaller, opportunities to learn from one another increase, but the value of imitating each other does not. Too much unity on the surface (where it's really more like uniformity) always turns out to involve some kind of domination and/or dependency. Belief in that kind of unity is what drove away the fascist scientists from Bohr's insightful talk.

Attempting to water down the Dalai Lama's appeal to the international community for help in securing the basic rights of his captive people, the Chinese regime cynically played a card which has often been played honestly and well, namely that this kind of "interference" would be an imposition of Western values on a non-Western people. His Holiness showed the flaw in that argument, using good Buddhist principles.

> All human beings, whatever their cultural or historical background, suffer when they are intimidated, imprisoned or tortured. . . . There should be no difference of views on this. We must therefore insist on a global consensus not only on the need to respect human rights world wide but more importantly on the definition of these rights. Recently some Asian governments have contended that the standards of human rights laid down in the Universal Declaration of Human Rights are those advocated by the West and cannot be applied to Asia and others parts of the Third World because of differences in culture and differences in social and economic development. I do not share this view and I am convinced that the majority of Asian people do not support this view either, for it is the inherent nature of all human beings to yearn for freedom, equality and dignity. . . . The rich diversity of cultures and religions should help to strengthen the fundamental human rights in all communities.

Indeed, even the august concept of human rights may not be vibrant enough to make us hear the cry of these basic needs. Speaking in the context of the struggle for animal welfare, Mary Midgley writes that the biosphere "is the whole of which we are parts, and its other parts concern us for that reason. But the language of rights is rather ill-suited for expressing this." Let us say rather that the drive to find happiness is close to the core of our being, and that is why it's identical in each of us. On the "heart level" there are basic needs and aspirations every human being has in common. We all have a need for community and service; we have an inalienable, universal need for respect — both to be accorded one's basic human dignity and to respect others ungrudgingly. There are, and must be, minor differences playing across the surface of this commonality. We need both to be fully realized as human beings.

There can only be one Michael Nagler (happily, some may think), and while there are certain things I think will make me happy as an individual (the opportunity to teach nonviolence, an occasional hike through unspoiled forests), my desire for happiness is the same as and has the same validity in every person, indeed in every blessed creature. Violence denies both this surface uniqueness and underlying identity. Nonviolence affirms both, at their respective levels. Active nonviolence — a calling for each and every one of us — uses both in its blueprint for loving community.

Today, as the world is torn by ethnic and pseudo-ethnic hatreds, it seems necessary to state and restate these truths, and cling to them, and act on them. Whether you take the traditional "realist's" explanation that what happened to Yugoslavia was a "burden of history" or the nonviolence advocate's explanation that it was the general rise of violent culture and the particularly ill-advised misuses of the mass media there, it is obvious that people caught up in such ferocious hatreds cannot remotely remember that they share an underlying unity with surface differences. They see only differences, which then take on monstrous proportions and finally bring about the condition that ethologist Eibl-Eibesfeldt called "pseudo-speciation," the illusion that those other than oneself aren't human. Today it is "criminals" and "terrorists," yesterday it was "communists," and who knows who may be the next group to be thrust beyond the pale of rights and the "discourse of reason," unless, as Einstein said, "We remember our humanity and forget all the rest."

Nonviolence is a way to remember. As a young activist friend of mine recently said, nonviolence is when you "humanize your enemy and let your 'enemy' humanize you." When you respond with courage and respect under duress, it raises your image, humanizes yourself in the opponents' eyes — and helps, in however small a way, to raise the awareness of humanness in the global culture. This elevated awareness, in turn, defuses some of the world's violence. Pick any conflict — in the Mideast, in the Balkans, in Africa, in America: the kind of unreasoning hate we see erupting around the world would not arise if our general worldview were not so dehumanized. There would still be problems like water rights and social advantages; but they would be just that — problems. You don't hate problems, you solve them.

And so the idea of the world as a machine had bad consequences, as Joseph Wright foresaw. It was a new idea when he painted "The Experiment" and still is relatively new in the sense that it replaced a myth humanity had held for countless centuries. Realizing this, many have thought — and I may seem to have implied — that what we need to do is bring back that myth. It won't be easy. Having spent much of my career studying and teaching myth, I am acutely aware that with the changes Wright was illustrating, myth itself has been weakened as a "learning strategy" and way of modeling our understanding of the world. Science became and remains, as my late friend Willis Harman often said, "the main knowledge-validating system of our culture."

This is not a problem for nonviolence, however. Gandhi himself constantly, and appropriately, presented nonviolence as a science in both the practical and theoretical senses of that term — that it could be practiced systematically and explained within the canons of human logic. From the science of nonviolence, as it develops and becomes widespread, will grow up again "the myth," in the non-pejorative sense of "the agreed-upon world-model," that there is life and consciousness interweaving all creation. After all, as Carolyn Merchant's study so well documents, it was because our forebears, in their zeal to industrialize, no longer *wanted* to believe that Earth was alive, that they rejected that concept as a primitive, animistic, superstitious belief. Today we want to know again that life is sacred. And we can, once we have found a way to understand that it is whole, that beneath all the diversity we see lies some kind of unity that we do not. This development will have more revolutionary consequences for human well-being than the Scopes trial.

Epilogue

If you are deemed worthy of peace, you will
rejoice at all times. Seek understanding, not gold.
Clothe yourself with humility, not fine linen. Gain
peace, not a kingdom.
— St. Isaac of Syria

T hese are exciting times," writes Vandana Shiva in
her book, *Stolen Harvest: The Hijacking of the Global
Food Supply.*

As the examples in this book show, it is not inevitable that
corporations will control our lives and rule the world. We
have a real possibility to shape our own futures. We have an
ecological and social duty to ensure that the food that
nourishes us is not a stolen harvest. . . .

We have the opportunity to work for the freedom and
liberation of all species and all people. Something as simple
and basic as food has become the site for these manifold and
diverse liberations in which every one of us has an opportunity to participate — no matter who we are, no matter where
we are.

The examples that excite Dr. Shiva, who was one of India's leading
physicists before she became one of the world's leading environmental
activists and thinkers, are cases of spirited resistance by ordinary Indians
— grass-roots, usually village-based, often consciously Gandhian — to
the piracy of Earth's food resources by major transnational corporations.

Several things about this struggle merit her enthusiasm.

For one thing, and it is not lost on her or many of the "uneducated" villagers, this is a life-and-death matter, ripe for nonviolent attention. Recall that two of Gandhi's key campaigns were about concrete, basic staples of life: cloth and salt. From the theft-through-privatization of salt, which is a basic enough staple of life, similar world forces have now moved on to the Earth's seeds. By marketing "terminator" seeds which will not reproduce, and crafting international trade agreements that force farmers to buy them, and by other means, corporations such as Monsanto hope to make world farmers as dependent on them as they ever were on colonial regimes of yore. Before, exploiters had to wait until crops grew or salt washed up on shore before confiscating them in the name of whatever structures of authority they concocted; now the same shortsighted greed, more globally organized and more scientifically sophisticated, has got its hands on the reproductive resources of Nature herself.

One of the reasons violence can't win out in the long run is, quite simply, we don't really want it to. Violence gets vulnerable when it goes too far because when it does the violent themselves recoil. Then it's only a matter of, once again, "compelling reason to be free." And so we are witnessing setbacks to the seemingly inexorable multinational corporate advance, setbacks that occurred when it crossed the line from exploiting people, which is bad enough, to exploiting the very nature from which people derive life. It is noteworthy that these setbacks are taking place even in this age of insensitivity, when we might have thought that many people have become virtually blind to life and nature in their one-pointed focus on machines and money.

Violence inevitably goes too far. When it does — when people are pushed from poverty into destitution, when their last hope of fulfillment has been robbed, or when, in their colossal arrogance, man lays claims to nature in such a way that people living on that part of nature are starved or dispossessed — they fight back.

How makes all the difference. The resistance to nature-theft has also, like the resistance to political freedom, gone both ways. Ecological struggles have been both violent, as with the early efforts of Earth First!, or nonviolent, as with the famed Chipko movement in North India. Another reason Dr. Shiva is enthusiastic about these resistance movements is that they are committed to nonviolence, and — something new since Gandhi's time — are a grass-roots reality answered by a much greater "top-down" awareness of nonviolence than was possible in his day. UNESCO graced the start of the millennium with an ambitious "Culture of Peace" program; the parent body has declared the first millennial decade to be a Decade of Education for a Culture of Peace and Nonviolence — exactly the right focus. There have always been good fights, but rarely were they fought in a commensurately good way. If these times are exciting, it is because the new way, the way consistent with the goal, is gaining power.

My friend Lee, a highly skilled physician's assistant, recently moved out to join our community in California, bringing her delightful deep Baton Rouge accent and all her compassion and experience. Lee found herself a nice position in a small medical practice; but shortly after she joined the pleasant, semi-rural operation in Sonoma County that practice was "acquired" by a healthcare corporation. Not one of the most rapacious; in fact, it was the Seventh Day Adventists, who have fine hospitals dotted around the state. But Adventists or not, they thought like a corporation. Within weeks, all the nurses were fired. The staff were now "personnel," not doctors or nurses, and the new managers started ordering them around and issuing directives that dropped like a guillotine between them and their patients, mostly friends they had served for years, making their work tedious and demeaning. Lee is sticking it out, for now. She hopes the senior doctor will come back — when he recovers from his heart attack.

That's corporate medicine. Corporate journalism is no different. Neither is corporate coffee (though, at time of this writing, one major chain has agreed to sell "Fair Trade" coffee, which greatly helps small growers, mostly in Central and South America). As I said earlier, I don't even want to talk about corporate education. Chain bookstores are a particularly nasty threat to diversity, and perhaps it should not surprise us. As Ivan Illich pointed out some time ago in a stunning and oft-re-printed article, violence always compromises diversity. What are we doing?

Partly, I suppose, it's a Western thing. "At millennial intervals Western civilization has made an attempt to organize itself as a world-empire, as a world-church, or as a world federation." Why not a world corporate network? Because when they get to be that big, corporations lose — let's be precise: the people in them lose — sight of the larger picture and humane values. They end up doing anything for profits (there are some exceptions to this, but only some), and they won't even be aware of what they're doing to the earth and the people in their way, such is the size and complexity of it all. And because it just isn't right to corporatize people, not to mention nature; it's too great an offense against diversity. So the corporate world order will one day have to go the way of the world empire, the world church and the top-down world federation. Dr. Shiva's enthusiasm is that she may be seeing that day's dawn. As she often says, "I think the movement is stronger than it realizes and that corporate rule is more vulnerable than we imagine."

Shortly before he passed away, the much-missed E. F. Schumacher, author of *Small is Beautiful,* came to Berkeley, and I had him in to talk to my students. His first remark as he looked around the featureless, underground classroom was, "Look how much trouble we've taken to get away from light and air so we can spend so much money to pipe them in again." I remembered this a few years later when a Russian chess master was pitted against a computer. This computer had been dubbed "Hal," if I recall. I was not fooled. Along with practically everyone else, I rejoiced when the wretched machine went down in ignominious defeat. In high school my friends and I had often sung "John Henry" to approximate guitar chords and more enthusiasm than musicianship. John Henry, the legendary "driver" of railroad ties, was pitted against the new steam drill everyone secretly hoped would not outdrive him.

> John Henry, he drove his fourteen foot.
> Steam-drill, it drove only nine,
> Lord God, Steam-drill, it drove only nine!

But think about the absurdity of it all. Who built the nasty steam drill/computer in the first place? Did it arrive from Mars, or slouch up on land from a jurassic swamp? Why do we work so hard to do something we hope will fail? I have no answer to that question, but I do know one thing: it means that we are not as committed to bleaching the world of life and diversity as we think we are, and that gives us hope that the corporate Goliath has a soft forehead. I'm sorry, has a soft heart that can be won over by the modern David's nonviolent witness.

Wisdom Refound

The Chipko ("hugging," as in tree-hugging) movement began in the 1960s when Sunderlal Bahuguna, a Gandhian coworker, helped mobilize the villagers of the Uttarkhand district of the lower Himalayas to resist the government-inspired deforestation that had left the forest bereft of its native trees and the villagers not only bereft of their livelihood but helpless before each season's disastrous floods. To a significant extent, the villagers, mostly women, have recovered control of their lands, and their message has spread far beyond the Garhwal slopes to be a hope to nonviolent environmental movements everywhere. I said the Chipko movement began in the 'sixties; but you could also say it goes back centuries. In truth, it was only brought back to life in the 'sixties by the Gandhian spark: women and men had sacrificed themselves *en masse,* and successfully, when the Maharaja of Jodhpur came for the trees in 1731. It was reborn on March 27, 1973 when someone at a village meeting, possibly an old man, remembered an important piece of folk wisdom. "When a leopard attacks a child the mother takes the onslaught on her own body."

It is not a coincidence, of course, that the Chipko Andolan ("movement") has indigenous roots. Nor is it only environmental struggles that have mined this resource. Many parts of the search for a nonviolent future offer examples of thinkers and activists discovering wisdom that industrialism had shunted aside, particularly criminal justice. Many cultures had much more restorative concepts of reconciliation in place before industrialism overtook them, and are seeking to reassert them against their industrial overlay. It is happening from Canada to New Zealand, where the Victim-Offender Reconciliation Program (VORP) has combined modern restorative approaches with Maori ones to bring about a marked reduction in recidivism among young people. Closer to home, Hon. Robert Yazzie is the Chief Justice of the Navajo Nation. Like many of his community, he only discovered after graduating from Oberlin and the New Mexico School of Law, that an alternative to the galling "vertical" system of justice that relies on hierarchies and power and aims at punishment (and produces alienation) was right at his doorstep. Much of what he says about "horizontal" Navajo concepts echoes what we have been saying throughout this book.

> Navajo concepts of justice are related to healing because
> many of the principles are the same. . . . Navajo healing
> works through two processes: first, it drives away or removes
> the cause of the illness; and second, it restores the person to
> good relations in solidarity with his or her surroundings and
> self.
>
> Navajo justice . . . favors methods which use solidarity to

restore good relations among people. Most importantly, it re-
stores good relations with self.

In the restored, and restorative Navajo system there are third-party
mediators chosen by the community to bring about reconciliation between the community and the offender. The mediators are called "peacemakers." They are chosen because of their marked reverence for life, and,
to make Pepinsky and Quinney's dream of "criminology as peacemaking" complete, the new legal institution set up for them is called the
Navajo Peacemaker Court.

It is unwise to romanticize about the unspoiled past, no doubt. Many
of the conflict avoidance mechanisms developed in pre-industrial societies are unworkable in our enormous, European-based national entities
and, in some cases, collapsed when they encountered them. But it would
be even more unwise to ignore gems of traditional wisdom that glitter in
societies across the world. We can use them to brighten our own approaches to conflict resolution, peace, criminal justice, sports (many cultures had noncompetitive ones), the environment and anything else where
alienation is a problem.

The effort to recover these useful culture-ways will be — it is to
some extent already — itself an act of healing, for the relationship between the pre- and post-industrial worlds of this planet has been severely
disruptive.

We can be perfectly urban and yet preserve the spirit of culture-
ways humanity enjoyed when people were not yet as torn as we are from
the source and purpose of life. Somewhere in Georgia in the early part of
the 1990s two white youths killed a black youth, and the Southern Poverty Law Center helped bring them to justice. The mother of the dead
boy was there in the courtroom when they were tried and convicted. One
of those young men broke down on the stand. He looked at her and said,
sobbing, "I only hope that someday you'll be able to forgive me."

She said, "Son, I've already forgiven you."

"Lay hold of goodness, not justice," writes Saint Isaac of Syria. "Have clemency, not zeal, with respect to evil."

Three things can help us systematically follow what that mother did, so that we can participate in the great project of liberating life from violence, as Vandana Shiva says, "no matter who we are, no matter where we are."

(1) When William James wrote his classic essay on "the moral equivalent of war" in 1911, he definitely had *part* of the right idea, that the only way to take the inevitability out of war was to give young people something else to do with their restless energy. But what?

> If now — and this is my idea — there were, instead of military conscription, a conscription of the whole youthful population to form . . . a part of the army enlisted against Nature. . . . They would have paid their blood-tax, done their part in the immemorial human warfare against nature; they would tread the earth more proudly.

It is sobering to realize how in half a century the "immemorial" struggle against nature turned out to be a shockingly wrong way to approach life. What could have saved James from the error? If he had known that nonviolence is a law threading through *every* relationship. The nonviolent writ runs everywhere; we have to start right from the imagery of our minds and spread outward to include everything that lives. As an Indian sage said, "If we don't see God in all, we don't see God at all." No substituting a war on nature for a war on people; no substituting vicarious television violence for real violence — not if you want to know real peace. Among many groups and organizations that have picked up the echo of nonviolence today, one that tries to achieve this universality is the Seamless Garment Network, and I like that image. It reminds me of

Pepinsky's one of "weaving combatants, weakest victims first, back into a social fabric," and Stuart Cowan's call to "the great work of reweaving the human economy, process by process, product by product, industry by industry, back into the Earth economy."

That's what we need: a seamless nonviolent ethic towards all life and a nonviolent praxis for every life-threatening problem.

(2) Remember that means and ends are one and indivisible. Some still see no contradiction in using violence to protect the earth, the unborn, or the lab animal in its cage. We can sympathize, but these reactions are self-defeating (as Earth First! discovered from experience). Spiking trees, bombing clinics, hurling insults at researchers or parading around with gruesome photos of lab animals being tortured — those means spread the poison they are intended to defeat. Taken to extremes they would be like Ted Kaczynski blowing up people with technology to defeat technologism. It was on this note that we began this book: that *we have to be against not this kind of violence or that kind of violence, but violence.*

It is a big demand, but the time is ripe. After the terrorist attacks on the U.S. embassies in Africa in 1998, the kneejerk reaction swiftly followed: bomb somebody. This time, though, the press here and there felt visibly uncomfortable. There was a headline that read, as I recall, "Strikes: Futile but Essential." Are you OK with that logic? Neither is anyone else, really.

(3) And thirdly, *remember that nonviolence is a science.* We do need the naive profundity Flaubert appreciated in Wright's painting. We need to look at life with the sensitivity of children and to protect it with the sophistication of very well informed adults — the innocence of doves and the cunning of serpents. In the modern age which, for better or worse, we inhabit, we will not succeed by doing nonviolence on a hunch (though we'll get further than being violent on a hunch). We need a compelling logic that both lights up the path and reveals pitfalls. Imagine if we thought, for example, that the parable of that forgiving mother in

Georgia meant we should let all those who offend against life walk free. Not at all. We forgive totally in our hearts (or strive for that ideal), but when someone's violence is out of control they – and we – have to be kept out of their own harm's way. Yes, forgive, for your own sake if none other. Yes, use forgiveness to rehumanize and reconcile. But even then our nonviolence will not be complete unless we follow through and ask ourselves, all right, what caused this problem? Where are the unseen connections here? What can we do to stop such horrors happening again?

Paul and Annie are as down-home as you can get. When I spent two days on their farm in Central Michigan — two days without store-bought food or mass media — I learned a lot about community-supported agriculture. For the Community Farm they've run for a decade or more is no mere family operation, nor is it a for-profit business (though Paul and Annie are quite well off, within the range of their sensible needs). Both committed meditators, these founders of Community Farm (think *færm*, in the broad "a" of the North Midwest) have given birth to an institution as important as it is unpretentious, for it represents a parallel economic universe that is happening, they told me, in scattered pockets all over North America. On farms, in communities, in vegetarian coops and sometimes enclaved in the wilds of a big city, people who are often barely twenty are walking away from the money economy and its values not unlike the way we did in the 'sixties — only with a lot more practical knowhow. Paul and Annie may look folksy, but they also travel the world lecturing on the new/old science of biodynamics.

The nonviolence of Community Farm goes deep, Annie explained. "There's the whole practice of replenishing the earth as you live off it, so that while you get your nutrition *it* gets more nourishing, not less." It occurred to me that this goes even beyond "sustainable." And later, helping Paul and Annie feed, water, milk and talk to their four cows (I did pretty well on the milking, for a Brooklyn boy) I was deeply impressed with their relationship with animals. "We have no idea how much we've lost," my friend Steve later reflected. "Apartheid wasn't just in South Africa, and it isn't just about people." By removing animals from our streets and from our sight, by relegating them to zoos and circuses, we lose, they lose, and even the economy loses. Violence gains. As the philosopher Porphyry, the first in the West to write extensively about vegetarianism, said, "For he who abstains from [harming] every thing animated . . . will be much more careful not to injure those of his own species. . . . But he who confines justice to man alone, is prepared, like one in a narrow space, to hurl from him the prohibition of injustice."

What I visited those two days was nonviolent agriculture. As Annie put it, "We don't hate — not the aphids, the viruses or even the rats." Which doesn't mean they tolerate the rats. It was one thing when the sleek rodents ate the cow's grain and their own vegetables, but when they started trotting out their families to meet the visiting children ("Oh look, Mommy, what an interesting woodchuck!"), Paul and Annie had to do something. They did something, but they didn't hate. They used poison — once, in an emergency (the children, after all), and then they tried an ancient, improbable remedy that seemed to me like non-violent witchcraft (biodynamic farmers call it the "woo-woo factor"), and it worked. There's not a rat in sight. But that's not the most important thing. "Even if we had gophers," Annie predicted, "we wouldn't hate them."

These are exciting times.

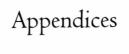

Appendices

Notes and References

CWMG = The Collected Works of Mahatma Gandhi. New Delhi: Government of India, CD-Rom version (see Resource list, p. 326). Most quotations from Gandhi are drawn from this source. Where they are also in readily available books that source will be listed in addition.

Introduction

MÁRQUEZ, page 11: Weisman, Alan. 1998. *Gaviotas: a Village to Reinvent the World.* White River Junction, Vermont: Chelsea Green. Back cover.
SURPRISE RAIN FOREST, page 11: Op. cit., pp. 14 and 175f.
LUGARI, page 15: Op. cit., p. 33.

Chapter One: Hard Questions, Hard Answers

ARENDT, page 18: Arendt, Hannah. *On Violence.* New York: Harcourt, Brace & World, 1969, p.6.
GANDHI, page 18: CWMG, Vol. 53, p. 354 (*Harijan* 4/14/46, p. 90).
ELLUL, page 18: Ellul, Jacques. *Contre Les Violents.* Vienna: Le Centurion, 1972, p.7.
FOURTEENTH CENTURY TEXT, page 20: Johnston, William, translator. *The Cloud of Unknowing.* New York: Image, Doubleday, 1973, p. 129.
BURTON, page 22: Burton, John W. *Violence Explained: the sources of conflict, violence and crime and their prevention.* Manchester: University of Manchester Press, 1997, p. 10.
DAVITZ STUDY, page 24: Davitz, Joel R. "The Effects of Previous Training on Postfrustration Behavior," *Journal of Abnormal Social Psychology* 47 (1952) pp. 309-315.
NGUBANE, page 26: Ngubane, Ben. AP wire report, July 27, 1998.
BRITISH PSYCHOLOGICAL SOCIETY, page 27: Sobel and Ornstein. "Bad News on TV is Bad News All Around," *Mental Medicine Update,* IV.1, (1995), p.1.
CURBING VIOLENT EMOTIONS, page 28: Goleman, Joel. "Today's Lesson: Curbing Kids' Violent Emotions," *San Francisco Chronicle,* March 5, 1992, pp. D3, D6.
SCHORR, page 29: Schorr, Daniel. "TV Violence: What We Know But Ignore." *Christian Science Monitor.* September 7, 1993, p.19.
MANDELA, page 29: Brink, André. "*Time* Magazine's 100 Leaders & Revolutionaries of the 20th Century." *Time* 151, no. 14 (1998), pp.188-190.

MANDELA, page 29: Here I am drawing on Meer, Fatima, *Higher than Hope: the authorized biography of Nelson Mandela.* New York: Harper & Row. (1990), pp. 218ff.

MANDELA AND DE KLERK, page 30: Daniszewski, John, "Mandela, de Klerk debate," AP story in the *Santa Rosa Press Democrat*, April 15, 1984, p. A5.

GANDHI, page 31: CWMG, Vol. 75, p. 409.

FAILED COUP, page 32: Remnick, David. "Dumb Luck: Bush's Cold War," *The New Yorker*, Jan 25, 1993, p.105 (my emphasis).

ALEXANDER PRONOZIN, page 32: E-mail from Peacemedia section of Peacenet conference on September 28, 1991.

YUGOSLAVIA'S VIOLENCE, page 34: British independent TV journalist Gaby Rado on location, quoted in the *Washington Spectator*, February 1st, 1994, p. 2.

TWELVE-YEAR-OLD, page 34: This quote and the next from a Sonoma County school newsletter called *Kid Konnection*, July, 1994, p. 21.

BERRY, page 35: Berry, Wendell. *Standing by Words*. San Francisco: North Point, 1983, p. 65.

ANCIENT INDIAN CLASSIC, page 37: Isha Upanishad, verse 12 (my translation).

TEENAGER TO CLINTON, page 37: Richard Magee, quoted in *(YO) Youth Outlook* for September 11-15, 1995, p. 6.

GREEK PHILOSOPHER, page 37: Heraclitus, fragment B 45: "You will never reach the limits of the soul [or, life principle], travel as far as you will by any road: so deep is its meaning" (my translation).

YOU'RE A MACHINE, page 38: Sanders, Robert. 2000. "Berkeley, LBNL Scientists Snap First 3-D Pictures of the 'heart' of the Genetic Transcription Machine." *Berkeleyan* (January 19-25, 2000) p.3]

HUSTON SMITH, page 38: Quoted in Glazer, Steven. *The Heart of Learning.* New York: Jeremy P. Tarcher/Putnam, (1999), p. 218.

THE POSSESSED, page 40: Dostoevsky, Fyodor. *The Possessed (a.k.a. The Devils).* New York: The Heritage Press, 1959, p. 571. Though this sentiment is put in the mouth of an unlikely character, there is no doubt Dostoevsky himself subscribed to it.

SOCIAL WORKER, page 40: Conniff, Dorothy. "Day care: a grand and troubling social experiment," *Utne Reader* (from *The Progressive*), May/June, 1993, p. 67.

Chapter Two: Hope in Dark Times

KAREN RIDD STORY, page 41: Mahoney, L. and Eguren L. *Unarmed Bodyguards: International Accompaniment for the Protection of Human Rights.* West Hartford, CN: Kumarian, (1997), p. 176. I am also drawing on verbal reports from several PBI workers (the story was well known in PBI circles before Mahoney and Eguren's important book appeared).

BOULDING, page 44: Boulding, Kenneth E. *Three Faces of Power.* Newbury Park, CA: Sage, 1989. The following quote is on p. 10.

WILLIAM BLAKE, page 45: Erdman, David V., editor. *The Poetry and Prose of William Blake.* Garden City, NY: Doubleday, 1970, p. 36.

AUGUSTINE, page 45: *City of God* XIX.12, my translation and emphasis.

VIOLARE, page 46: Lewis, Charleton, and Short, Charles. *A Latin Dictionary.* Oxford: Oxford University Press, 1962, under *violare.*

LUSSEYRAN, page 47: Lusseyran, Jacques. *And There Was Light.* New York: Parabola, 1987, p. 178.

GALTUNG, page 49: Galtung, Johan. "Violence, Peace, and Peace Research," *Journal of Peace Research,* Vol.6: No.3 (1969) pp. 168ff. Galtung restated this definition several times elsewhere, with minor changes.

AUGUSTINE, page 50: *Confessions* I.xviii; my translation.

MEDICAL EVIDENCE ON FORGIVENESS, page 50: For some bibliography, see Worthington, Everett, editor. *Dimensions of Forgiveness: Psychological Research and Theological Perspectives.* Radnor, PA: Templeton Foundation Press, 1998, and McCullough, Michael E., Kenneth I. Pargament, and Carl E. Thoresen, editors. *Forgiveness: Theory, Research, and Practice.* New York: Guilford Press, 2000.

MAFIA MURDER TRIAL, page 51: Tuesday, July 8, 1997, p. A4, citing an article from the *Los Angeles Times.*

POINTING FINGERS OF BLAME AT PEOPLE, page 54: cf. Ivie, Robert L., "Metaphor and the Rhetorical Invention of Cold War 'Idealists,'" *Communication Monographs* 54, (1954) pp.165-181.

NURSE JOAN BLACK, page 54: This AP story from the *Los Angeles Times* for Aug. 11, 1993, p. B7.

PROTHROW-STITH, page 55: Prothrow-Stith, Deborah. *Harvard Alumni Gazette,* April 23, 1992, sec. Q&A, p. 23. Following quote from p. 24.

SWAMI RAMDAS, page 57: Ramdas, Swami. *Ramdas Speaks,* Vol. III. Bombay: Bharatiya Vidya Bhavan, 1957, p. 149.

"NONVIOLENCE" IN ENGLISH, page 59: See Pam McAllister, *You Can't Kill the Spirit: Women and Nonviolent Action.* Philadelphia: New Society, 1988, p. 9. The reference here is to Western writers: the word appeared earlier, of course, in Gandhi's English writings or translations.

SANSKRIT NEGATIVES, page 59: Compare the following quote from Roshi Jiyu Kennet, "Buddhism states what the Eternal is not. (I use the term Eternal rather than God. God has the implication of being a deity with a beard and a long stick.) It does not state what it is because if it did we would be stuck with a concept. Buddhism states specifically what we know for certain. It will not state that which is taken on faith.

We can find this out for ourselves . . . but we cannot state what it is. Friedman, Lenore. *Meetings with Remarkable Women*. Boston & NY: Shambala, 1957, p. 168.

WOMEN'S SUFFRAGE MOVEMENT, page 60: Hunt, James D. *Gandhi and the Nonconformists*. New Delhi: Promilla, 1986, pp.54ff.

GANDHI, page 60: This quote and the next from CWMG. 1999, Vol. 34, p. 94: originally *Satyagraha in South Africa*, p. 103.

"GANDHIAN TACTICS: I.E., PASSIVE RESISTANCE", page 62: Friedman, Robert. I. "An Unholy Rage," *New Yorker*, May 7, 1994, p. 54. Friedman's claim is misleading in another respect as well: the settlers' actions he cites are only symbolic. As we'll see in chapter four, this isn't Gandhian either.

DE WAAL, page 63: de Waal, Frans. *Peacemaking Among Primates*. Cambridge, MA: Harvard University Press, 1989, p. 1.

FIVE MILLION TEEN VOLUNTEERS, page 64: Bailey, Bill. *America's Good News Almanac*. New York: Simon and Schuster: Pocket Books, 1996, pp. 40-42.

GANDHI, page 65: CWMG, Vol. 34, p. 267.

COMPELLING REASON TO BE FREE, page 65: Pyarelal. *The Epic Fast*. Ahmedabad: Navajivan, 1932, p. 35.

GEORGIA STATE PRISON, page 67: Jones, Brandon Astor. "Cell 38," *New Internationalist*, No. 294, (1997) p. 35.

ARENDT, page 67: Arendt, Hannah. *On Violence*. New York: Harcourt, Brace & World, 1969, p. 80.

MARTIN LUTHER KING, page 67: Frady, Marshall, "The Outsider, II," *New Yorker*, March 10, 1992, p. 70.

GANDHI, page 68: These two quotes respectively from CWMG, Vol. 30, pp. 66f and Vol. 9, p. 392.

"NEW PHYSICS", page 69: See chapter 8 for more on this strange similarity between "new" physics and nonviolence.

PEPINSKY, page 69: These two quotes from Pepinsky, Harold E. *The Geometry of Violence and Democracy*. Bloomington, IN: Indiana University Press, 1991, pp. 44 and 127.

GANDHI ON HISTORY, page 70: Gandhi, M. K. *Hind Swaraj, or Indian Home Rule*. Ahmedabad, Navajivan, 1938, p. 70.

DE WAAL, page 71: Op. cit., p. 233.

CALIGULA, page 72: Crossan, John Dominic. *The Historical Jesus: the Life of a Mediterranean Jewish Peasant*. San Francisco: Harper Collins, 1991, pp. 130-132. Following quote from p. 136.

EASTER ISLAND MESSAGE, page 74: Young, Louise B. "Easter Island: Scary Parable." *World Monitor*, August 1991, p. 45.

Chapter Three: "No Power to Describe"

BIRMINGHAM INCIDENT, page 79: Lynd, Staughton. *Nonviolence in America*. Indianapolis: Bobbs Merrill, 1966, pp.525f. (See below for the new edition of this valuable resource).

"NONVIOLENT MOMENT", page 80: Mirsky, Yehudah. "Jewish Perspectives," In, *Perspectives on Pacifism*. David R. Smock, editor. Washington, D.C.: U.S. Institute of Peace, 1995, p. 23. I cannot subscribe to Mirsky's commonplace interpretation of nonviolence as passive, but I otherwise recommend this perceptive article.

YOU FEEL THE PAIN, page 80: From the film, *A Time for Justice*. Teaching Tolerance: Atlanta.

EILEEN EGAN MUGGING, page 81: *San Francisco Examiner: Parade.* "I Refuse to Live in Fear," Sunday, Oct. 23, 1994, pp. 22f.

RESCUERS, page 82: Fogelman, Eva. *Conscience and Courage.* New York: Anchor Doubleday, 1994, pp. 6 & 59.

BERTA PASSWEG, page 83: Henderson, Michael. *All Her Paths Are Peace: Women Pioneers in Peacemaking*. West Hartford, CN: Kumarian Press, 1994, p. 162.

GANDHI, page 84: CWMG. 1999, Vol. 5, p. 335 (*Satyagraha in South Africa*, p. 100). For Cardinal Sin, cf. Stephen Zunes, "The Origins of People Power in the Philippines," Zunes, Kurt and Asher, editors. *Nonviolent Social Movements: a Geographical Perspective.* Oxford Blackwell, 2000, p. 151.

MENAND, page 84: Menand, Louis. "The War of All Against All," *New Yorker* March 14, 1994, p. 74.

GANDHI, page 84: Easwaran, Eknath. *Gandhi the Man.* Petaluma, Calif.: Nilgiri Press, 1978, p. 92 (=CWMG, Vol. 35, p. 365).

DUTCH RESCUER, page 85: Fogelman. Op. cit., p. 228.

SUE SEVERIN, page 85: Personal Communication with the author.

DANISH RESCUERS, page 86: Flender, Harold. *Rescue in Denmark.* New York: Simon & Schuster, 1963; this and following quotes from pp. 144, 149 & 148.

SCOTT PECK, page 88: Peck, M. Scott. *The Different Drum: Community Making and Peace.* New York: Touchstone: Simon and Schuster, 1987, p. 35.

NEHRU BEATING, page 89: Nehru, Jawaharlal. *An Autobiography.* C. D. Narasimhaiah, editor. 1936 (Oxford paperback, 1991). Delhi: Oxford, p. 91.

THICH NHAT HANH, page 90: Nhat Hanh, Thich. *Love in Action: Writings on Nonviolent Social Change.* Berkeley: Parallax Press, 1973, p. 71.

LUNCH-COUNTER SIT-IN, page 90: Personal communication with the author from David Hartsough.

BLACK TEENAGER, page 92: Weston, Kevin. "Why I don't pack," *YO* (*Youth Outlook*), Winter 1994, p. 4.

AMERICANS IN HEBRON, page 92: *Michigan Peace Team Bulletin*, Spring, 1998, p. 2.

RESONATING IN OUR EARS, page 93: P. V. Narasimha Rao, quoted in *India News*, October 1, 1994.

EDICT FORTY OF ASHOKA, page 93: Nikam, N. and McKeon R., translators. *Edicts of Ashoka*. Chicago: University of Chicago Press, 1959.

MEISTER ECKHART, page 93: Perry, Whitall N. *Treasury of Traditional Wisdom*. Cambridge, U.K.: Quinta Essentia, 1971, p. 533.

LIVINGSTON, page 94: Livingston, Robert. *Sensory Processing, Perception, and Behavior*. New York: Raven Press, 1978, p. 8.

A REAL YOGI, page 95: Ritajananda, Swami. *Swami Turiyananda*. Madras: Sri Ramakrishna Math, 1963, pp. 172f.

JOE MONTANA, page 95: Cohn, Lowell. "Montana Was Cool in the Eye of the Storm," *San Francisco Chronicle*, January 24, 1989; Special Souvenir Section, p. 2.

WILLIAM JAMES, page 96: James, William. *Principles of Psychology*. Reprinted in *Great Books of the Western World*. Chicago: Encyclopedia Britannica, 1952, pp. 274f.

MEDITATION EAST AND WEST, page 96: Borg, Marcus. *Jesus: A New Vision*. New York: Harper & Row, 1987, pp. 43f.

KRISHNA AND ARJUNA, page 97: Bhagavad Gita VI. vv. 34f (my translation).

MR. AND MRS. VOS, page 98: Fogelman. Op. cit, p. 178.

NO POWER TO DESCRIBE, page 101: Gandhi, M. K. *All Men are Brothers*. Ahmedabad: Navajivan, 1960, pp. 111f. This quote seems not to be in CWMG.

Chapter Four: "Work" versus Work

JEWETT AND LAWRENCE, page 103: Jewett, Robert and Lawrence, John S. *The American Monomyth*. Garden City, NY: Anchor Doubleday, 1977.

FACTS ABOUT GUNS IN THE HOME, page 104: Kellermann, A. L., and others. "Gun Ownership as a Risk Factor for Homicide in the Home," *New England Journal of Medicine* 329, no. 15, (1993) pp. 1084-1091; also Somerville, Janice, "Gun Control as Immunization," *American Medical News*, January 3, 1994, p.7.

COSTS OF GULF WAR, page 105: This figure from the U.N. Compensation Commission can be found at the site, www.onog.ch/uncc/claims/e_claims. The cost to the allies was $60 billion, not counting subsequent interventions on behalf of the Kurds or the continuing military costs.

BRITTAIN, page 106: Brittain, Vera. "Massacre by Bombing," *Fellowship* March, 1944, p. 50. Note p. 51: (her emphasis), *it is the infliction of suffering, far more than its endurance, which morally damages the soul of a nation.* This article was reprinted by *Fellowship* in 1996 and may be obtained from the Fellowship of Reconciliation. (see resource list). For the studies done after the war, see Ernest R. May, *"Lessons" of the Past.* New York: New York University Press, 1973. See esp. p. 141f for striking cases of bombing having opposite results from those intended.

PATHAN BOMBING, page 107: Tendulkar, D. G. *Mahatma: Life of Mohandas Karamchand Gandhi.* New Delhi: Government of India, 1951, p. 39.

ARMY AND MARINES USE VIDEO GAMES, page 108: see Grossman, Lt. Col. Dave, and Degaetano, Gloria. *Stop Teaching Our Kids to Kill: A Call to Action Against TV, Movie and Video Game Violence.* New York: Random House, 1999, and Kara Platoni, "The Pentagon Goes to the Video Arcade," *The Progressive,* July, 1999, p. 27.

NOUWEN, page 108: Henri J.M. Nouwen, "Saying No to Death," in Walter Wink, editor, *Peace is the Way,* Maryknoll, New York: Orbis Books, 2000, p. 144.

COL. GROSSMAN, page 109: Grossman, Lt. Colonel Dave. *On Killing: The Psychological Cost of Learning to Kill in War and Society.* New York: Little, Brown and Company, 1996; Grossman, Lt. Col. Dave, and DeGaetano, Gloria. *Stop Teaching Our Kids to Kill: A Call to Action Against TV, Movie and Video Game Violence.* New York: Random House, 1999.

WALTZ, page 109: Waltz, K. N. *Man, the State, and War: A Theoretical Analysis.* New York: Columbia University Press, 1959 (1964), p. 231.

DETERRENCE OR BRUTALIZATION, page 110: Bowers, Wm. J. and Pierce, Glenn, "Deterrence or Brutalization: What is the Effect of Executions?" *Crime & Delinquency* 26, no. 4, (1980) pp. 453-84. Twenty years have not changed this. According to Steven Mesaner, criminologist at SUNY Albany, "It is difficult to make a case for any deterrent effect" from recent FBI statistics: see R. Bonner and F. Fessenden, "Death penalty not factor in homicide rates," *Santa Rosa Press Democrat,* September 22, 2000, p. A16.

SR. PREJEAN, page 110: Prejean, Helen, C. S. J. *Dead Man Walking: an Eyewitness Account of the Death Penalty in the United States.* New York: Random House, 1993, p. 232.

TEEN WITH BACKPACK, page 110: Weston, Kevin. "Why I don't pack," *YO (Youth Outlook),* Winter, 1994, p. 4.

SALT SATYAGRAHA, page 113: Nanda, B. R. *Mahatma Gandhi.* Delhi: Oxford University Press, 1958, p. 167. One other peculiarity deserves mention: the architect of the whole Salt Satyagraha, Gandhi, had sworn off salt at that period!

ROSENSTRAße, page 115: Jochheim, Gernot. *Die Gewaltfreie Aktion: Idee und Methoden, Vorbilder und Wirkungen.* Hamburg-Zurich: Rasch und Röhring Verlag, 1984, p. 262.

STOLTZFUS BOOK, page 117: Stoltzfus, Nathan. *Resistance of the Heart: Intermarriage and the Rosenstrasse Protest in Nazi Germany.* New York: Norton, 1996.

SAINT OF AUSCHWITZ, page 119: Lorit, Sergius C. *The Last Days of Maximilian Kolbe.* New York: New City Press, 1988, pp. 15f.

SHOCK TO WHOLE CAMP, page 120: Treece, Patricia. *A Man for Others.* San Francisco: Harper and Row: San Francisco: Harper and Row, 1982, p. 178.

WILL TO LIVE, page 120: Frankl, Viktor E. *Man's Search for Meaning: An Introduction to Logotherapy.* Ilse Lasch, translator. Boston: Beacon Press, 1959, p. 102. My editor, Bernadette Smyth, kindly brings to my attention that the women generally fared better at the camps than the men, not because they were treated any more humanely by their captors but because they took better care of each other: picking lice from children's hair, talking to one another, touching, building community so as to give one another more will to live.

NON-VIOLENCE IN WWII, page 122: For other examples of non-violence in WWII, see Roger S. Powers, William B. Vogele, editors, *Protest, power, and change: an encyclopedia of nonviolent action from ACT-UP to women's suffrage.* New York: Garland, 1995, and Muller, Jean-Marie, *Vous avez dit, "pacifisme"?: de la menace nucleaire à la defense civile non-violente.* Paris: Cerf, 1984, esp. pp. 251f, 265 & 279.

LAW OF SUFFERING, page 125: CWMG Vol. 54, p. 48 (*All Men Are Brothers*, p. 118).

INDIAN INFLUENCE ON CIVIL RIGHTS MOVEMENT, page 127: Kapur, Sudarshan. *Raising Up a Prophet: the African-American Encounter with Gandhi.* Boston: Beacon, 1992.

PENN'S LETTER, page 128: Lynd, Staughton, and Lynd, Alice. *Nonviolence in America: a Documentary History.* Maryknoll, New York: Orbis, 1995, p. 2.

SEVENTY YEARS OF PEACE, page 129: Trussell, John B. B.. *William Penn, Architect of a Nation.* Commonwealth of Pennsylvania: Pennsylvania Historical and Museum Commission, 1983, p. 37.

THE "GREAT LAW", page 129: This fact and the next from Brinton, Howard Haines. *Friends for 300 Years: The History and beliefs of the Society of Friends Since George Fox Started the Quaker Movement.* Wallingford, PA: Pendle Hill Publications and the Philadelphia Yearly Meeting of the Religious Society of Friends, 1965, pp. 151f and 79.

GANDHI, page 130: CWMG, Vol. 79, p. 199.

ASHOKA'S CONVERSION, page 131: Basham, A. L. *The Wonder that was India.* Calcutta: Rupa & Co, 1967, pp. 53-55.

GAVIOTAS AND GUERILLAS, page 133: Weisman, Alan. *Gaviotas! A Village to Reinvent the World.* White River Junction, VT: Chelsea Green, 1998, pp.112f. Paolo Lugari himself was once kidnapped by the M-19 guerilla faction, but after two days they released him, exhausted by his energy and enthusiasm (ibid, p. 101).

PETRA KELLY, page 136: Kelly, Petra. *Thinking Green!* Berkeley, Calif.: Parallax Press, 1994, pp. 57f.

SCHMEHLING AT LE CHAMBON, page 138: Hallie, Philip. *Lest Innocent Blood be Shed.* New York: Harper & Row, 1979, pp. 275, 245 and 114.

THEATER BUT NOT SYMBOL, page 140: Gandhiji became a master of the theatrical: his goats in London, the pinch of salt put in his tea with the Viceroy: note that both objects were quite concrete. A case could be made that some of the protests against the Prince of Wales's visit in 1919 were symbolic, but then the whole visit was. To my knowledge, no *proactive* measure of Gandhi's was an empty symbol at any time in his long career (and Arun Gandhi, the Mahatma's grandson, has confirmed this). It's interesting that many symbolic statements made by the peace movement are attempts to mon imentalize acts of extreme evil: Hiroshima, Auschwitz, etc. One wonders whether this is consistent with the Gandhian spirit of constructivism and "seeing no evil."

TWO KINDS OF POWER, page 140: CWMG, Vol. 30, p. 66.

WEAKNESS OF THREAT, page 141: Tyler, Tom R. *Why People Obey the Law.* New Haven: Yale University, 1990.

SZENT-GYEORGYI, page 141: Szent-Gyeorgyi, Albert. *The Crazy Ape.* New York: the Philosophical Library, 1970, p. 44.

WORKING TOGETHER OVERCOMES HOSTILITY, page 142: Sherif, M. *In Common Predicament.* Washington, D.C.: Public Affairs Press, 1966.

STUDIES PROVE MEDIA INFLUENCE BEHAVIOR, page 144: Grossman and Degaetano, op. cit., p. 127.

"NONVIOLENCE" IN *HIGH NOON*, page 145: Fellman, Gordon. *Rambo and the Dalai Lama.* Albany: State University of New York Press, 1998, p. 20.

MY REAL POLITICS, page 146: Pyarelal, and Sushila Nayar. *In Gandhiji's Mirror.* Delhi: Oxford University Press, 1991, p. 268.

Chapter Five: A Way Out of Hell

DRUG USER PROFILE, page 149: Browning, Frank. "Drug Users Defy Stereotypes," *Pacific News Service*: 4:6, 1992, p. 3.

COOPERATIVE INSTITUTIONAL RESEARCH STUDY, page 150: This study was covered by, among others, William Raspberry in the *International Herald Tribune* for 7 February 1988. Similarly, young suicides among Australia's aboriginal communities are predominantly "those who feel and think"; see Michael Gordon, "A Journey Into a World Apart," reprinted from *The Age* in *World Press Review*, September 2000, p. 16.

YOUNG ADDICT, page 151: *YO*, January/February 1997, p. 7.

COST OF WAR ON DRUGS, page 153: *San Francisco Chronicle*, November 10, 1997. The "war" cost $60 million in 1968 before escalating to these levels, with no appreciable difference in result.

QUINNEY, page 153: Pepinsky, Harold E. and Quinney, Richard. *Criminology as Peacemaking.* Bloomington: Indiana University Press, 1991, p. 3.

MORRIS, page 153: Morris, Ruth. *Penal Abolition: the Practical Choice.* Toronto: Canadian Scholar's Press, 1995, p. 5.

MARTIN LUTHER KING, page 153: Washington, James M., editor. *Testament of Hope.* San Francisco: Harper & Row, 1986, p. 243.

WATERSHED MOMENT, page 154: Schiraldi, Vincent. Quoted in *UC Focus* (University of California, Berkeley) 8, no. 6, 1994, p. 1.

SHARON ROBERTS, page 157: Roberts, Sharon. "Ex-Offenders Aid World of Disabled," *New York Times*, February 4, 1990, p. Y33.

MORRIS, page 160: op. cit., p. 33.

GANDHI, page 160: CWMG: This and following quote from Vol. 19, p. 466.

DR. TREBACHER, page 161: Trebacher, Arnold. Interview in the *Pacific News Service* editorials for June 24-28, 1991, p. 2.

RESTORATIVE JUSTICE, page 161: From the syllabus of Prof. Pepinsky's course, CJUS P202, "Alternative Social Control Systems," Spring 1996.

AVP, page 163: This and the following quotes from Lila Rucker's chapter, "Peacemaking in Prisons: a Process," in Pepinsky and Quinney, op. cit., pp. 174, 177, & 175. Rucker is quoting various authorites.

TINGLES OF EXCITEMENT, page 164: ibid, p. 172. In fact, "correctional" would be a step forward, in some places. The purpose of the California penal system was explicitly changed from correctional to punitive in 1976. According to a Sonoma County official I interviewe˙ twenty years later, this "regressive" change had no visible impact on the state's crime rate. We now have a system which in fact frequently makes non-violent offenders into violent ones.

PSEUDO-SECURITY, page 166: Morris, op. cit. This and the following quote from pp. 44, 46 and 45.

WILBERT RIDEAU, page 168: Woodbury, Richard. "A Convict's View: 'People Don't Want Solutions,'" *Time* magazine, Aug 23, 1993., p. 33.

MASSACHUSETTS WOMAN, page 168: Webster, Katherine. "Verdict, guilty; sentence, literature," *Santa Rosa Press Democrat.* May 31, 1994, p. A6.

KING SPEECH, page 169: King, Martin Luther. "Why I am opposed to the war in Vietnam," delivered in Atlanta, 3rd Sunday in April, 1967.

MAN CANNOT FLOURISH, page 170: Friedman, Meyer and Ulmer, Diane. *Treating Type A Behavior — and Your Heart.* New York: Ballantine, Fawcett Crest, 1984, p. 196.

HEW STUDY, page 170: Deepak Chopra, quoted in *Noetic Sciences Review*, No. 28 (Winter, 1993) p. 19.

AFRIKANER FAMILIES, page 170: Quoted in the *Pacific News Service*, August 9, 1992, p. 6.

CULT MEMBERS, page 170: From a *San Francisco Chronicle* editorial, Friday, March 18, 1997, p. A24.

FRANKL, page 171: Frankl, Viktor E. *Man's Search for Meaning: An Introduction to Logotherapy.* Translator Ilse Lasch. Boston: Beacon Press, 1959, p. 101.

NINETY-ONE-YEAR-OLD, page 172: Midlarsky, E. and Kahana E. *Altruism in Later Life.* Sage Library of Social Research. Thousand Oaks, Calif.: Sage Publications, 1994, p. 79.

EINSTEIN, page 172: Einstein's letter was reprinted in the *New York Times*, March 29, 1972.

ARCHBISHOP ROMERO, page 175: Romero, Oscar. *The Violence of Love: the Pastoral Wisdom of Archbishop Oscar Romero*; compiled and translated by James R. Brockman. San Francisco : Harper & Row, 1988, p. 81.

MOTHER TERESA, page 175: Benenate, Becky & Durepos, Joseph, editors. *No Greater Love.* Novato: New World Library, 1997, pp. 94f.

Chapter Six: The Sweet Sound of Order

GANDHI, page 177: CWMG, Vol. 79, p. 309.

HANDS WITHOUT GUNS, page 179: Working Assets mailer, May 1998.

DR. ROBÈRT, page 179: Mailer reprinted from Spring, 1997 *Wingspread Journal*, The Johnson Foundation.

GANDHI, page 181: CWMG, Vol. 34, p. 42 (*Satyagraha in South Africa*, p. 43).

GANDHI, page 181: CWMG, Vol. 10, p. 283 (*Hind Swaraj, or Indian Home Rule*, p. 60).

GANDHI, page 186: CWMG, Vol. 24, p. 77.

GANDHI GRANDDAUGHTER, page 186: Conversation with Tara Bhattacharjee, published in the East Bay newsletter *Gandhi Mela* VII (1995), p. 19.

WORKING TOGETHER, page 187: Sherif, M. *In Common Predicament.* Washington, D.C.: Public Affairs Press, 1966.

TOYNBEE, page 189: Quoted by B. R. Nanda in *India News*, October 1, 1994, p. 11.

GANDHI, page 190: This and following quote from Tendulkar, D. G. *Mahatma: Life of Mohandas Karamchand Gandhi.* New Delhi: Government of India, 1951, pp. 123 & 115.

OTHER PARTS OF CONSTRUCTIVE PROGRAMME, page 190: Those programs were, 9: Women, 14: Kisans (peasant farmers), 15: Labour, 16: Adivasis (indigenous peoples — still a contentious issue in India), 17: Lepers, and in a sense one could count 18: Students. The pamphlet, *Constructive Programme, Its Meaning and Place* was first published in 1941 and is still available from Navajivan Press in Ahmedabad as well as outlets in the U.S. (See Resources).

NYC POLICEMAN, page 198: This and following quote from Marie Winn, *The Plug-In Drug*, New York: Viking Press, 1980, pp. 193 & 197.

BRONFENBRENNER, page 199: Bronfenbrenner, Urie. "The Origins of Alienation," *Scientific American* 231, no. 2, 1974, p. 61.

SUSAN ATKINS, page 200: Orlick, Terry. *Winning through Cooperation: competitive insanity, cooperative alternatives.* Washington: Acropolis Books, 1978, p. 79.

THURMAN INTERVIEW, page 202: This and the following quote from Tendulkar, 1952, *Mahatma,* Vol. 3, pp. 50 & 51.

THE WEISSERS, page 204: Levy, Daniel. "The Cantor and the Klansman," *Time* magazine, February 14, 1992, pp, 14f. There is now a book on this dramatic episode: Watterson, Kathryn. *Not By The Sword.* New York: Simon and Schuster, 1995.

LARRY TRAPP TESTIMONY, page 205: Ibid, p. 14

ELIAS JABBOUR EXPERIMENT, page 206: Communicated by e-mail from Patti Malin, Coordinator, Institute for Global Communication, Dec. 8, 1997.

JAN ØBERG EXPERIMENT, page 206: E-mail from the Transnational Forum on April 30, 1998. This excellent resource can be communicated with and browsed at http://www.transnational.org.

THINGS DEGRADE, page 207: Marshall, Ian and Zohar, Danah. *Who's Afraid of Schrödinger's Cat?: all the new science ideas you need to keep up with the new thinking.* New York: Morrow, 1997, p. 139.

ENCYCLOPÆDIA BRITANNICA, page 207: Britannica® CD Deluxe Edition © 1994-2000 Encyclopædia Britannica, Inc., under "chaos." The *Britannica* wryly adds, "the idea that a system cannot spontaneously become better ordered but can readily become more disordered, even if left to itself, appeals to one's experience of domestic economy."

KING EPIPHANY, page 210: Garrow, David J. *Bearing the Cross: Martin Luther King, Jr. and the Southern Christian Leadership Conference.* New York, 1986, p. 58; next quotes pp. 58 & 60. We might note in passing that the threatening phone call had the exactly opposite effect that the callers intended; and that this was even more true of the bombing: in response, the Montgomery Improvement Association increased its demand from a polite form of "separate but equal" to outright desegregation of public buses, and generally steeled their resistance (ibid, p. 61). That's how violence usually "works," when it's stood up to.

ANTHROPOLOGICAL THEORY, page 211: This theory of scapegoating and "mimetic violence" had its first major appearance in French in 1972, then was translated by Patrick Gregory in 1978 as Girard, René, *Violence and the Sacred,* Baltimore and London: Johns Hopkins University. See also Girard's *Job, the Victim of His People,* London, Athlone Press, 1987. The latter is highly recommended as an accessible introduction to the main points of Girard's theory.

GANDHI: CWMG, Vol. 56, p.163.

KING ON MONTGOMERY BOYCOTT, page 212: King, Jr. Martin Luther. *Stride Toward Freedom.* New York: Harper and Row, 1958, p. 111. Following quote from p. 71.

Chapter Seven: A Clear Picture of Peace

GLENN SEABORG, page 215: Seaborg, Glenn T. "Premonitions After the Bombs," *Bulletin of the Atomic Scientists*, 41, no. 11, 1985, p. 33.

ROBERT MCNAMARA, page 218: Lazlo, Ervin and Yoo, Jong Youl. *World Encyclopedia of Peace*. Oxford: Pergamon Press; 1986, Vol. 3, p. 350.

NONVIOLENCE FOR DEFENSE, page 219: Steven Huxley, in *Civilian-Based Defense* newsletter for August, 1992, p. 4.

GANDHI, page 219: Prabhu, R. K., and U. R. Rao. *The Mind of Mahatma Gandhi*. Ahmedabad: Navajivan, p. 458. Cf. CWMG, Vol. 31, p. 482, uttered much earlier (1925): "The conviction is daily growing stronger that there is no peace for India, and indeed for the world, save through non-violence."

PHYSICIST I.I. RABI, page 219: Quoted in Nuclear freeze mailer from 1982.

EMERSON, page 221: Emerson, Ralph Waldo. "War," quoted in Arthur and Lila Weinberg, editors, *Instead of Violence: Writings by the great advocates of peace and nonviolence throughout history*, New York: Grossman Publishers, 1963, p. 379.

E. P. THOMPSON, page 222: From the essay, "Protest and Survive," in E.P. Thompson and Dan Smith, editors, *Protest and Survive*, Harmondsworth: Penguin, 1980, p. 52.

THE BUDDHA, page 222: Easwaran, Eknath, translator. *The Dhammapada*. Petaluma, Calif.: Nilgiri Press, 1990, p. 88.

D.W. GRIFFITH, page 224: Rogin, Michael P. *Reagan, the Movie and Other Episodes in Political Demonology*. Berkeley: University of California, 1987. p. 192.

SHIRO AZUMA, page 225: quoted in the *San Francisco Chronicle*, August 18th, 1998, p. A 11.

"WAR CRIMES", page 225: As one who believes war itself is avoidable, and therefore a crime, I suspect and always put quotes around this notion.

ARENDT, page 226: Arendt, Hannah. *Eichmann in Jerusalem: A Report on the Banality of Evil*, New York: Penguin Books, 1987, pp. 85f.

COGNITIVE DISSONANCE, page 227: Cf. Mahoney, L. and Eguren L.. *Unarmed Bodyguards: International Accompaniment for the Protection of Human Rights*. West Hartford, Conn.: Kumarian, 1997, p. 36.

CAROL COHN, page 228: Cohn, Carol. "Sex and Death in the Rational World of Defense Intellectuals," *Signs* 12, no. 4 (1987), p. 687.

UNESCO LANGUAGE, page 228: *UNESCO News* 5:2 (February 20, 1998) p. 8.

GENERAL MEJÍA, page 229: Mahoney and Eguren, op. cit., p. 32.

MIKE MCCULLOUGH, page 230: Quoted in the *Utne Reader* for March-April 1997, p. 71. Cf. McCullough's book, *To Forgive is Human*, InterVarsity Press, 1997. The full quote, incidentally, begins, "the old theory was that if you're angry, you need to express it. But expression actually makes it worse, and imagery . . ."

POWER OF LANGUAGE, page 230: This field has gotten a good deal of well-deserved scholarly attention. See, for example, George Lakoff and Mark Johnson, *Metaphors We Live By* (University of Chicago, 1980), and of particular interest, Lakoff, "Metaphor and War: The Metaphor System used to Justify War in the Gulf," 1991; draft obtainable from lakoff@cogsci.berkeley.edu.

CUSS CONTROL ACADEMY, page 231: Sampson, Ovetta.. "Curse of the Word," *Santa Rosa Press Democrat*, May 16, 2000, pp. D1f.

BILL KENNEDY, page 233: Advertisement for the U.S. Monetary War College, *Insight* (June 9, 1990), p. 27.

Chapter Eight: Fighting Fire with Water

GANDHI, NOT INDIA'S PROBLEM ONLY, page 240: Tendulkar, D. G. *Mahatma: The Life of Mohandas Karamchand Gandhi*, Vol. 2. New Delhi: Government of India, Publications Division, 1951, p. 237; second quote from CWMG, Vol. 57, p. 107 (Pyarelal. *The Epic Fast*. Ahmedabad: Navajivan, 1932, p. 133).

GANDHI, "BLASPHEMY", page 241: CWMG, Vol.74, p. 194 (Prabhu and Rao. *The Mind of Mahatma Gandhi*. Ahmedabad: Navajivan. 1967, p. 128).

TIME TO CONFRONT THE RAJ, page 241: Walker, Charles C. *A World Peace Guard: an Unarmed Agency for Peacekeeping*. Hyderabad: Academy of Gandhian Studies, 1981, p. 3. This little book was one of the first writings on the peace-team movement.

GANDHI, page 241: CWMG, Vol. 73, pp. 24f.

ATTRACTING JAPANESE ATTACK, page 242: Tendulkar, op. cit., Vol. 6, p. 75. Following quote from p. 10.

WILD PATHAN, page 243: Easwaran, Eknath. *Nonviolent Soldier of Islam: Badshah Khan, a Man to Match His Mountains*. Petaluma: Nilgiri Press, 1999; these two quotes from pp. 107 & 195.

KISSA KANNI MASSACRE, page 245: Ibid, pp. 122f.

ISLAM AND NONVIOLENCE, page 246: Paige, Glenn, and others. *Islam and Nonviolence.* Honolulu: Matsunaga Institute for Peace, University of Hawai'i, 1993; see also Michael Nagler, "Is There a Tradition of Nonviolence in Islam?" in J. Patout Burns, editor, *War and its Discontents: Pacifism and Quietism in the Abrahamic Traditions.* Washington, D.C.: Georgetown University Press, 1996, pp. 161-166.

HELP THE AGGRESSOR, page 246: *Complete Sahih Bukhari: A Collection of the Hadith in Sahih Bukhari.* Vol. 3, Book 43, Number 624.

BADSHAH KHAN, page 247: Easwaran, op. cit. p. 183.

GANDHI, page 248: CWMG, Vol. 54, p. 286 (Prabhu and Rao, op. cit., pp. 452f). Thermopylae is the narrow mountain pass where, in 480 B.C.E., a small Spartan army under Leonidas died to the last man trying to hold off a vastly greater Persian force.

GANDHI, page 249: CWMG, Vol. 82, p. 167 (Tendulkar Vol. 6, p. 69).

EASY TO SAY IT WOULD NOT HAVE WORKED, page 250: The absence of evidence does not seem to prevent skeptics from decrying the scheme now, any more than it did at the time: "Gandhi held to his belief that nonviolence could defeat the Japanese, despite their lack of the inhibitions derived from English-speaking public morality [sic]. This belief, *fortunately for the Indians*, was never tested in practice." D.C Watt, in Alan Bullock & R. B. Woodings, *20th Century Culture*, New York: Harper and Row (1983), p. 256 (my emphasis). Even most of Gandhi's Congress believed the myth — and we now know that it was purely a myth — that British arms were the only thing standing between them and the Japanese.

ALGERIA, 1962, page 251: Unless otherwise indicated, these references are from an article on "Nonviolent Interventions" by Alberto L'Abate in *Peace Courier* for March, 1994, p. 2.

ENRILE AND RAMOS, page 251: Zunes, Stephen. "Unarmed insurrections against authoritarian governments in the Third World: a new kind of revolution," *Third World Quarterly* 15, no. 3, 1994, p. 417.

INSTITUTIONS, NOT BORDERS, page 252: Compare the Greek philosopher Heraclitus: "Citizens should be as zealous to defend their institutions as they are their walls" (Fragment B44, my translation).

HANS SCHOLL, page 255: Scholl, Inge. *The White Rose: Munich 1942-1943*. Ohio: Wesleyan University, 1970, p. 95.

THE ASSASSINATIONS STOPPED, page 257: Moser-Puangsuwan, Yeshua and Weber, Thomas. *Nonviolent Intervention Across Borders: A Recurrent Vision*. Honolulu: University of Hawai'i, 2000, p. 138. UN (armed) peacekeeping has been much more dangerous. By way of example, fourteen Indian troops with UNEF in the Sinai were killed and twenty wounded in a single engagement in 1967: "So far as [the Israelis] were concerned, anybody in uniform facing them was an enemy" (Rikhye, Indar Jit, and others, *The Thin Blue Line;* New Haven: Yale University [1974], p. 61).

PATTY MOTCHNICK, page 256: Moser-Puangsuwan and Weber, op. cit., p. 14.

QUAKER PEACE AND SERVICE, page 256: Mahoney, L. and Eguren L. *Unarmed Bodyguards: International Accompaniment for the Protection of Human Rights.* West Hartford, CN: Kumarian, 1997, p. 216.

PBI "TEAM" OF ONE, page 256: Moser-Puangsuwan and Weber, op. cit., p. 13.

FRENCH PEACE-TEAM COORDINATOR, page 258: Le Meut, Christian. Interview in *Non-Violence Actualité* (February, 1994), p. 10.

SRI LANKAN INCIDENT, page 258: Peace Brigades International. Report: Sri Lanka Seminar, 1992 (unpublished). Available from Bob Siedle-Khan, PBI, 59 E. Van Buren St. #1400, Chicago IL 60605.

MARGE ARGELYAN, page 258: Argelyan, Marge. "Walking the Talk of Nonviolent Intervention," *Signs of the Times* (CPT newsletter) VI, no. 1, 1996, p. 2.

BISHOP TUTU, page 260: Speech by Bishop Tutu on January 2, 1993, on National Public Radio; cf. Robert Siegel, editor, *The NPR interviews*, 1994. Boston: Houghton Mifflin, 1994, p. 213.

UN PEACEKEEPING, page 262: For a good account (without my nonviolence analysis) of UN and other recent attempts to get military intervention to serve humanitarian purposes, see Thomas G. Weiss, *Military-Civilian Interactions: Intervening in Humanitarian Crises*, New York: Rowan and Littlefield, 1999.

KIGALI INCIDENT, page 262: From a letter by Elise Boulding to "Colleagues Concerned with International Nonviolent Peace Services" on June 10, 1994.

JOE LOYA, page 263: Loya, Joe S. "How Cops Are Turned," *Cleveland Plain Dealer*, August 26, 1997.

E.M. FORSTER, page 264: Forster, E. M. *A Passage to India.* New York: Harcourt, Brace and Co., 1952, p. 11.

INDIAN SHANTI SAINIK, page 264: Weber, Thomas. *Gandhi's Peace Army: the Shanti Sena and Unarmed Peacekeeping.* Syracuse: Syracuse University Press, 1996, p. 133.

VIOLENCE CORRUPTS, page 265: These quotes respectively from Chris Hedges, "What I Read at War," *Harvard Magazine* (July-August, 2000) p. 61, and *Housman's Peace Diary* for 1998, Stony Creek, Connecticut: New Society Publishers.

NONVIOLENCE ORDERS, page 266: Esquivel, Adolfo Perez. *Christ in a Poncho: Testimonials of the Nonviolent Struggles in Latin America.* New York: Orbis Books, 1984, p. 127.

RANDY BOND, page 266: from the *Michigan Peace Team Bulletin* 2 (1998), p. 8.

CHRONIC LACK OF RESOURCES, page 268: Moser-Puangsuwan and Weber, op. cit., p. 320.

KONRAD LORENZ, page 270: Lorenz, Konrad. *On Aggression.* Marjorie Kerr Wilson, translator. New York: Harcourt, Brace & World, 1966, p. 284.

MEN BENT ON WAR, page 271: Walsh, Gerald G., and others. *St. Augustine, City of God.* New York: Image, 1958, pp. 451, 457.

PEACE IS THE QUEST, page 272: Ramdas, Swami. *Ramdas Speaks*, Vol. III. Bharatiya Vidya Bhavan, 1957, p. 43.

Chapter Nine: Children of Earth — Toward a Metaphysics of Compassion

OUTRAGING THE MUTE EARTH, page 274: At line 22 the poet himself had told us that Achilles was "dishonoring brilliant Hector in his fury," thus putting the dead body and the earth, with their complementary sets of symbolic resonances, into close parallelism, and bringing his own voice into resonance with the god's.

WHO WILL HEAR . . ., page 275: The subtitle to the German edition of Sri Eknath Easwaran's *The Compassionate Universe*, Berkeley, California: Nilgiri Press, 1989.

IN AN IRAQI HOSPITAL, page 275: E-mail of May 24,1998 entitled, "To Feel What Ima Feels," by Kathy Kelly of the Voices in the Wilderness, and reproduced with her permission.

FLAUBERT, page 278: From the Metropolitan Museum exhibit catalogue, 6 September - 2 December, 1990, p. 58.

WHO UNDERSTANDS CHILDREN, page 278: These statistics respectively from "Every Fifth Child," in *Bread for the World* newsletter, 4:2 (March, 1992) and the Op-ed page of the *San Francisco Chronicle* for March 28, 1994.

BOHR IN 1938, page 283: Rhodes, Richard. *The Making of the Atomic Bomb*. New York: Simon & Schuster: Touchstone, 1988, p. 243.

GERMAN BROCHURE, page 285: Respectively *Gewaltfreiheit* or "freedom from violence" (German is one of the few languages with a positive translation of "nonviolence") and *Selbstdarstellung*. This is the 1994 brochure of a regional Educational Project for Peace Work (Fränkisches Bildungswerk für Friedensarbeit e.V.).

JOHAN GALTUNG, page 285: Galtung, Johan. "Violence, Peace, and Peace Research," *Journal of Peace Research*, No. 3, (1959) pp. 167-191. Cp. Aldous Huxley, *Means and Ends* (London, 1937) p. I: "the free development of each will lead to the free development of all."

THE DALAI LAMA, page 286: Speech at Non-Governmental Organzations, United Nations World Conference on Human Rights, Vienna Austria, 15 June, 1993 (available at www.tibet.com/DL/vienna.html).

ONE DEATH IS A TRAGEDY, page 286: This quote is variously attributed to Goebbels and Stalin; see Soloman, Norman. "Wizards of Media Oz: Behind the Curtain of Mainstream News," E-mail to (www.labridge.com/change-links/GOODGRIEF.html).

NONVIOLENT LOGIC, page 286: St. Augustine, *Confessions* vii.12, (my translation). The embedded quote is of course Genesis I.31.

ORWELL, page 287: Orwell, George. *A Hanging*, in Ian Angus and Sonya Orwell, editors, *The Collected Essays, Journalism and Letters of George Orwell*, London: Secker and Warburg, 1968, p. 46.

TALMUD AND KORAN, page 287: Respectively, Mishnah Sanhedrin IV, 5 and Koran 5.35.

RABBI KOOK, page 288: Kook, Abraham Isaac. *The Lights of Penitance, the Moral Principles, Lights of Holiness, Essays, Letters, Poems*. New York: Paulist Press, 1978, p. 6.

THE DALAI LAMA, page 290: This comment of His Holiness's is also from 1993, and may be found at www.tibet.com/DL/vienna.html.

MARY MIDGLEY, page 290: Midgley, Mary. *Evolution as a Religion*. London: Methuen, 1985, p. 157; cf. 153: "Words like *rights* and *duties* are awkward because they do indeed have narrow senses approximating to the legal, but they also have much wider ones in which they cover the whole of the moral sphere . . . 'Animal rights' may be hard to formulate, as indeed are the rights of man. But 'no rights' will not do. The word may need to be dropped entirely."

Epilogue

VANDANA SHIVA, page 294: Shiva, Vandana. *Stolen Harvest: the Hijacking of the Global Food Supply.* Cambridge, Mass.: South End Press, 2000, p. 4.

IVAN ILLICH, page 297: Illich, Ivan. "The Delinking of Peace and Development," *Alternatives* VII:4 (1981), 409-416.

WESTERN THING, page 297: Wright, Quincy. *A Study of War.* Chicago: University of Chicago Press, 1965, p. 1043.

EARLY CHIPKO, page 298: Weber, Thomas. *Hugging the Trees: the Story of the Chipko Movement.* New Delhi: Penguin, 1989, pp. 92f; following quote from pp. 40f.

INDIGENOUS RESTORATIVE JUSTICE, page 299: For more on this and other 'culturally appropriate' aspects of the new justice paradigm, consult the site www.restorativejustice.org.

JUSTICE YAZZIE, page 299: Yazzie, Robert Hon. "Life Comes From It: Navajo Justice Concepts," *New Mexico Law Review* 24, 1994; this and following quote from pp.180f & 186.

SAINT ISAAC OF SYRIA, page 301: Isaac, Saint. *The Ascetical Homilies of St. Isaac the Syrian.* Brookline, Mass.: Holy Transfiguration Monastery, 1984, p. 246.

WILLIAM JAMES, page 301: James, William S. *The Moral Equivalent of War,* in *Memories and Studies.* New York: Longmans, Green & Co, 1911, pp. 290f.

STUART COWAN, page 302: Cowan, Stuart. "A Design Revolution," *Yes!,* summer, 1998, p. 30.

PORPHYRY, page 304: Taylor, Thomas, translator. *Porphyry on abstinence from animal food.* New York: Barnes and Noble, 1965, p. 140.

Resources and Opportunities

Happily, the world of nonviolence — the organizations that do it and the books and articles about it — is expanding so rapidly now that a complete list of such resources would require a separate volume. I cannot close, however, without giving at least a sample of this richness (I trust that other worthy organizations, writers and people will forgive their omission).

Meditation

First things first. There are many methods of meditation abroad, but I can speak responsibly only of the one I know and practice, which is spelled out in *Meditation* by Sri Eknath Easwaran (Nilgiri Press, various editions). For more information about this highly popular book or other resources and projects of the Blue Mountain Center of Meditation, check our web site, www.nilgiri.org, or call (800) 475-2369.

Nonviolence

The venerable Fellowship of Reconciliation (FOR), based in Nyack, NY but present most everywhere, has been publishing *Fellowship* and promoting the learning and the doing of nonviolence for decades. Through FOR, and their international arm (IFOR), one can contact denominational organizations like the Jewish or Buddhist Peace Fellowship around the world. More recent, but somehow at the center of things, is Nonviolence International, set up in Washington, D.C. by Mubarak Awad. Worthy of note for its "broad spectrum" rejection of violence in all forms is the Seamless Garment Network. My own outfit is called METTA (an acronym, but also the Buddhist term for "loving-kindness," or nonviolence) and we specialize in education on nonviolence in all its applications. A like-minded Franciscan-based organization is Pace e Bene. All of us accept tax-deductible donations, by the way; and here is some contact information:

Fellowship of Reconciliation
P.O. Box 271
Nyack, NY 10960-9988
www.forusa.org

Nonviolence International
4545 42nd Street N.W.
Washington, D.C.
(202) 393-3616, or nonviolence@igc.org

METTA
PO Box 183
Tomales, CA 94971
www.mettacenter.org

Pace e Bene
1420 West Bartlett Ave.
Las Vegas, NV 89106
(702) 648-2281

A good hub for religious and secular nonviolence groups:
The Other Side
300 W. Apsley
Philadelphia, PA 19144
(800) 700-9280, or www.theotherside.org/resources/nv/index.html.

For insightful commentary into European events from a nonviolent perspective, an excellent site is: http://www.transnational.org/new/index.html.

Some recent books on nonviolence (see also under "peace armies," below):

Zunes, Stephen, Kurtz, Lester R. and Asher, Sarah Beth, editors. *Nonviolent Social Movements: a Geographical Perspective.* Oxford: Blackwell, 1999. See also Zunes' article, "Unarmed Insurrections Against Authoritarian Governments in the Third World: a New Kind of Revolution. *Third World Quarterly* 15.3 (1994): 403-26.
    A reference book for many historical events is, L. Kurtz et al., editors, *Encylopedia of Violence, Peace & Conflict* (3 vols.). Another is Powers and Voegele, *Protest, Power and Change* that we cited above (see notes to chapter 4). Consult also now the book by Peter Ackerman and Jack DuVall, *A Force More Powerful,* and the PBS documentary with the same title by Steve York, for documentation of civil uprisings of (hyphenated) non-violent character of the last century. A more selective, and dramatic, treatment is the film *Power of the People* (a.k.a. *Where There is Hatred*) by Zev Ilan.
    There are a number of fine essays by various writers and activists in two recent collections: Walter Wink, editor, *Peace is the Way,* Maryknoll, New York: Orbis Books,

2000, and G. Simon Harak, editor, *Nonviolence for the Third Millennium*, Macon, Georgia: Mercer University Press, 2000.
Any works by Elise Boulding, e.g. her recent *Culture of Peace*, or *Nonviolence of the Brave*, come highly recommended.

There are two recent manuals of interest:

Ken Butigan and others, *From Violence to Wholeness*, for those wishing to experiment with a more nonviolent life-style (available from Pace e Bene), and Michael Nagler, *The Steps of Nonviolence* for those who find themselves in a major dispute or conflict and wish to resolve it nonviolently (available from FOR).

Gandhi

As you've gathered from the references to this book, the *Collected Works of Mahatma Gandhi* is now on CD-Rom, and it is available from www.gandhiserve.com or, in the U.S. from Arun Gandhi's institute, (901) 452-2824, Gandhi@cbu.edu. Prior to reading those 90+ volumes in any form, however, I recommend *Gandhi the Man* by Sri Eknath Easwaran and also his *Nonviolent Soldier of Islam*, as superb introductions. Both are available at Nilgiri Press (see above under **Meditation**). Contact METTA for other suggestions.

Books by and about Gandhi can be purchased directly from Greenleaf Books, Canton ME 04221 (that's all you need), (207) 388-2860, or from South Asia Books in Columbia, MO. (573) 474-0116.

In addition to the present volume, Berkeley Hills Books has brought out a series of five books by Gandhi for which I have written extensive introductions: *Book of Prayers*, *The Way to God*, *Vows and Observances*, *Prayer*, and *The Bhagavad Gita According to Gandhi*. Contact them by email at jpstroh@berkeleyhills.com, or call (888) 848-7303.

Restorative justice

In addition to the books cited in chapter five, for a good overview with full use of indigenous models, see Jim Consedine, *Restorative Justice: Healing Effects of Crime* (Lyttleton, New Zealand: Ploughshare, 1995). the film *Doing Time, Doing Vipassana* documents a bold experiment to teach prisoners to meditate that began in one of India's largest penal institutions and has spread all over the world. The ordering information:

Vipassana Publications
P.O. Box 15926
Seattle, WA 98115
Fax: (206) 522-8295 sales@vrpa.com

Yes! magazine for fall 2000 is dedicated to restorative justice, and one can also consult Howard Zehr, *Changing Lenses*, Scottdale, Pennsylvania: Herald Press, 2000 for additional resources — or just search on "restorative justice" on the internet for a trove of sites. But don't miss the Prison Ashram Project run by Bo and Sita Lozoff's superbly named:

Human Kindness Foundation
PO Box 61619
Durham, NC 27715
(919) 304-2220, or www.humankindness.org.

Alternatives to Violence Project (AVP)
Bill McMechan, International-Network Convenor
PO Box 157
Hastings, Ontario
K0L 1Y0 CANADA
(705) 696-2153, or mcmechan.avp@sympatico.ca

Victim-Offender Reconciliation Program (VORP)
19813 N.E. 13th Street
Camas, WA 98607
(360) 260-1551 Voice(360) 260-1563 FAX
Email: martyprice@vorp.com

"Peace armies" (see chapter seven)

Here I will just cite the two headquarters of the recent effort to "mainstream" nonviolent intervention, Peace Brigades International, Christian Peacemaker Teams and the other groups working in the field can all be reached through them (and in Moser-Puangsuwan and Weber, below):

PeaceWorkers   Mel Duncan
721 Shrader Street   801 Front Ave.
San Francisco, CA 94117   St. Paul, MN 55103: (651) 487-0800
(415) 751-0302, or www.nonviolentpeaceforce.org

The major books on this key development have been cited above:
Moser-Puangsuwan, Yeshua and Thomas Weber. *Nonviolent Intervention Across Borders: A Recurrent Vision.* Honolulu: University of Hawaii, 2000.

Mahoney, L. and Eguren L. *Unarmed Bodyguards: International Accompaniment for the Protection of Human Rights.* West Hartford, CN: Kumarian, 1997.

Weber, Thomas. *Gandhi's Peace Army: the Shanti Sena and Unarmed Peacekeeping.* Syracuse: Syracuse University Press, 1996.

New paradigm thinking on the environment, economies of justice, etc.

The "classic" nonviolent environmental struggle is the Chipko Movement, for which a place to start is Thomas Weber, *Hugging the Trees: the Story of the Chipko Movement.* New Delhi: Penguin, 1989.

The Positive Futures Network based in Bainbridge, WA and their journal, *Yes!* is one good way to stay in touch with new thinking on organization and the economy, lifestyle, etc.

Of many books that try to explain the new physics to laypeople, I personally got the most out of Nick Herbert, *Quantum Reality.* New York: Anchor Doubleday; 1985.

This may also be a good place to mention the cooperative paradigm in biology, and for that I will cite as representative F. B. M. de Waal, *Peacemaking Among Primates.* Cambridge, Mass., Harvard University, 1989.

A representative writer on alternative economic models is Hazel Henderson, and one might consult her *Paradigms in Progress: Life Beyond Economics.* San Francisco: Berrett-Kohler, 1991-1995.

Finally, if I may plug a friend's book, treat yourself to the forthcoming *Kindred Spirits: Stories, passions and portraits from the heart of community,* by Laurie Harrison and Greg Ewert (Anacortes, WA: Island Time Press, 2000).

Index

MICHAEL N. NAGLER is Professor Emeritus of Classics and Comparative Literature at the University of California, Berkeley. He is the founder and chairperson of the University's Peace and Conflict Studies Program, and currently teaches courses in nonviolence and meditation. Dr. Nagler is the author of *America Without Violence*, and, with Eknath Easwaran, an English edition of *The Upanishads*, as well as numerous articles on classics, myth, peace and mysticism. He lives in Tomales, California.

AMR287·M-CA
20

619 726 8199

726 8199

Janet

619 726 8199 Janet